WHITE TIGER

White Tiger

An Autobiography of
Yang Xianyi

The Chinese University Press

White Tiger: An Autobiography of Yang Xianyi
  By Yang Xianyi

© The Chinese University of Hong Kong, 2002

ISBN 962–996–046–X (paperback)
      962–996–070–2 (hardcover)

THE CHINESE UNIVERSITY PRESS
The Chinese University of Hong Kong
SHA TIN, N.T., HONG KONG
Fax: +852 2603 6692
      +852 2603 7355
E-mail: cup@cuhk.edu.hk
Web-site: www.chineseupress.com

Printed in Hong Kong

Contents

Illustrations

Foreword

For many, Yang Xianyi needs no introduction at all. For those in the West who struggled to study Chinese literature in the 1950s and 1960s, he and Gladys were already at that time a living legend. Without them and their prolific output of translations I don't know how we would have managed. For many of those same people, when they later arrived in Beijing, he and Gladys became a wonderful source of hospitality and friendship. They certainly treated the five members of my own family (three of them rather small and unruly) with extraordinary kindness and generosity when we first arrived in China in the autumn of 1980.

This delightful memoir of his gives a rare insight into the survival (against all odds) of a courageous, witty and principled individual during the often harsh first half-century of Chinese "liberation". It is a wonderfully candid and entertaining self-portrait of an intellectual under communism, and as such deserves to be read by many who are not directly involved in Chinese studies. Such readers may not know who Yang Xianyi is. His own self-descriptions are so modest, he wears his learning so lightly, that they may not realize quite what a distinguished person they are dealing with. He belongs, along with Qian Zhongshu and Yang Zhouhan (both of whom feature in his memoir, and both of whom are alas now dead), to what will certainly come to be regarded as the last generation of great cosmopolitan Chinese men of letters. All three studied at Oxford before the war, absorbing in their different ways European culture, ancient and modern. What made them so special, so different from subsequent generations of Chinese scholars visiting the West, was that they were all three at the same time so deeply versed and literate in their own classical literature.

Of this trio, Yang Xianyi is the most playful and mischievous, both as a person and as a scholar. Rumour has it that in the early eighties, when China was being subjected to a series of rather unpleasant campaigns to root out "Spiritual Pollution" (i.e. to suppress any form of free-thinking self-expression), he would get on the phone to one of his group of like-minded friends and say loudly and provocatively (knowing that his phone was likely to be tapped), "Where shall we go and get polluted tonight?" As this autobiographical memoir shows, he has little tolerance for nasty political nonsense of any kind. In the hopeful decade after the end of the Cultural Revolution, several of China's younger writers came to respect him as a free spirit, a kind, but shrewd, critic, a wise mentor and friend.

His wisdom is informed by an insider's knowledge of a system in which he has survived (and suffered), and at the same enlivened by a sharp and cultivated sense of humour. I recall a piece of very useful advice he gave me, when I first arrived in China. If we ever got into any sort of trouble, he said, I should mention *The Story of the Stone* (the classic eighteenth-century novel, which both he and Gladys, in Beijing, and David Hawkes and I, in Oxford, had for several years been in the process of translating). He knew that this book, indeed the mention of its title alone, possessed talismanic powers (even with members of the Public Security Bureau). I once had occasion to resort to this piece of cultural name-dropping. It worked.

His caustic insight and humour are at the service of a natural sense of decency and integrity. That is why he spoke out so strongly (and so articulately) after the Tiananmen fiasco of 1989. "We won't execute these fascists. We just want them to step down." The words were delivered in impeccable English, and with a wry humour that only served to enhance their force. They spoke eloquently for the cause of freedom in China.

People respect what Xianyi says, because it is free of cant, and because he sees the funny side of things, while all the time preserving a deep sense of what is right. He has always been a deeply patriotic Chinese intellectual, and remains to this day a firm believer in the basic values of socialism (which have little to do with the functioning of an institutionalized, corrupt party state). This refreshingly honest sense of knowing and saying what he believes comes through strongly in this memoir. As does his love of sharing ideas with friends over a glass. In the words of the great medieval poet Tao Yuanming (as Gladys and Xianyi translated him over fifty years ago):

> Sometimes he was provided by his friends
> With wine, if he their problems would untie.
> And when the cup was filled he drained it straight,
> And when advice was asked would not refuse.
> But sometimes he would not his counsel give,
> For unjust cause his gift would not abuse.
> For when a wise man is desired to teach,
> He will not err by silence or by speech.

There is a quality of mellowness and warmth, an uncanny gift for friendship, that pervades both this memoir and Yang Xianyi as a person. I only really knew him during the two years we were in China, and have not seen him for nearly twenty years. The last time I spoke to him on the phone was in that first week of June

1989. But I have kept a photograph hanging on a wall of my study, taken in the early 1980s, when he and Gladys were visiting David and Jean Hawkes at their remote farmhouse in the Welsh hills. The weather was bitterly cold, and the two scholars (who had just met for the first time) had retreated into the snug parlour, for a glass of malt whisky. They are both sitting there smiling, Xianyi with a cigarette in his hand, his glass on the table in front of him, and next to it a copy of *Last Exit to Brooklyn*.

John Minford
Fontmarty, February 11th, 2002

Plate 1. Yang Xianyi, the son of the Bank of China's head in Tianjin, mid 1920s.

Plate 2. Yang Xianyi in Oxford.

Plate 3. In Nanjing, 1940s.

Plate 4. In Beibei, 1944 (photo taken by Sir Cecil Beaton).

Plate 5. Yang Xianyi and Gladys Yang in Lushan, 1955.

Plate 6. The children: (from left) Ye,
Ying and Zhi, 1952 or 1953.

Plate 7. At the backyard of Foreign Languages Press, late 1970s.

Plate 8. In Oxford, early 1980s.

Plate 9. A convivial couple.

Plate 10. A knotty problem solved.

Plate 11. In Canberra, 1992.

Plate 12. Giving a speech at the Chinese University of Hong Kong, 1994.

Plate 13. Buying watermelon at the free market in Beijing. Yang Xianyi has a good reputation as *maizhu*.

Plate 14. Doing his grocery.

Plate 15. In his study at home, late 1980s.

Plate 16. Chinese chess, flexing the mind.

Plate 17. Yang Xianyi, the founder of Panda Books, at a Panda exhibition in Oxford University, 1990 or 1991.

Plate 18. Receiving an honorary Ph.D. at the University of Hong Kong with Mother Teresa, 1993.

Plate 19. Classic pose.

Plate 20. Still prefers his typewriter.

Plate 21. Sitting in his favourite chair at home, the foreign experts' apartment in Friendship Hotel, 1998.

Plate 22. In his apartment at Wuluju in the west suburbs of Beijing, 2000.

Plate 23. A courageous and witty individual,
a patriotic and principled intellectual.

1

I Was Born

I was born on January 10th, 1915, which by the lunar calendar reckoning was the 27th of the eleventh month of the previous year and that was the Year of the Tiger. My mother told me later that before she gave birth she had a dream, and saw a white tiger leap into her lap. That, according to the fortune-teller, was an auspicious as well as unlucky sign: the boy would grow up with no brothers and his father's health would be endangered by this birth, but he would have a distinguished career after going through many misfortunes and dangers. I don't know whether my career can be considered distinguished or not, but I certainly was my mother's only male child and my father died of illness when I was only five years old. And I have passed through many troubles in my past seventy odd years. So the fortune-teller could say that his guess was not too far wrong.

October 1911 marked the founding of the first Chinese Republic with Dr. Sun Yat-sen as the first president. I was born four years after that. The Qing (Manchu) dynasty was overthrown. China was no more a moribund feudal empire, but stepping into the modern world. However, old ideas and old customs die hard. When I was born, the world around me looked just the same as it had several decades earlier. It was still a semi-feudal, semi-colonial country. The Qing dynasty began its decline before the Opium War of 1840. By the end of the nineteenth century the Manchu feudal rulers had already lost their vigour, and the government was run mainly by Han officials. As history had it, Yuan Shikai and a number of other officials in North China actually forced the last emperor, Puyi, to abdicate. They then asked Dr. Sun Yat-sen from the south to head the first Chinese Republic. So from the beginning, North China was in the hands of a number of ex-Qing dynasty officials and generals. My grandfather had been a fairly high Qing provincial official and some of my grand-uncles were close colleagues and friends of Yuan Shikai and that lot of North China high officials. At that time my father was head of the Bank of China in Tianjin. The bank was a government bureaucratic capitalist organization and my father as its president helped those early North China warlords with its money. So my father, though not a high official, was on close terms with all those early North China government heads.

I remember that when I was a small child I had a yellow silk short jacket which, in the old days, could only be worn by one of the young princes of the Manchu imperial family. It was a present from the Yuan Shikai family. Yuan Shikai, being the main person to oust the last emperor, after Dr. Sun Yat-sen's early death made himself the president of the republic, then attempted to make himself emperor, but died before he could reach his goal. After Yuan's death the succeeding presidents of our young republic were all ex-Qing officials or generals from North China, and my family was connected with most of them. So much for my old family.

My father had three wives, the third of whom was considered a concubine, not a real mistress of the house. My mother was number two. She was first bought by my father as a concubine, but as the first wife had no son and my mother, at that time only a girl of eighteen, gave him his first male offspring, she came to be considered the second mistress of the house. When I was small, I had to call my father's first wife mother too, so I had two mothers. The Number One Mother came from northern Jiangsu Province, from Huaian, which is in the Huai river valley, north of the Yangtze. My grandfather was once the governor there. She came from an old-fashioned wealthy family. Although she gave my father several children, most of them died soon after birth, leaving only two girls. The eldest daughter, my half-sister, had an unhappy life. She was not allowed by her mother to go to a modern school. She only had a family tutor who taught her the Confucian classics, and she learned to write classical poems at home. She had an unsuccessful marriage, was soon divorced, then eloped with a young servant. That man extorted a lot of money from the family, so the family ransomed her back, and she remained a lonely woman, living at home all her life, until she died of cancer in the 1950s. I and my two younger sisters nicknamed her "the princess". The second daughter was not permitted to go to school either and she died in her teens of tuberculosis. She was a gentle and kind girl. I felt very sorry for her. Number One Mother also died of cancer in Tianjin in the early fifties.

I had another half-sister, the daughter of my father's third wife. She was two years younger than me. After my father's death, her mother decided to leave the Yang family and marry someone else who worked in a theatrical company. So she took her daughter with her and went away. We had no more connection with them, except that many years later we heard that this half-sister had become a Beijing opera actress. Some people say her name appeared in some newspaper. Both the mother and daughter must have died long ago.

My mother had, besides me, two more daughters. Both my two

sisters are younger than me. Actually the youngest was born after my father's death. The eldest was, for many years, a professor in Beijing Normal University, teaching Chinese literature, but is now retired. The younger used to teach English in Nanjing. She is also a writer and has published various poems and essays.

I have only some very vague recollections of my father. He was rather short, but solidly built. He was the eldest of my grandfather's eight sons. My ancestral home was in Sizhou (now called Sixian) in northern Anhui province. Though my grandfather became the governor of Huaian in northern Jiangsu and moved the family there, we still considered our ancestral home to be Sizhou. My father spent his early years in Huaian, then was sent abroad to study in Japan. Towards the end of the Qing dynasty, many officials with more enlightened reformist ideas liked to send their sons abroad to study. All my grandfather's eight sons studied abroad, in England, France, the United States, and Japan. Though my father spent several years in Japan, I heard he didn't do much serious study but spent most of his time with geisha girls. Anyway I remember my mother showed me once, when I was still very young, some of the love poems he wrote in classical style to one of the geisha girls when he was in Japan. She kept those poems for many years after his death, but later I think she destroyed them. After my father came back to China as a young profligate, he was also addicted to opium. Then he decided to break his opium pipe, and turned his life around. Grandfather helped him to get the post of director of the Bureau of Telegraphs in the north-east, then the presidency of the Bank of China in Tianjin. He became an astute and skilful financier and probably the most prominent capitalist in Tianjin in those days. Unfortunately he died too young, in his fifties, of typhoid, leaving his widowed wives a lot of money. He was probably the wealthiest trustee of the Tianjin Bank of China. I still remember when I was only seven or eight years old, although my father had been dead for several years, I had to go to one of the bank trustees' meetings as his representative, and many of the much older trustees, who had been my father's old friends and colleagues, praised me for my intelligence and good manners.

I only have a few vague impressions of my father because he died when I was only five years old. I remember one of his hobbies was practising darts in the front courtyard. Those darts were not the darts people play with in English pubs. They were heavy steel darts, about four or five inches long, with sharp points, quite lethal weapons. He would throw them at some target ten or twenty feet away, usually a wooden board marked with a bull's eye. The points of those darts would pierce the wooden board. He was quite good at it. I suppose this was one of the weapons people used in the old days to protect themselves against brigands or other villains.  Another hobby of his was singing Beijing opera, but one of his favourite hobbies was playing with fighting crickets in the autumn. Chinese crickets are a kind of insect like the grasshopper. They have strong jaws and strong forelegs and like to fight and wrestle each other. Chinese people like to keep and train them every autumn for fighting contests. This pastime started in the late Song dynasty and went on through the Ming and Qing dynasties. My father used to buy hundreds of such fighting crickets every autumn and gave the better ones colourful, high-sounding names like "Prince of Golden Jaws", "Invincible King", and the like, and he would train them to fight. I remember that after my father's death, there were still hundreds of exquisitely made pottery cricket cages thrown away in our garden. Though in his late life he had long given up smoking opium, he still smoked cigars and cigarettes. They were all foreign, the cigarettes usually British and the cigars usually Dutch. He also liked drinking French cognac and other foreign liquor. Once I took half a bottle of his cognac from the cabinet, and poured most of the contents into a large earthenware goldfish urn in the front garden. I enjoyed watching the goldfish all drunk, seemingly dancing in a tipsy sort of way until they expired, floating in the water. This happened long after my father's death, and since no one would touch those liquors in the cabinet, this mischievous prank went undetected.

My father left his widowed wives a lot of money, all deposited in the bank, plus several landed estates in Tianjin. The Number One Mother and my own mother did not understand the banking business, and our family maintained a high standard of living after his death. Much of the family wealth was squandered in this way. Two of my uncles later cheated us of large sums of money by pursuing some speculation scheme and losing it all. The family servants also stole many things. During the Japanese occupation of Beijing and Tianjin, most of our bank deposits were converted into Japanese puppet government currency. With the Japanese surrender, such currency became waste paper and by the time of Liberation in 1949, practically all of our bank savings were gone. The landed estates in Tianjin were sold and the family's fortune all disappeared. My mother kept a small sum of money and some jewels.

When I decided to come back to China in 1940, North China was still in Japanese hands, so I did not go to Tianjin but went to Chongqing in the interior. My mother also left Tianjin to join me in Chongqing. So I myself never witnessed the final bankruptcy of our house in Tianjin. Number One Mother remained in Tianjin until the very end. She died of cancer before Tianjin was liberated by the Chinese Communists. My own mother actually went back to Tianjin after the Japanese surrender, to help Number One Mother settle affairs, sell the remaining properties, and send away most of the servants and maids. But I stayed at that time in Nanjing in the south and did not go back to North China. I only revisited Tianjin in 1952 on my way to Beijing after Liberation. By then Number One Mother had already died. My own mother and my younger sister finally left Tianjin and joined me in Beijing after I had settled there after Liberation in the early fifties.

But before all this, my old family lived in a big and rather ugly mansion in the Japanese concession in Tianjin. In those days there were large areas of Tianjin under the jurisdiction of various foreign powers: the Japanese concession, French concession, British concession, and German concession. The German concession had been abolished after the First World War and incorporated into the British concession. These foreign concessions were better administered and had a more modern look and feel than areas under Chinese administration. They were, in fact, foreign colonies in China, and many foreign communities, mostly business people, lived in them. But many wealthy Chinese families in Tianjin preferred to live in these foreign concessions too. Our house was situated on a street called Garden Street. There used to be some Japanese shops and a Japanese Shinto shrine nearby. Our house actually consisted of several courtyards in a larger walled area. Inside the main gate was the front courtyard with rooms occupied by servants. On the right was the family reception hall where the master of the house met and entertained his guests and visitors. Further to the right was the inside courtyard, with the main two-storeyed building where the mistresses and family lived. There was a fair-sized garden in front, with two big pomegranate trees in flower pots, as well as two large earthenware urns containing live goldfish placed just before the inner doors leading to the rooms. There were also several plots of flower and trees. I enjoyed playing in the garden by myself as a child. I used to watch ants fight, and

chased dragonflies. Later I played with air-pistols there. Behind the main building in which the family lived, there was another small backyard, with maid-servants' quarters to the left, and a back door leading to an alley outside and to the right. The front reception hall was also a two-storey building. It had an inner chamber on the right. My family tutor used to live there. In the reception hall there was hardwood old-fashioned furniture, some bronze sacrificial vessels, and on the wall hung scrolls of paintings and calligraphy. There was no staircase leading upstairs. The upstairs rooms were connected instead by a wooden corridor to the main family living quarters on the right. These rooms were occupied by my elder second half-sister after she contracted tuberculosis. Her mother felt that her illness might be contagious, so she had to stay there alone until she died. During her illness she only had one maidservant looking after her. I was discouraged from visiting her often, though she was very fond of me. She was usually very sad and lonely, but she never complained. She was in solitary confinement all the time.

Behind the front courtyard and the reception hall, there was another courtyard. It was occupied by my grandfather's concubine and her family. After his retirement from office, my grandfather came to Tianjin and lived with his eldest son, my father, till he died. My grandmother died early and my grandfather's concubine was much younger. She stayed in our house in a separate courtyard until she died in the early 1930s. My two mothers did not get on well with her, so we very seldom visited her and her family. She had a son whom we called "young uncle", but this boy was rather a bully, several years older than me, and I usually shunned him. Later he went to Hong Kong and I heard that he became a freelance photographer and film-producer. But my family never had any more relations with him.

Our family decided to sell this old house in 1931, after the Japanese army seized the three north-eastern provinces and encroached on Tianjin. The Japanese concession came to be considered unsafe, so our family moved to the French and later British concession. The old house was later divided into three houses and sold to three different families. When I left Tianjin in 1934, our family was in the French concession. In 1937 when the Sino-Japanese War broke out and the Japanese army seized north China, setting up a puppet government, our family moved to the British concession. I was in England at the time.

2

As a Child

As a child I never went to kindergarten or primary school. As I was the only son, my Number One Mother would not allow me to go outside to school until I was twelve, fearing somebody might kidnap me or I might meet with some awful accident. So I had to study at home with a family tutor. I first had a couple of private tutors when I was six or seven, but they were all unsatisfactory. Then my family found a good scholar, a poor gentleman named Wei who had a most unfortunate life. He passed the county examination when the Yihetuan or Boxer Uprising started. Some foreigners were killed, and troops sent by the eight foreign powers attacked Tianjin and Beijing. His house was destroyed in a fire and his wife and child died, leaving only himself. So he came to Tianjin to earn his living as a tutor for several wealthy families. One of my uncles introduced him to our family and he stayed in our house for several years, teaching Chinese classics to the children until he became ill in his old age and returned to his own district to live with one of his nephews. He died two years later when he was over seventy. I liked this old tutor very much. He was always very serious and dignified, and very kind to me. He considered me his best pupil and had high expectations of me for the future. First he taught me the Confucian classics, and then works by other important Chinese classical writers. He was fond of writing poems in the classical styles, so he also taught me how to write poetry. Soon he found I could write as well as he could, and he was delighted. He left me several volumes of his own poems as a momento when he left, but unfortunately I lost those manuscripts in the later war days, so those poems were never published.

In my early teens I also read a lot of old anecdotes and tales, and a goodly portion of popular Ming and Qing prose romances and novels. In those days there were book-vendors coming to the different wealthy households to sell entertainment books for the mistresses and young family members to read in the evenings, so I used to buy many such volumes, including early detective stories and pornography. In China, by the early twenties there was already a movement for literary reform. In 1919 the famous May 4th Movement occurred, which was against foreign imperialism and anti-feudal in character and advocated science and democracy. Many modern bookshops appeared in Tianjin at that time selling works by such new writers as Dr. Hu Shi, Zhou Zuoren, and Lu Xun. I used to ride in my family's rickshaw, accompanied by one of my young servants, to these bookshops to buy books. I would read them greedily. Because of my feudal family background and the classical education I was receiving, in my early teens my views on Chinese culture were rather conservative. Although I read these works of modern Chinese literature greedily, I was dubious about literary reform and the use of the vernacular in place of the classical language. I remember once, when I had an essay-writing class in my first year of school, I wrote an essay attacking Hu Shi's proposal for literary reform, claiming that our classical language was far superior. Of course later I gradually came to change my views, but I was still fond of the Chinese classical language and sceptical about

the validity of modern Chinese poetry. The writings of Zhou
Zuoren and Lu Xun, however, were the exception. I was very
fond of the writings of these authors, both for their thought content
and for their concise, clear language — even though they wrote in
vernacular Chinese.

The beginning of our present century saw China at a crossroads.
Should the country return to feudalism? Move forward to reform
or revolution? Embrace Western modern ideas brought in by foreign
imperialist powers? My family was typically semi-feudal and semi-
colonial. My ancestors were Qing dynasty officials. My grandfather
and three of his brothers had all passed the imperial palace
examination as Hanlin Academicians and had served as high
provincial officials. So they were typical feudal literati and
bureaucrats. On the other hand, my own father and several of my
uncles had all studied abroad and greatly admired the Western
countries, especially England, France, Germany, and America.
Brought up with this background, I first received a Chinese
Confucian education, but by the time I was twelve or thirteen, my
mother finally succeeded in persuading Number One Mother to
allow me to go to a modern middle school for further study. The
school they chose for me was a British missionary school in the
French concession called the Tianjin Anglo-Chinese College
(TACC), which was fairly close to our house.

I first attended a preparatory class for a year, then did six years
of regular study, making seven years in all. I had to take the one
preparatory course for a year because certain courses in that school,
like English literature, physics, chemistry, world history, geography,
and mathematics, were all taught in English, with English textbooks,
by English missionary teachers. My family feared I might have
difficulties. Actually I had more than enough knowledge of English
and mathematics at that time, and my Chinese was above the

required standard. For that reason I usually got top marks in school without much effort, leaving me a lot of time to spend on outside readings. My two younger sisters and younger half-sister also went to a foreign missionary school. It was an American missionary school called the Keen School. Their missionary teachers insisted on giving them Christian names, so they became Amy, Lucy and Vera. I resisted having a foreign name. When my old missionary teacher said that if I wanted to study in England I must adopt an English name, I answered: "In that case I'll be Julian, after Julian the Apostate." Actually my teacher probably did not know who this Julian was, so he did not take offence. I only happened to know about this Roman emperor from reading a novel by some East European writer translated into English. It was probably by the Polish writer Sienkiewicz, whose novel about the Roman emperor Nero and his era, *Quo Vadis*, was well known and already available in a Chinese translation at that time. Actually, later when I went to England, I found that there was no such rule, and that I had no need to adopt a Christian name. So I still registered myself as Yang Hsien-yi (nowadays spelled as Yang Xianyi). At the time, the officer at the police station thought that the last syllable of my given name was my surname, so he addressed me as Mr. Yi.

The old family tutor who taught me the Chinese classics stayed on with us for a few more years after I entered school, but I no longer had my daily lessons with him. My family then thought I must have another tutor to teach me English and mathematics at home, so that I could do well in school. They found a woman who was the wife of a doctor trained in Japan. She was then in her thirties, barely more than a dozen years older than myself. Her English was fluent and she could read French. She was very fond of French romantic literature. She had adopted a Christian name too, Sarah. Because she was rather unhappy with her married life, she was rather lonely and had decided to get out and become the private tutor in a family. My mother got on very well with her, until she sensed that I was too intimate with her and that she was rather infatuated with me. I think my mother feared a family scandal. This was probably one of the reasons why she decided to let me go abroad to study. After I went to England, Sarah wrote me several long romantic letters, complaining of her unhappy life. I never wrote back. Later I heard she committed suicide by taking an overdose of sleeping tablets.

The middle school I attended, TACC, was not far from our house. It was founded by the London Missionary Society which was Congregational. My future wife's father, J. B. Tayler, used to teach there, but by the time I entered that school, he had already moved on to teach at Yenching University in Beijing. We never got to know each other at the time. Because it was a missionary school, every morning at ten o'clock we had to attend a Christian service for half an hour. We sang Christian hymns and read the Bible in English. Very few of the students actually became Christians. We all went there because it was rather a good school, with good Chinese and English teachers. Of course the English teachers were all earnest Christian missionaries with English university degrees. In a way I rather enjoyed reading a bit of the Bible every morning. We were usually taught from the New Testament, but I enjoyed reading the Old Testament with all its interesting stories of incest and murder, and good poetic passages. When the teacher was giving the sermon, I would be reading the Book of Isaiah or Hezekiah, or the Book of Song of Solomon instead. I also enjoyed singing hymns loudly, to exercise my lungs. Though I never became a Christian, I learned some knowledge of Western culture and literature through this experience and it was useful.

I enjoyed most of my school lessons. I was well above other

students in English and Chinese literature and I enjoyed learning mathematics, physics, chemistry, geography and history. I liked proving certain theorems in plane geometry and adding in the end Q.E.D. (*quod erat demonstrandum*) because it was a good exercice in logical reasoning. I also enjoyed doing laboratory work in my chemistry classes, mixing sulphuric acid with potassium phosphate and other compounds. Before fifteen or sixteen, I was rather interested in physics, and wanted to be an inventor. I tried to produce a perpetual motion machine, some sort of metal ball that would go on revolving and revolving. Of course this runs counter to the simple law of friction and I finally gave up after having wasted a lot of time. By the time I was in senior middle school, my interest in the physical sciences had waned, and I turned back to English and Chinese literature and ancient history.

From my English textbooks, I had already learned some passages of prose by Ruskin, Goldsmith, Addison, Swift, and others, and a bit of English poetry by Sir Walter Scott, Wordsworth, Grey, Shelley, Byron, and Keats. But most of my reading in Western literature was done outside school. There was a bookshop selling foreign books at that time in the French concession. The bookshop was called the Xiuhe Bookstore. It was owned by a man from Fujian province named Lin Xiuhe. He had probably learned his trade in Hong Kong because he was rather intelligent and modern-minded and knew how to order his books from abroad. I would go to that book shop every other day during the week to browse through his books and buy some, or go through his various book catalogues and order books through him. Books from abroad would arrive promptly within two months and I could pay in Chinese currency. At first I was interested in children's and juvenile books, tales by the Brothers Grimm, Hans Christian Andersen, Oscar Wilde, Lewis Carroll's *Alice in Wonderland, Through the Looking*

Glass, Barrie's *Peter Pan*, Stevenson's *Treasure Island*, Jules Verne's *Twenty Thousand Leagues Under the Sea*, and the like. I found some of Rider Haggard's adventure stories fascinating. Later I read a lot of Alexander Dumas's historical romances, like the D'Artagnan series from *The Three Musketeers* to *The Man in the Iron Mask* and *The Son of Porthos*. By the time I was in senior middle school, I could read books in English very quickly, and I read a lot of Western literature in English and in English translations. At that time, quite a bit of European and American literature had been translated into Chinese as well. I find it almost impossible to give a list of the books I read then. Usually I read a book or two daily and was thus able to cover most of the best-known European and American novelists and poets. I became very fond of ancient Greek literature too, in English translations, and as I could not find a teacher to teach me Greek in Tianjin, I wanted to go abroad to study it. This was one of the factors which motivated me to go and study classics at Oxford.

At that time I began to be interested in politics too, and I felt intensely patriotic. I read the Italian reformer and revolutionary Giuseppe Mazzini's book *The Duties of Man* in an English translation, and wanted to take him as my model. After I went to London, I bought his entire works in English translation and read them avidly. I found them in a second-hand bookshop in Charing Cross. In those days before the Second World War, one could find all sorts of odd books in English in those bookshops between the Charing Cross and Tottenham Court Road. But this jumps ahead of my story and I must relate more about my early years and how I eventually went to England.

3

Young Chinese Students

Young Chinese school students, during the late twenties and the early thirties, had very strong feelings against foreign oppression. Already 1923 there was a movement to ban the buying of Japanese goods, because during the reign of Yuan Shikai, when the young republic had just been founded, there had been a secret treaty with Japan giving the Japanese various concessions and special privileges in China. When this became known to the public, there was a great uproar and the treaty was annulled. In 1925 another such movement took place in Shanghai, this one organized by students and workers. On May 30th of that year, the British police in the concessions opened fire and massacred some students and workers. This came to be called the "May 30th Incident", and every year after that Chinese students and civilians would commemorate it as a day of national shame. So when I was a junior middle school student, I and other students would organize a strike, refusing to attend classes given by English teachers. We did that at least twice. The school would be paralysed and our English principal, Dr. Hart, was furious. The school authorities threatened to dismiss all the students involved, but since I was a ringleader and refused to be an exemplary student, and since my family was wealthy and well-known in Tianjin, it all came to nothing in the end. I, however, gained prestige with my fellow classmates.

In 1931, the Japanese army stationed in the north-eastern provinces of China attacked local Chinese garrisons and began their occupation of that region. So the puppet state of Manchukuo ("The Manchu Kingdom") was set up in Changchun, and the deposed Qing dynasty's last Manchu emperor was made the puppet head of a puppet state. Patriotic Chinese forces were organized in the four provinces of the north-east to resist the advance of the Japanese forces of aggression, but the central government under Chiang Kai-shek had its hands full fighting the Communists in central and southern China and did nothing to support the patriotic forces. All of China was in an uproar, especially north China, against this Japanese aggression. I and several dozen of my classmates at school started military training every morning before classes, coached by a retired army officer whom we paid with our pocket money. During that winter we persisted, for two or three months, in doing military exercises on the school grounds. Of course this was futile, and gradually our group dwindled and finally we gave it up. But I stayed on till the very end. I usually went to school early, more than half an hour before classes began, and my family did not know about this, or at least they did nothing to stop my foolish gesture. But I and other students and teachers contributed money to the guerrilla forces in the north.

The year after, in 1932, the Japanese started to make trouble again in Shanghai, attacking the local garrison, the Nineteenth Route Army. There was bitter fighting between the Chinese and the Japanese aggressors, that lasted for more than two months in Shanghai. Every day we avidly read the newspapers for war reports, and whenever there was news of a successful exchange, we passed the good news around to friends and neighbours and shouted with joy. All China sent contributions of money to the Shanghai front to help our patriotic soldiers. The central government again did nothing to help. Finally the Nineteenth Route Army had to withdraw from Shanghai. The Japanese, however, were not yet ready to occupy the Yangtze valley. They still had to consolidate their gains in the north-east. So they signed a truce and withdrew from Shanghai for the time being. I was then in the first year of my senior middle school. During this period, as the Chinese people's patriotic feelings were running high, sporadic fighting would break out between the local police force and Japanese rogues in Tianjin. So our family decided, for safety's sake, to move out of the Japanese concession into the French concession.

Apart from juvenile and hotheaded patriotic activities, my main interest at the time was reading and writing poetry. I read much Chinese classical poetry, from the earliest periods to modern times. Poetry with patriotic content, from the end of the Qing dynasty, by writers like Huang Zhongxian, Kang Youwei, Liang Qichao, and others made a strong impression on me and I wrote poems imitating their style. I remember that one poem I wrote on an Italian marble lion, which I had bought, mentioned the founding of the Italian republic and Giuseppe Mazzini, comparing Italy with China. I lost this poem later on. Another poem, on snow, was inspired by Shelley's "Ode to a Skylark". In that poem I compared falling snowflakes to poetry, to music, to warriors, and to revolutionary martyrs. I ended the poem with lines expressing my wish that I could some day sacrifice myself to revolution, to wipe clean the world still full of filth. Such is the juvenile fancy of a boy in his teens — I was then only seventeen — but it showed my early fervent patriotic and revolutionary feelings, and it probably showed the path I was going to take in later years. I still have this poem. It was sent back to me some years ago by a former classmate, together

with whom I would write poems. He had made a copy, and so these many years later it returned to me.

I was at that time also reading a lot of Western poetry. In the beginning I was interested in the American poet Longfellow and the English poet Tennyson because they were the easiest to read and understand for a young Chinese student, then I read Byron and Shelley and others of the Romantic period. Towards the end of my middle school days I was mainly interested in French poets like Baudelaire, Valéry, Rimbaud, Gautier, and Mallarmé. Many young Chinese intellectuals seemed to be especially interested in that period of French literature for some reason or other. I had known quite a few friends who felt like that. I remember one book I liked at that time was Gautier's novel *Mademoiselle de Maupin*, which could not be considered as any sort of great literature. At the same time I tried to translate some poems I liked into classical Chinese. I remember one of the earliest attempts at translation was some poems by Longfellow, then some songs from Shakespeare's plays, like "Full Fathom Five Thy Father Lies" from *The Tempest*, then some poetic fragments of Sappho, the Greek poetess. Of course the latter was from an English translation since I knew no Greek at that time. This was the beginning of my interest in literary translations. I forgot to mention there was also Milton's "L'allegro" and "Il Penseroso", which, I also translated into classical Chinese verse.

I remember one amusing episode which happened in 1933 when I was eighteen. We then had a new Chinese principal for our school. Formerly the school principal had been British, an old missionary teacher named Dr. Hart. But by that time the local Chinese authorities had decided that the school must be Chinese and we should have a Chinese principal. So the school decided to invite a Mr. Huang Zuolin to be the new principal. Huang was then just back from England. He was a student from Manchester. He had studied drama at university. He only stayed at our school for little more than a year. Later he went back to study Western theatre at Cambridge, then came back to China again as a university professor and later became an authority on theatre and one of China's best stage directors. He is still living, now in his eighties. He is a very good man, a man of moral integrity. I know him well and have a great admiration for him. During that year when he was principal at my school, I had one confrontation with him. I was the leader of a student strike commemorating the day of national disgrace. He came out as the newly appointed principal, telling us to end the strike or face the consequences. I defied him. Later on, of course, we students realized he was a good man and the matter was closed. During that year in Tianjin he wrote a historical play in English about the Warring States period when the King of Wu was enamoured of a beautiful woman called Xi Shi and lost his kingdom in the end. The play was put on stage at some experimental theatre for two or three performances and only for a limited audience. The actors and actresses were all amateurs with no theatrical experience. They had to be able to speak English and were all youngsters selected from different schools. The girl who played the part of the heroine Xi Shi was called Madeleine Zhang, the fiancée of a classmate of mine called Robert Li. I was given the part of a soldier who came to demand the king's surrender before he committed suicide. This was the first and only occasion when I acted in a play on a stage. I still remember that I only had one line to speak, obviously a very minor part. When I, the soldier, rushed on stage with sword in hand, I spoke sternly to the king in English, "Put down your sword, sir. There is no need for bloodshed." Then the king, glaring at me wildly, realized the hopelessness and fell on his sword and died. Later when I was a student at Oxford, I

visited Huang in Cambridge and mentioned this episode as a joke and we both had a good laugh over it.

In 1934 I graduated, ready to enter Chinese university. At that time China had several good universities. In Beijing the most prestigious universities were Tsinghua University, Peking University, and Yenching University. I wanted to study at Tsinghua University or Peking University, but Yenching University had its entrance examination earlier and Yenching, being an American missionary university, had a special relationship with my school. A good student from my school needed only to have tests in English, mathematics, and an I.Q. test. I took the test, and the examiners thought my I.Q. and English were excellent and said I could skip the first year and enter university as a second year student. I wanted, however, to take the other entrance examinations to Tsinghua and Peking Universities, but something else happened that changed the whole plan and made me go to England instead.

4

To Journey Abroad

To journey abroad for study was hardly part of my plans at the time. But there was an old English teacher in my school named C. H. B. Longman. He taught physics and other subjects and his wife taught English literature. Both of them were very fond of me, considering me their favourite student. Mr. Longman that year decided to take a holiday back to England. He planned a roundabout trip, going across the Pacific to see America, then travelling overland to the East Coast and taking another boat across the Atlantic to reach London. He offered to take me to London and find me a private tutor there to study Greek and Latin before entering an English university. One of my classmates, a boy named Robert Li, wanted to go with me to study in England too, so I was to have reliable companions all the way. My mother thought it was a good idea. My family had plenty of money, and the exchange rate for foreign money then was very favourable: I could exchange four yuan for one pound. Later one needed eight yuan or more for one pound. So financially I did not have to worry. My family could easily pay for my English education for several years. At that time in the early thirties, air travel was rare if not impossible, and most people went abroad by sea. I remember that at that time the fastest passenger ships across the Indian Ocean were two Italian liners, the Conte Verde and Conte Rosso, but we booked our tickets on a Canadian liner. It was one of the Empress boats, but I have since forgotten its name, either the Empress of Japan or the Empress of Russia. This boat took nearly a month from Shanghai to Vancouver, a few days longer than the Italian liners. But we were in no hurry, and we could see Japan and Hawaii on the way. It was summer when we had our passports and tickets ready, and we set off by train to Nanjing and then Shanghai for the boat. My mother and my English tutor Sarah accompanied me all the way. There was also our family's old servant Pan Fu, who was in a way the family steward. He was to look after the ladies and the young master, attending to all their needs. My classmate, Robert Li, came along with his fiancée Madeleine Zhang, who was going to the United States to stay with her uncle, then the Chinese consul in the States. Nothing much happened during the train journey. We were well looked after all the way, but this was my first journey outside Tianjin and everything looked novel and exciting. When we were small, my younger sisters had been to the seaside in Beidaihe with my uncle once or twice, but I was never allowed to leave Tianjin for fear of accidents or kidnappers, because I was the only male offspring. We first arrived in Nanjing, were met by some former family servants and relatives and stayed there for a couple of days, then continued our journey to Shanghai. I remember when we arrived in Shanghai it was very hot. Fortunately we were put in one of the best hotels and there was air-conditioning, so it was quite comfortable. Air-conditioning was still rare in those days in north China, and I found it very interesting.

I met Mr. and Mrs. Longman on the boat as well as my classmate Robert Li and his fiancée Madeleine. The Canadian liner then set sail, first stopping in Kobe, Yokohama, and Tokyo in Japan and we went ashore each time to see these cities. Since the Sino-Japanese

War had not yet started, even though there was some feeling of hostility towards the Japanese, we were able to roam around a bit without mishap. Tokyo in those days still looked rather crowded and shabby after their last earthquake. Kobe and Yokohama looked more prosperous, and we found some very beautiful scenic spots with pine trees and rocks. After Japan, our boat went on to Hawaii. Honolulu only had one long and beautiful boulevard with American shops and other conveniences. Behind the main boulevard were shabby quarters where the natives lived. We visited one nice aquarium and enjoyed the sub-tropical atmosphere. The Hawaiian people were very hospitable to us as tourists, and we were loaded with flower garlands and cheap and delicious fresh pineapples. We took a lot of pineapples to our boat and enjoyed eating them for days.

After the trip to Hawaii, as we were nearing the West Coast of the States, a quarrel began in our group. Mr. Longman, the old missionary, felt that as our guardian on the journey he was morally and physically responsible for us. He had never been to the United States himself and had quite a prejudice against the lack of morals in the United States. Since the uncle of my classmate Robert's fiancée was the Chinese consul in America, Madeleine said her uncle would take us around to the American casinos and cabarets for sightseeing. Mr. Longman was against the idea. He said that as long as he was our guardian, he would not let us do anything irresponsible before we reached England. Madeleine could go with her uncle if she liked, but I and Robert must stay with him all the time, to keep ourselves safe from the American gangsters and prostitutes. We argued and argued with him but he was adamant, and he was rather rude to Madeleine, forcing her to tears. Robert said nothing, but I flared up and openly denounced him as a despot, saying that in the future we would not listen to his words any more. We parted then in anger. The gentle Mrs. Longman could do nothing to save the situation. This quarrel persisted all the way into America. So I was no longer on speaking terms with the Longmans. Even after we arrived in England, and Mr. Longman found us a hotel and got me a private tutor and we parted, I was still resentful of him. I never visited them in England nor wrote a letter to apologize for my behaviour. I must have hurt the old couple very much, for they were really very fond of me. I was then rather headstrong, and in my family, since I had always been the young master, I would not suffer myself to be bullied by anyone. It might also have had something to do with the Chinese people's feeling that all Western imperialists wanted to bully us, and at that time I shared that feeling very much. I think now that I was rather unfair to old Mr. Longman and this is one incident which I recall now with some regret.

We arrived in Vancouver and from there went straight to Seattle, leaving Canada and entering U.S. territory since Seattle was just next door to Vancouver. In Seattle we were met by Madeleine's uncle and spent a couple of days there. Madeleine's uncle took us sightseeing and we enjoyed seeing all the open space and woodlands. Seattle was a beautiful city, with a good climate. I cannot remember doing much else there, except eating some would-be Chinese meals in a small would-be Chinese restaurant. From Seattle we went on to Yellowstone Park and the Rockies. All these excursions had been carefully planned beforehand by Mr. Longman in Tianjin. We stayed in cabins or cottages set up for college students or tourists, nowadays probably called hostels. We saw the hot springs and other scenic spots. I specially enjoyed walking by myself in the Grand Canyon, taking in all the magnificent scenery. After three or four days in Yellowstone Park, we travelled east to Chicago, where the World's Fair was to be held that year. Mr. Longman, who had never been to the States, only thought of Chicago as a city of gangsters, an impression he must have received from Hollywood films seen in Tianjin. He would not have wished to have seen that city except for that World's Fair. We spent nearly a week at the World's Fair, visiting pavilions organized by Eastern European and Islamic countries and eating strange Greek and Spanish foods. We felt as if we were doing a grand tour of the whole world.

I especially remember spending one evening in an open-air theatre, listening to the famous Italian conductor Toscanini giving his interpretation of a Beethoven symphony, whether the Fourth or the Fifth, I do not now remember. This was the first time I went to listen to a Western symphonic orchestra. Later in London I went to many concerts, but this was the first occasion. Of course I had already had some musical education in Tianjin before, but at that time I could only enjoy short pieces such as Beethoven's minuets, Schubert's "Ave Maria", Schumann's "Träumerei", Debussy's "L'après-midi d'un faune", Ravel's "Bolero", and the like. All those I had learned to appreciate through listening to gramophone records. I also remember an Italian opera company had once visited Tianjin, probably in 1932 or 1933. They gave several performances, and I went to practically all of them. Their repertoire had included "Rigoletto", "La Bohème", "Madame Butterfly", and others. Since then I had developed a taste for Italian opera, but I had always preferred Puccini to Verdi and others. There was an Italian serenade I had especially liked. It was Toselli's "Serenata", which starts with the words, "Like a golden dream in my heart...." Of course I don't suppose it was from an opera anyway. But no more about my early education in Western music. I am digressing from my subject and must come back to our tour in the United States.

5

From Chicago to London

From Chicago's World Fair we went on to Niagara Falls. It was of course entirely Mr. Longman's idea to see the Falls. It was certainly spectacular, but I was not too impressed by it. The thing that made the strongest impression on me during that visit was seeing so many American Indians selling souvenirs or lolling around aimlessly. They certainly looked like a poorer class of people and appeared rather apathetic and unhappy. In Tianjin I had seen many poor people, many with much more wretched lives. But since these Indians were physically different from the white people, especially the colour of their skin, they struck me with the idea that they were second-class citizens. So although the United States boasted of her wonderful democracy, I felt there was still social inequality and injustice for their national minority people. This is not just an after thought. I felt rather strongly about it at the time and I had the same feeling later in New York, when we went to see the American writer Alexander Woolcott and found him to have a Negro servant. Although I had many servants in Tianjin, I always was on familiar terms with them, and they were all Chinese just like me. It had never struck me in the same way. I do not mean this as a criticism of the American social system. Rather I am just recording the impressions of a nineteen-year-old Chinese boy. Maybe at that time I had too idealistic and preconceived an idea of America's democracy, thinking it would be more perfect. In China we had a very bad record of the barbarous treatment of the minority peoples by the Han Chinese. In the past, tens of thousands of them had been massacred. Still, never having witnessed such acts myself, when I saw the social injustices that existed in the America I had idealized, it came as a bit of a shock.

From Niagara Falls we went on to our last stop in America, New York. I was very impressed by all the skyscrapers there. I found them more fascinating than Niagara Falls. They were not beautiful, rather they were ugly and imposing, like a nightmare. It was all very glittering and modern, not like our dusty and rather old fashioned north China. We visited all the tallest skyscrapers, the Empire State Building, the Chrysler Building, Times Square. We first stayed in a small hotel and then moved to the International House on Riverside Drive, a large hostel for foreign students, with self-help meals in a canteen, and cheap. The surroundings were quiet and far from the fashionable parts of the city and the crowds. Madeleine's uncle took Robert and myself to some cabarets. Mr. Longman took a cold and aloof attitude towards this but did not interfere. He never went with us to those "decadent" places. Madeleine's uncle also took us to call on his friend, the well-known American writer Alexander Woolcott. This writer had just written a popular book of essays called *While Rome Burns*, which was very well reviewed. Madeleine gave me a copy of the book, but I never read it. I was not familiar with American literature and at that time had only read some of Mark Twain's stories and Washington Irving's *Sketch Book* and *The Alhambra*, and some Edgar Allan Poe. We went to Woolcott's house, were greeted by a Negro servant dressed in livery, but the master was out and not returning for some time. So I never met this famous writer.

I remember one amusing episode when I was staying at the International House on Riverside Drive. There was a nice park within walking distance from the guest-house. I usually took a stroll there in the morning or sat under a tree watching the squirrels darting here and there on the grass or on the trees. One morning, as I was watching some squirrels in the park before my breakfast, a shabbily dressed man came up. He was less than medium height, looking rather furtive and worried. He walked past me, glanced back, then came back again. At first he hesitated, then suddenly came up to me raising both fists in a boxer's stance. I was staring at him because he looked rather suspicious. When he put up his fists, as if to attack me, I involuntarily raised my fists too, shielding my face in self-defence. He suddenly grinned, as if we had greeted each other in silence and understood each other. He put down his fists and said: "Hi, buddy! You're just the guy I want. How's about I make you a proposition?" I replied: "What proposition?" trying to behave like an American gangster in a Hollywood film. He explained he was "in a fix". He was the manager of a boxing contest to take place in New York that evening. It was only to be a featherweight contest, the opponents being a black man against a white man. Unfortunately the black boy had got a fever in the morning and could not appear that evening. So he had to find a substitute. It was to be a put-up show, with the white boy defeating the black boy, not really hurting him. When he saw me put up my fists in self-defence, he felt that he had found "the right guy" and wanted to offer me a "proposition": take the place of the black boy. Then he would have a "Chink" instead of a "Nigger", and that would be good box-office. I was offered "two hundred bucks", for which I thanked him but firmly declined, saying I was just

passing through, on my way to England to study and did not want to get involved in a boxing contest. He was disappointed and went away. Two hundred U.S. dollars in those days was probably quite a handsome offer, but being a rich man's son, it meant nothing to me. Anyway I could hardly return to my guardian Mr. Longman with a bloody nose or broken jaw. Thus I missed my chance to take part in a boxing contest in America.

Our ten-day tour of New York was over. Robert and I had to continue on with the Longmans to England, leaving Madeleine behind with her uncle. She was to continue her studies in America. Before our departure, Madeleine was tearful but tried to put up a brave countenance. She said over and over again that we must both write her often and not forget her. She told me especially that I must see that Robert wrote to her every month, if not every week. She said wistfully: "When shall we three meet again?" to which I replied with the line from Shakespeare's *Macbeth*: "In thunder, lightning or rain", and we laughed. Actually we never met again after that. After we arrived in England Robert wrote to her every month at first but then got more and more interested in playing tennis and chasing cabaret girls. Soon he did not write her any more. Robert did not succeed in passing his entrance examination to Cambridge until two years later. By then, in 1936 or 1937, Madeleine had gone to live in Santiago, Chile, her uncle having been appointed ambassador or minister to Chile by the Kuomintang government. She was desperate and wrote me letters urging me to persuade Robert to go see her in Santiago. Robert visited her there once and they decided to break off their engagement. I heard later that she married an American. Robert did not get his degree but decided to stay on in England. I don't know whether they are still alive. The last time I saw Robert in England, his health was very poor. That was eight or nine years ago.

From New York we boarded another boat to cross the Atlantic to Southampton and London. The journey took us some time. Nothing much happened during the trip and I found it very dull. I only remember playing chess once or twice with an old English doctor. During the whole journey, starting from the Pacific until this Atlantic journey, we seldom talked with other foreign passengers on board. I was still shy of speaking to strangers in English, but by this time, towards the end of the journey I suddenly found my confidence and started chatting with this Englishman when playing chess. After that I seemed to be able to speak freely and no longer felt tongue-tied.

The interlude during the Atlantic journey afforded me the opportunity to jot down some reminiscences of the previous few weeks. I wrote them in English, in a series of essays, and concocted a small volume. I was reading D. H. Lawrence's two volumes of travel essays at the time. One was called *Twilight in Italy* and the other *Sea and Sardinia*. I liked these essays very much and while writing my own, I consciously imitated their style. I gave my volume the title in Latin *Terra Marique* (By Land and Sea). This was because I had just begun trying to learn some Latin, and Caesar's *Gallic Wars* was the first book I read. The phrase *terra marique* appears many times in that work and I remember thinking it appropriate for my essays. Now it seems to me rather childish and ridiculous, but at that time I was rather proud of my meagre knowledge of Latin and wanted to show it off. I posted this manuscript back to my sister Amy, but later on it was lost. I can't remember now what I wrote in that little book. My sister later told me that I seemed to be in love with Madeleine.

6

First Impressions

First impressions of London were that it was a depressing place, perhaps because when we arrived it was getting dark. London at that time was polluted, and to my mind's eye, shabby. The train was old-fashioned and not very clean, and the whole city seemed wrapped in fog, dank and chilly. It was certainly a let-down compared with the glittering New World. We first stayed in an old hotel called the Royal Hotel on Russell Square. Mr. Longman later took me to a private tutor to study Latin and Greek. This tutor, whose name I now can't remember, taught me Greek, but he had a colleague teach me Latin. They both had that down-and-out look of poor scholars. They could not have been earning very much at tutoring, for I did not see or get to know any other students. My Greek tutor was an Oxford graduate, so when I first met him he asked me:

"Do you want to go to Oxford or Cambridge? They are the two best universities."

"Which is the better university?" I asked.

"Why, Oxford of course. But it is harder to get in," he replied.

"Then I'll go to Oxford." And so it was decided. Robert was interviewed by another private tutor, so I do not know what he said. Later he stood for the entrance examination to Cambridge.

My intention was to go to England to study Western classics, Greek and Latin, because at that time I was fascinated by the wealth of ancient Greek and Latin literature, having read Homer, the Greek tragedies, Livy, a bit of Plato's dialogues, as well as Vergil and other works in English translation. In Tianjin I could not find any one to teach me such subjects, as I think I have already mentioned. Only in the spring of 1934 could my family find me an old Greek merchant who had agreed to give me an hour or two every week for the study of Greek. This lasted only two months, for that man knew no classical Greek, only modern Greek, so I only memorized the Greek alphabet, a bit of grammar, and one or two passages from the Greek New Testament. I learned a bit of Latin grammar from a Latin primer by myself. When I went to London, I found I had to start more or less from the very beginning.

My private tutor was very conscientious and every morning I had to go to his place from my hotel by the London underground to take my two-hour tutorial. He would assign me exercises which I would do at my lodgings every evening for another two or three hours or more before and after supper. The written exercises consisted of translating simple sentences from English into ancient Greek, and translating short paragraphs of ancient Greek into English.

I don't remember where my tutor lived, but it was quite some distance from my place, so travelling to and fro and doing my lessons and exercises more or less filled my days. I hardly had time for anything else: occasionally I managed to look at and buy a few books from second-hand bookshops between Russell Square, Charing Cross, and Tottenham Court Road. As I mentioned before, when we first came to London, we stayed in a small hotel on Russell Square, but by the time I started my lessons, I had moved to a boarding house for foreign students nearby, owned by an English couple. I paid my board and lodging every week, as this was more convenient than staying in a hotel, though not necessarily cheaper. My landlady and her husband were a greedy and miserly lower middle-class couple. I don't think the meals they gave the students were anything as good as hotel food. My Greek tutor was a good, honest Oxford graduate, but unlucky in his career. I remember he had a ruddy, round face and always wore a threadbare tweed jacket. He smoked a pipe incessantly, which looked none too clean, and he had rather dirty fingernails.

My Chinese classmate Robert had by then moved to some other lodgings, probably introduced to him through Madeleine's uncle. Though I rather disliked my boarding house, it had one redeeming feature. There were two or three other foreign students boarding there, and among these boys, there was one I particularly liked,  and we saw eye to eye. He was a Romanian student named Paul Zotta. By then I was rather tired of my classmate Robert Li's company. Robert had interests different from mine. He was crazy about tennis and theatrical people, while I preferred spending my time reading. Paul Zotta, however, was a bookworm too, so we had much in common. Together we bought many books from the second-hand bookshops and read anything we could lay our hands on: Plato, Aristotle, Bacon, Schopenhauer, Nietzsche, Bergson, Berkeley, and Sigmund Freud; some anthropology, including Frazer's *Golden Bough*, as well as Greek mythology and religion; and ancient history and literature. Paul Zotta and I were interested in more or less the same books, and we exchanged books, reading them late into the evenings after doing our homework. Paul always felt I had the more active mind, so he said I was D'Artagnan and he Porthos, after Dumas' *The Three Musketeers*. But there was no Aramis or Athos. Paul was sent to England by the Romanian government and said he was a royalist, attached to somebody high in a ministry. But we never discussed these things in detail and were not very interested at that time in European politics. We got on very well for nearly a year in that boarding house. In the spring of 1935, after I took the entrance examination to Oxford, I changed my boarding house to another place in Maida Vale in the western part of London. Paul by then had probably returned to Romania. After that we never met again, but in 1938 or 1939, he wrote me one letter from Europe, still remembering our former friendship and reminding me of that comparison to D'Artagnan and Porthos. Then there was silence. I don't think I ever replied to his letter. I still think fondly of him and that period. He was then my only friend.

Nothing much happened during that winter of 1934, apart from preparing for my examination and reading books. It may be that I first went to visit Paris by myself, or it could have been in 1935, the next year. I don't remember now. As for looking for second-hand books in Charing Cross and Tottenham Court Road in the late afternoon, I only remember buying a whole set of Giuseppi Mazzini's works and a whole set of Heine's works in English translation and a whole set of Jules Verne's novels in French. I read Mazzini and Heine quickly, but I don't think I read all of Jules Verne's novels. I found it rather hard to try to read them in French and decided to leave them for the future. However, during that period, my reading ability of French never improved so I never read them in their original language. I remember that by accident I got rather interested in collecting a few first editions. One evening as I left the tube station on my way home, I went into a small second-hand bookshop near Russell Square and found a little volume of verse in a corner. It was only marked three pence, so I bought it. The name of the poem was "Lara". There was no name of the writer. It was printed anonymously in 1814 or thereabouts.

I thought it sounded familiar and decided to find out who was the writer. I discovered it was one of Byron's early poems and a first edition for only three pence! I was delighted. After that I would occasionally go in to look for first editions of English books, hoping to make more unexpected finds. I collected several nineteenth-century first or second editions, including one of Dickens' novels, one by Shelley, and some by later poets, but I found them rather expensive and soon gave up the hobby. I later gave several of these first editions to an English friend, Tony Durrell, but never again did I find an anonymous first edition as cheap as three pence.

After working hard at Greek and Latin for five months, in the spring of 1935 I went up to Oxford for the entrance examination. At that time it was difficult for an Asian or African student to enter Oxford. There were only one or two vacancies for them in certain colleges. The college which accepted me was Merton College which was the earliest of the Oxford colleges, but Christchurch, Balliol and Magdalen were probably better known. I passed the written test without too much difficulty, and then I had to have an interview. The Dean or Examiner who interviewed me asked me:

"How long have you been studying Greek and Latin?"

"I have studied them for five months under a private tutor in London."

"What? Only five months? Then it must be a fluke.… Well, Mr. Yang, you know our English boys have usually had seven or eight years of Latin and Greek before they enter college. Although you've passed the test, your Greek and Latin could not be solid enough. We strongly advise you to postpone entering college for another year. You'd better study more Greek and Latin for the course. Besides, our quota for Asian students this year is limited to one person, and we already have another candidate, a Mr. Zhang (or

Wu) from Canton, who is studying history. We shall accept you for 1936 Michaelmas Term (i.e. Autumn)."

So my fate was sealed. I had to wait another year to enter Merton. During this year I was at a loose end. I did not want to pay another year for my tutorials and I did not want to stay in the same boarding house. So I moved to another boarding house in west London, in Maida Vale, where Robert was also staying. But I was not to stay in London very much this time.

7

An Excursion in Europe

An excursion in Europe was an option that appealed to me very much during this interlude. At that time it was quite cheap to live in Europe, with a very favourable exchange rate. One pound sterling was worth about four hundred French francs. So I decided to spend most of the summer of 1935 through spring 1936 in Europe. During that period I went to Paris at least twice. I cannot now remember the exact dates. I remember I went once with Robert and some other Chinese students for a fortnight or more and took them around because I had already been there before so could act as their guide. I got to know some parts of Paris very well. I really liked Montmartre and Montparnasse and the Champs Elysées. I did a bit of sightseeing in Paris, visiting the Louvre, the Eiffel Tower, and even going to Versailles to see the garden and palace. I remember that I went to the cemetery of Père Lachaise at least twice, being interested in the graves of Oscar Wilde and some French writers. At the time I was interested in the legend of Abelard and Heloise. I also wanted to see the wall where the communards were killed at the end of the Paris Commune, because I had read Karl Marx's articles on the event and was very moved by them. I suppose this was my first introduction to Marxism. Outside Paris and its environs, I remember spending about a month in Lausanne and the French speaking parts of Switzerland. I spent more than ten days in Lausanne at the university to improve my hearing and reading ability in French. I attended some lectures there, but found them too advanced and did not manage to improve my knowledge of French very much. In Paris, however, I did attend some lectures given by several famous French sinologues like Maspero and Granet. Because they were lecturing on ancient poets, subjects with which I was familiar, my comprehension was much better. I remember that in Lausanne I had two French books with me which I read with interest. One was the French writer Renan's *Vie de Jésus* and the other was Pierre Loti's *Vers Ispahan*, his travel essay on Persia. I spent several weeks with a Swiss family in Switzerland, whether it was in Geneva or somewhere else I cannot remember. I got a lot of good milk and cream, but this did not improve my knowledge of French very much. I went once to see the Chateau Chillon on a rock over the river where Byron wrote his poem "The Prisoner of Chillon". I went to some ski spots in the Alps for a day or two, but I did not try skiing, and I only did a little mountain climbing, nothing arduous, in the snow, just to get a sense of the Alps. I even went to the abbey where they produced the famous sweet liqueur, Chartreuse, and bought some chocolates, but this might have been as late as 1937. My memory of those days, as I roamed aimlessly around France and Switzerland, is very blurred. I cannot now recall the dates, since I never had the habit of keeping a diary.

In the summer of 1935, I decided to go on an organized Mediterranean cruise. I made my booking with a London travel agent, Thomas Cook. I booked a first-class ticket, which was unnecessarily extravagant, but at that time I felt I had plenty of money to burn and wanted to make the pleasure cruise as comfortable as possible. The cruise included Gibraltar, Algiers,

Lisbon, Sicily, Malta, Greece, and the Aegean, Istanbul, and Egypt, lasting nearly a month all together. As a first-class passenger, I had to dress properly every night for dinner. I wore a bow tie with stiff shirt. All this I thought was rather fun. I learned how to do a bow tie quite easily. My companions were all wealthy British and foreign professionals who were cordial and pleasant. The journey went smoothly and I saw the usual things and sights laid on for the tourists. I bought little souvenirs in Gibraltar and saw the monkeys on the hills of Algiers and was surrounded by a lot of urchins asking for money from the tourists. They stretched out their hands and cried: "Dinero! Dinero!" and I answered with the few Spanish phrases I had learned: "No tengo dinero", which made them all hoot with laughter, repeating after me, "No tengo dinero!" It was all fun. In Sicily I remember sharing half a bottle of chianti with an old fat Portuguese merchant in the shade outside a cafe when a waiter came over and asked, first pointing at the old merchant and then at me: "Papa? Figlio?" and I answered: "Si, si" and we had a good laugh. I suppose wearing a Western suit, I could have been mistaken for an old merchant's son in spite of my slanting eyes. There is much in common between a Chinese and a Portuguese or Italian in terms of looks, and the colour of the skin is not too noticeably different.

In Greece I visited the Parthenon and the Piraeus, and had a pleasant meal in a garden, with lots of figs, olives, and wine on Mitylene or Lesbos, the home islands of Alcaeus and Sappho. I took back to the ship a huge bottle of local sweet wine and got quite drunk on it. The trip to Istanbul was a little disappointing. I was mistaken for a Japanese using a fake Chinese passport. The Turkish authorities in those days were very suspicious of Japanese spies for some reason or other and could not understand why a young Chinese student would want to go to Istanbul, most

Chinese students in those days being so poor. So they kept me on board the ship and would not let me go ashore for half a day. I only had a few hours to rush through the main mosques and museums.

We had about three days in Egypt so I stayed in a hotel in Cairo and visited the Sphinx and the Great Pyramids nearby, and thoroughly enjoyed myself. The best hotel in Cairo at that time was the Mena House, but I chose a cheaper middle class hotel. It was either called the Metropol or the Semiramis. I would go back to the hotel and refresh myself with a bath and cool drink after trotting around or riding a camel in the dust and sultry sun. I bought myself some fake scarabs and a beautiful, old curved dagger with an ivory handle and intricate designs for five pounds at the bazaar. But the most memorable adventure was going out at night  to the desert with a hired guide. I think on that occasion I started after nine in the evening. I was riding a big Arabian horse with the guide following me. We wandered on, passing the pyramids in the desert. The moonlight made everything look magical and unreal. Then the Egyptian guide said he was good at fortune-telling. If I would give him a piece of silver to make a sign on the palm of his hand, he would tell my fortune. So I gave him a half-crown piece and he made the magical sign. Naturally the money disappeared into his pocket. He then told me how he could see before his eyes the sea. He was viewing a scene over the Atlantic. There, a beautiful English maiden with golden hair was pining for me. We had not yet met, but we would do so in the near future, and there would be wonderful things and many adventures awaiting us. Anyway he babbled on and asked for more silver. I was amused by all this trickery but did not give him another half-crown. Near midnight we went to an open-air cafe and a show. We had some sweet, rather sickly flavoured cool drink and watched a swarthy Egyptian woman do a belly dance. Naturally I paid for the drink and the show. It cost me a couple of pounds all together I suppose, but it was worth it. The night in the desert and the moonlight made it a haunting, unforgettable experience.

Our stop at Lisbon was another amusing experience. I went one night to a place called Cintra where there was a famous casino for roulette gambling. Although I had been to some Western-style gambling places before — in Tianjin I had already been once or twice to the race course to bet on horses, and in London I had been to a dog-racing stadium and in the north of England had bet on horses at a minor horse-racing track — I had never tried roulette. This was my first and only occasion. As soon as I entered the casino, I was greeted by a young girl who spoke English. She was quite young, well-dressed, and pretty. We chatted and I bought her a drink. Then I went and changed five pounds worth of chips. We went to the roulette table where some other people were already gambling. I asked her what was her favourite number and she said: "Seventeen." It might have been her age but I did not think so. She was quite young, but looked experienced. She was probably quite a few years older than me, though less than thirty. Anyway she was not a girl of seventeen. I took my whole pile of chips and put all the money on Red Seventeen. The croupier who was chanting: "Messieurs et mesdame, faites vos jeux" before, now chanted again "Rien n'a va plus", and set the roulette wheeling. It stopped at a number but alas not seventeen, and the croupier swept my bet away. I smiled at the girl and said it was not my lucky day and that I had had a tiring day and must have an early rest, since my boat would be leaving early next morning. So I said goodnight and left, going back to my hotel. If I had won through some fluke, I might have spent more time with her to squander the money, but I was not interested in the game. I only played it for the experience, not by nature being a gambler.

There were probably many other places I visited in Europe during that year, but I have since forgotten them. Anyway I spent the year fooling around and did not do any serious reading. But I did not spend all my time on the continent and spent quite some time in London, getting to know the city better, and like it. I bought a seasonal ticket to Queen's Hall where I could enjoy good concerts given by the London Philharmonic Orchestra. The conductor was usually Sir Henry Wood, but sometimes Sir Thomas Beecham. I did not have a great love for music. I only attended for my musical education. Music, after all, was an important part of Western culture. So I learned to appreciate many Western symphonic works, but some had a greater appeal for me than others. I did not much enjoy Bach and Beethoven and never liked Mozart much. I much preferred listening to Handel, Brahms, and Mendelssohn, and Chopin's piano pieces, Tchaikovsky, and some later musical works by Debussy, Ravel, Rimsky-Korsakov, and Stravinsky were more to my liking. Maybe this was because at heart I was still an oriental, not a European.

8

Politics

Politics are always a part of the life of almost any young college student. In London, near Russell Square, there was Gower Street, and at that time there used to be a Chinese institute there. This was not strictly speaking a Kuomintang Chinese Embassy organization, but it was under the sponsorship of overseas Chinese citizens and Chinese students in London. Of course it had close contacts with the embassy. I was introduced to that place by other Chinese students and through this institute I got to know more Chinese students. Chinese students at that time could be classified into three categories: self-supporting students like myself, students who were in England on scholarships, or Kuomintang government-sent students. The self-supporting students were mostly rich men's sons and most did not study seriously, preferring the life of pleasure. As for the second group, at that time there was the Boxer Indemnity Fund, money returned by foreign powers after they had extorted it from China following the Boxer Rebellion. That fund was used to send good students abroad, and these students usually worked hard and did well in their studies. As for those sent by the Kuomintang government, most of them were sent to spy on other Chinese students and academically were not too qualified. They were usually treated with contempt by good students, and we used to call them "Blue Shirts". This was because of circumstances at that time in China. General Chiang Kai-shek and other generals in the south under Dr. Sun Yat-sen had begun their northward expedition against the northern warlords, but later in 1927 Chiang Kai-shek had turned against and suppressed the Chinese Communists, who were their allies. When Chiang Kai-shek made his compromises with the northern warlord forces and had control of northern China, he moved his capital to Nanjing and continued his suppression of the Chinese Communists and other revolutionaries. In the mid-thirties, with the rise of fascism in Europe, he emulated the style of those fascist leaders. Like Mussolini, Hitler, and Franco, who styled themselves as "Il Duce", "Führer", and the "Caudillo", he too had a title, "Generalissimo", and had some young followers who wore blue shirts, just like his European counterparts with their black shirts or brown shirts. I need not go more into these explanations, since this is well-known history. I had many friends among the self-supporting students and those on scholarships but I shunned the so-called "Blue Shirts" in London. In those days there was a Chinese student union too, which held conferences once a year. I was elected chairman one year — I don't know why, probably because I was well liked by many students and considered more knowledgeable than many others who were only staying in England for a few years and whose English was not very fluent. But I never did any organizational work for the union and just attended a few sessions. At that time in west London, at no. 50, Upland Park Road, Hampstead, there was a house belonging to a middle-aged Chinese professor and his wife. His name was Wang Lixi, or Shelley Wang. He had been a professor at a minor university in central or south China and a journalist. He was an historian, and a good and progressive intellectual. He had eccentric ideas, thinking the famous usurper and charlatan Wang Mang at the end of the Western Han dynasty, in the first century B.C., was a great reformer and revolutionary. At that time he was writing a thesis about Wang Mang at his house in London, having left China a year or more before to escape political persecution. He was not, however, a member of the Chinese Communist Party. Many Chinese students and exiles like him frequented his place so it became quite a social centre. There were two other Chinese intellectuals lodging with him. One was Professor Xiong Shiyi [S. I. Hsiung], who later wrote a play and staged it in London. It was called *Lady Precious Stream* and was based on a popular folk legend. It became quite a hit and ran for nearly a year at one of London's little theatres. The other individual, an ex-Kuomintang magistrate, was an artist. His name was Chiang Yee. Later he also became quite well known as a Chinese writer in London. He published a whole series of books on Chinese art, such as *The Mind's Eye*, *The Silent Traveller in London*, and others.  In 1935 I often went to Shelley Wang's house in the evenings, enjoying his company and making many Chinese friends there. Through them I learned much about the political situation in China, about the Kuomintang's campaigns against the Chinese Communists' Red Army and similar affairs. Later, after the war of resistance against Japanese aggression had started in 1937, Shelley Wang decided to go back to China as a wartime correspondent. He died of illness in the Chinese north-west near Xi'an. His wife is still living in Shanghai. She became a member of the Kuomintang Revolutionary Committee, a patriotic organization that is one of China's democratic parties. I too became, and still am, a member of the same organization.

In London during the winter of 1935, one wealthy old Englishman, whose name was Ernest Pittman, invited me to his club for dinner one evening. I first met him on the Mediterranean cruise I had taken earlier. In those days wealthy Englishmen and professionals usually spent their evenings in their own clubs. He belonged to the Royal Automobile Club. We had a good dinner, then chatted and played a game of chess. He said one of his sons had just bought an airplane for his own use, and suggested that I should get one too since it was then the fashion. He also asked what sort of car I had. I had to admit that I did not own one yet. This was the first time I went to dine in an English gentleman's club in London. Later in 1937 when the Sino-Japanese War broke out, I and some other Chinese students were organizing a rally in London, making speeches to denounce the Japanese aggression and collecting donations to aid the war effort. I sent an invitation to him and he came. As he was leaving after listening to the speeches, he saw me at the door standing with some other Chinese students holding a cap in my hand to receive donations. He looked very embarrassed as he greeted me and surreptitiously put a ten pound note in my cap. I thanked him. It must have been quite a shock to him to see his wealthy young Chinese friend behaving like a beggar. After that we never communicated. I was too busy with my anti-Japanese propaganda efforts anyway.

In the spring of 1936 I decided to move from London to Oxford. I found a lodging house there with some other English boys who were also preparing to enter college later that year. In those days the university rule was that a new student doing a regular B.A. degree must spend the first two years living inside the college compound. I stayed in this lodging house because I had to wait for the Michaelmas Term in the autumn. While at that lodging house I remember meeting a young English anthropologist named Tom Harrison who was organizing a social survey he called "Mass Observation". I enlisted myself in his experiment and went with him for several weeks visiting various families in Wales, Cornwall, and other places. Those families were usually poor, quite often just lonely old people. We would converse with them and heard a bit of the local folklore and superstitions about witches and dragons, and recorded our conversations. In this way I learned a considerable amount about English society. During that half-year I also got to know the small community of Chinese students in Oxford. At that time there were less than a dozen Chinese students attached to various colleges. Most were Chinese university graduates coming to Oxford to study for a B. Litt. degree or a diploma, which only took one or two years. Most had scholarships, but a few were privately sponsored by Chinese organizations or people with private funds. Among my closest friends was a Chinese historian, Professor Xiang Da, who had come to research the ancient manuscripts found in north-west China's Dunhuang caves. These had been brought to England by Aurel Stein and others and were kept in the British Museum. Xiang Da went to study these ancient documents every week in London, but he had his lodgings in Oxford because of its quieter atmosphere and cheaper cost of living. Another good friend was Lü Shuxiang who was studying philology. Yet another good friend was Professor Yang Renbian, who was writing a thesis on Saint-Just and studying the history of the French Revolution. I also knew Professor Qian Zhongshu very well. He was a good scholar of Chinese and European literature and his name is now well known in China, as the vice-president of the Chinese Academy of Social Sciences. He was staying in Oxford for two years with his wife Yang Jiang, who was a good writer. Of course there were many other Chinese who were my friends at that time, but to spare my readers the task of remembering these difficult Chinese names, I'll only mention these four or five. All such scholars were older than myself. So they all used to call me "Xiao Yang" (Little Yang).

I found that in England there was quite a lot of interest in Chinese

culture and Chinese political affairs, owing to the fact that a lot of people had been to China. These friends of China and Chinese students at the university had organized a China Society in the university. This society had some hundred-odd regular members paying annual subscriptions and attending organized meetings once or twice a week. The society had one president and one secretary to run the whole business and to keep minutes or records of their activities. After I went to Oxford, I was chosen to be secretary in 1936. I became president of the society in 1937, the following year, a post I kept until I left the university. Our meetings were usually organized lectures. We would invite scholars, British or Chinese, to give lectures, then invited our members to come to these lectures and ask questions. During these years when I was president, the Oxford China Society was very active, partly because of the Sino-Japanese War at that time. We had a lot of popular sympathy and support from English friends. I remember in 1937 when the war had just begun, we held a meeting discussing the future outcome of the war and many English sinologists partici-pated. Many people spoke, and some English and American scholars felt that it was hopeless for China to carry on resistance against the powerful Japanese war machine, and I argued with them. I said that in spite of the odds, China would triumph in the end, for we had the support of most people in the world. I quoted from one book I had just read. It was by an English woman writer Freda Utley, and the book's name was *Japan's Feet of Clay*. My talk won much applause. At that time there was also a Japan Society in Oxford, which was organized by Japanese students and financed by the Japanese embassy. Because it had some financial backing, they could hold dinner parties and did quite well and had more members than the China Society. I decided to pull most of their English members away and make them join our society instead. I started a campaign with the help of some of my English friends to have more interesting meetings and lectures concerning Chinese civilization, and after one or two months' work, the Oxford China Society's membership rose from about a hundred to more than one thousand, and many people who took part in the Japan Society's activities earlier came over to attend our meetings. This made the Japanese students in Oxford very angry, and I was very pleased with my exploit.

In the summer of 1936 I was invited by a young Swedish attorney named Peterson, or something like that, whom I had met during the Mediterranean cruise the year before, to visit Sweden. I spent about a month there. He took me to an opera, and I visited an archaeological museum and met the old sinologist Anderson, who was the one who found those red pottery utensils with black geometric designs in China's north-west, similar to those found in the Near East. He had the theory that ancient Sumerians were linked to China in prehistoric times. We also went to see a Chinese-style garden and palace built by one of the Swedish kings. I also visited Uppsala and Göteborg. This Swedish gentleman also gave me a couple of good dinners. At other times, in Stockholm I would take my meals in a popular cheap restaurant called the Norma and I learned to order food myself. In Stockholm I met a young Chinese scholar named Yang Zhouhan, who was helping Oswald Siren compile a book on Chinese paintings. I got to know him quite well. Later he also went to Oxford to take a course in English literature, then returned to China to become one of our best authorities on English literature at Peking University. He was a very good scholar and also translated some Latin classics into Chinese, including Ovid's *Metamorphoses* and Vergil's *Aeneid*. He died a couple of years ago of cancer, a great loss to our country.

Before I left Stockholm I went one day to a pleasure park in the

city called the Lido. I met a young girl who accompanied me in the park and who could say a few English sentences. We chatted and walked around quite happily, although I knew even less Swedish than her English. Before we parted, she asked me in Swedish: "Am I attractive?" I did not know the Swedish word for "attractive", so I did not know what she meant. However, I could guess it did not mean "ugly" or "unpleasant" or something like that, so I only mumbled "Ya, ya" in a rather lukewarm manner. Later I looked it up a dictionary and realized what she was saying. If I had understood her earlier, I might have answered in a more complimentary manner.

9

Autumn 1936

I n autumn, the college's Michaelmas Term began, and I moved into the college compound. In those days the college rules for new students were very strict. One could not entertain girl students within the college after certain hours in the evening, and if one went out, one must be back in the college compound by ten o'clock in the evening, after that the college gates would be closed. In England there have always been popular drinking bars serving beer, gin, and other alcoholic drinks and they are called "pubs" (public houses). Oxford students and their tutors often frequent such pubs. In the thirties there were restrictions forbidding students to go to such places after certain hours, and there were college officers called "proctors" chasing students out of pubs. Although I was never chased by a proctor, I tried and succeeded many times to return after hours, having to climb over the wall or to slide myself down a coal chute. Merton College had such a coal chute on Merton Street. One just pulled up a lid on the pavement and let oneself down the hole, sliding down into the coal storage room within the college. Young students always enjoy breaking rules and this was a very easy trick to learn from other students. Within the college compounds new students had living quarters known as "digs". I lived up a staircase in a flat consisting of a large study, a bedroom, and a pantry for servant and toilet, but there was no bathroom. Every morning I had to cross the quadrangle and run to the bathroom to have my bath. Each student had a servant called his "scout". My scout was a short middle-aged man named Howard. He was very good to me and I liked him very much. He would see to the laundry, polish my shoes every morning before I was up, have my clothes ready and ironed, and bring me hot water to wash and shave. He would also order my meals if I wanted to have breakfast, lunch, or dinner with friends in my rooms. But normally I would eat in the dining hall together with my teachers (the dons) and other students. Before such a communal meal, there was always a service spoken in Latin by the dons at the high table. We could order beer with our meals. College life seemed very medieval and quite enjoyable.

In those days an ordinary B.A. degree took three years to complete before final examinations, but the Honours School with Greek and Latin took four years. The first two years were spent studying Greek and Latin literature, then there would be one final examination for Honour Moderations (Hon. Mods.). After one took the Hon. Mods. one could take a course in philosophy or history, called "Greats". One could also avoid the "Greats" school and devote the last two years to some other subject, like foreign literature or English literature, before final examinations for the Honours B.A. degree. That was the course I took. I had two years of Greek and Latin literature at Merton, then took English literature. An Honours Degree was graded, and one could get a First, Second, Third, or Fourth. The final examination results were published in the leading English newspaper, the *Times*. My Greek and Latin tutor in Merton was a young man called Robert Levens, a very good man. Unfortunately he died young, in the fifties or sixties. He asked me to his home once for tea and gave me a book of Roman letters, which he had compiled, as a parting souvenir. I still have that book on my bookshelf.

I was never a good student. In middle school in Tianjin, my level of Chinese and English was far above the other students, so I never had to study hard or prepare for examinations. When I went to Oxford, although my foundation in Greek and Latin was very poor, I felt I had enough intelligence to cope with the examinations and did not study hard to get through. It never bothered me whether in the finals I got a high grade or not. For English students a high grade was quite important. To get a First could get you a good government job. But I knew even then that this degree mattered nothing to me at all. I was to go back to China and could always get a university job, whatever the degree or grade. I only studied Greek and Latin because I enjoyed reading the literature, but I never intended to be a grammarian. The Hon. Mods. course did require a fairly comprehensive knowledge of Greek and Latin literature, and put a lot of emphasis on the use of the languages. But I never paid too much attention to the required texts. When I first started the Hon. Mods. course, I had to read Homer first, which I found fairly easy because I enjoyed reading Homer, but I did not like spending too much time on writers like Isocrates, or Vergil, Horace, or Cicero. So I spent more time reading later writers like Athenaeus, Philostratus, Lucian, Apuleius, Petronius, and others, which were not required by the examiners. I remember when I went to my tutor Robert Levens for my first tutorial, I was asked to write an essay on some Greek or Latin writer as a test of my understanding and knowledge. I wrote an essay on the Greek poets Alcaeus and Sappho, making them patriots fighting against a despotic government and for democracy. I think Robert Levens probably was rather amused by my young enthusiasm and rather childish interpretation.

Soon after I entered college, I got into trouble with the college authorities. I made friends with some of the new students who were boys from the north of England, from Yorkshire and Lancashire, and they were a rather rebellious lot. One of these boys was Bernard Mellor, son of a brewer from Blackpool. Another was Fred Webster, the son of a butcher from Barnsley, Yorkshire. Another was Cyril Littlewood Heaton, who had a widowed mother, but I forget where he came from. There were others who joined our gang from time to time, like Terry Whitaker, a Welshman, and others. After drinking a lot of beer at night, we would get up to all sorts of antics inside or outside the college, pretending to be ghosts to frighten other gentler boys, and the like. I remember one night after Terry Whitaker got very drunk, he rode away on his bicycle, because he belonged to another college. Soon he came tottering back and said there was too strong a storm at sea, so he had to bring his ship back. Actually outside Merton there was a cobbled lane, and he had found it too hard to ride steadily on his bicycle. On another occasion one of the rival student gangs kidnapped Cyril Littlewood Heaton and took away all his clothes so he had to run back completely naked from another quadrangle. He was caught by one of the tutors and got severely reprimanded. I had a toy air-pistol, and we often took turns shooting at targets inside my study. One night, we opened a window and took aim at the street lamp on the other side of the college lane, trying to put out the light. However the glass of the lamp was too thick and though we made many chinks in the glass, it did not break. Just as we were trying to shoot out the lamp, the dean of the college passed by our window and we very nearly hit him on the nose. He was very startled and peeped in through the window and saw us sprawled on the floor on our bellies with the air-pistol. The next morning, the dean summoned me and demanded to know who was the culprit. I admitted that the air-pistol was mine, and took the whole responsibility. But the dean had seen the others, whom he already felt were bad students, so he insisted that the others must have put me up to it. Since I wanted to take the whole responsibility, he could do nothing. In the end he confiscated my air-pistol and fined me twenty pounds and the matter was closed. This incident occurred during the autumn of 1936, not long after I entered school. We probably spent the winter holidays of 1936 going between London and Paris. The Oxford school period was divided into three terms each year and each term lasted eight weeks. So more than half of the year I was on holiday away from Oxford. I never stayed in Oxford during the holidays.

During the spring holidays of 1937, I went with my new friend Bernard Mellor to stay in his home in Blackpool for a fortnight. His father was a local brewer, so I visited his brewery. I also visited a town named Barnsley in Yorkshire where another school friend Fred Webster lived, but this might have been early summer. I only stayed in his home for a few days. I remember going with him several evenings to the local pubs to drink beer and play darts with local workers. In July 1937 the Sino-Japanese War began and for some time there was fierce fighting in Beijing and Tianjin. North China was soon occupied by the Japanese, and the war spread to Shanghai and Nanjing further south. Whether by the time I was in Yorkshire the war had actually started or not, I cannot be sure, but anyway at that time there was much talk about the Chinese people's war of resistance against Japanese aggression. I remember one evening while playing a dart game with the local workers, I hit the bull's eye several times. The locals were really amazed. They made me stand on a table and shouted that if I wanted to go back to fight the Japanese, they would follow me and join my guerrilla army. It was a very moving occasion. Another incident I remember

when I stayed with Fred Webster in Yorkshire was one night when we went out drinking in the pubs, and were walking back late, about eleven p.m. The street was empty and quiet and we decided to take the street lamp back as a trophy. In those days a new type of street lamp had just been introduced. It was called the Belisha Beacon, Belisha being the name of a minister who introduced the beacon. It was round and looked like a football and had an enamelled white surface. Fred climbed up the pole and took the beacon down and we kicked it all the way home like a football. We decided to hide the trophy, but Fred's elder sister, who was still awake when we got home, spotted it. She was flabbergasted and felt the police would be after us. So she insisted we take it back, which we did, without causing any incident.

Apart from visiting my friends' homes in Lancashire and Yorkshire, I went by myself to the Lake District on a walking tour for a week. The Lake District is in the north of England, close to Scotland. For a small fee, one could go walking through the scenic spots and stay each night in a youth hostel, supplied with dinner and breakfast. For lunch one could just go to a hotel on the way. I learned to enjoy such walking tours a lot. Usually one walked fifteen or twenty miles a day with only a rucksack on one's back until the next hostel. The roads were usually good, and the people I met were friendly. It was a Spartan but healthy pastime. Between 1938 and 1939 I went on such walking tours in the Lake District at least three times, the last time being in the spring of 1939 with Gladys (later to be my wife) and the writer Xiao Qian, who was then a Chinese newspaper correspondent stationed in England. I remember one day walking from one youth hostel somewhere in the Lake District to another hostel, guided by a road map, but somehow we lost our way, so the journey took much longer. Gladys wept with fatigue, so in order to cheer ourselves up, we decided to sing marching songs loudly. We sang at the top of our voices, first the song popular in the First World War, "It's a Long Way to Tipperary", then some Scottish folk songs, like "Anne Laurie", "Loch Lomond", then some Christian hymns like "Onward Christian Soldiers", and they did seem to cheer us up as we walked on and on. Finally we reached our destination, after walking about twenty-five miles. It was a wearying walk, but how good we all felt afterwards.

10

Summer 1937

In summer 1937, I decided to go to some quiet and out-of-the-way place to do some serious reading of the classics, since the following spring I had to face the Hon. Mods. examinations, and so far I had been doing little work during my holidays or even during term-time. I at first thought of going to the Isles of Scilly, then I noticed in the newspaper that there was a fishing cottage in Lamona, in Cornwall near Penzance, where I could hire some rooms in a board-and-lodging place, and there I could be completely away from my friends and acquaintances. I wrote to the address given by the advertisement and ended up there. It was certainly a quiet place all right. The landlady was very nice and gave me good meals with plenty of local cream and honey and I had a comfortable old-fashioned bed. The landlady was a very quiet woman. She attended to all my meals and other needs but never bothered me at any time and never tried to make conversation. There was one local pub in Lamona. Whenever I went there the local fishermen who frequented the place would only give me a friendly nod, but would keep away from me shyly. They would eye me with curiosity but never ask any questions. I could not enter into any conversations with them because they all had strong local accents and a strange dialect I found difficult to understand.

They all talked among themselves about local affairs, about which I did not know the least. So I never made friends with any of them. Even the local cows on the meadows were shy and suspicious of me. I don't suppose they ever had a stranger like me in that lonely spot. After a few days spent reading Aeschylus and Xenophon, I got very bored. The nearest town, Penzance, was not within walking distance. A local bus went there only on certain weekdays, so I would go into Penzance a couple of times every week to buy detective stories, ghost stories, and thrillers to while away my boredom. I stayed there a whole month, during which time I read more ghost stories and thrillers than my required reading of the classics.

After my unsuccessful attempt to live the life of a hermit and do some serious reading, I decided to spend the remaining part of my summer holiday in Europe. I had always wanted to go to Italy. Even when I was in Tianjin I had great admiration for Giuseppe Mazzini, one of the founders of modern Italy. However Mussolini's invasion of Abyssinia gave me a bad impression. Abyssinia's fate reminded me of Japan's aggression in China. It was natural in those days for a young Chinese to sympathize with the oppressed and the weak and have a strong aversion to fascism, even though I was a wealthy man's son. So, when I went to England, I made up my mind not to go to Italy as long as Mussolini's fascist government was in power. Another country I had always felt like visiting was Spain. In Tianjin, in my middle school days I had read with great interest Washington Irving's *The Alhambra* in Chinese translation and Azorin's *Una Hora de España* in English translation, and I had longed to see Spain, especially Andalusia. Unfortunately in 1937 the Spanish Civil War had begun and going there was out of the question. I knew Professor Yang Renbian, who was doing a B. Litt. thesis on Saint-Just of the French Revolution. He told me that before he returned to China, he wanted to make a tour of Belgium, Holland and Germany, especially the Rhine Valley. So I decided to join him. We went first to Belgium, saw Brussels and visited some subterranean caves. Then we were off to Holland, where we visited the windmills and the quaint and colourful countryside. But most of our time was spent on a walking tour from Cologne to Dragon then Heidelberg and Coblenz to Berlin and Weimar. We noticed when staying in various small hotels that Adolf Hitler's portrait was hanging in most places. This manifestation of the cult of the individual left me with a strong impression. It was the first time I had seen a living person worshipped as ancestor or god. Of course after Liberation I got used to seeing Chairman Mao's portrait hung up everywhere in China, but at that time I felt it was a bizarre idea. Before I left China, the northern warlords never commanded so much respect, and the Kuomintang Generalissimo Chiang Kai-shek's influence had not yet reached Tianjin. But this time in Germany there was already a feeling of lawlessness in the air. Young storm troopers were marching down the streets carrying huge banners. In Heidelberg I enjoyed visiting that ancient university, which looked in many ways like Oxford (I forgot to mention earlier that in Holland I also visited the university town of Leiden which also reminded me of Oxford). But in Heidelberg, too, the young German students also began to look unruly. I saw some of them getting very drunk, a couple having a contest with sabres, trying to slash each other's cheek, and one boy opening his fly to piss in front of some girls. I am not suggesting that all Heidelberg boys behaved like that at that period, but I did find such drunken disorder in the university in broad daylight rather disgusting and menacing. In Berlin, my friend Yang Renbian left me and went back to Paris. I stayed on for a few more days. One evening I bought a ticket which cost only one Reichmark to watch a pageant in an open-air

theatre. The pageant itself was nothing interesting, just something legendary and historical glorifying the German nation. It started with some Nordic gods, like Odin, marching down the stage, then some Aryan heroes, like the Greek and Trojan Hector and Achilles, then some Teutonic knights, and so on. It was all colourful and very boring. But just as the show was about to begin, there was a stir near the entrance and some people came in. I saw a little man looking rather huddled up in a dark brownish raincoat and walking a little jerkily, like Charlie Chaplin. He was surrounded by some bodyguards and going to the front seats. As soon as he came in, many people in the audience stood up, some even giving the Nazi salute. Some of my neighbours were obviously tourists from England. They either stood up hesitatingly, thinking it the polite thing to do, or remained seated. I remained seated too. This was the one and only occasion on which I saw Adolf Hitler at a fairly close distance. I don't think he stayed very long watching the pageant. He left soon after seeing a bit of the show, and his entourage went with him. He probably only went there to make a public appearance.

Nothing else interesting happened in my Germany trip. I got back to England with a walking stick covered in little badges marked with names of German towns of the Rhine Valley. It was a souvenir of this walking tour. There was, however, one small incident which I remember happening at the German frontier. I was leaving Germany by train. My friend Yang Renbian had left several days earlier, so I was travelling by myself. It was nearing midnight as the train reached the frontier, and many of my fellow passengers were dozing off to sleep. I suddenly realized that in my hurried departure, I had forgotten to get a German exit visa. It was too late to do anything about it. If they discovered I had no exit visa, I might be sent back to Berlin to complete the procedure. I decided to follow the other passengers' example, so I pretended to be asleep. When the guard turned up, I had my hand already in my pocket on the passport while feigning sleep. Without opening my eyes, I took the passport out, opened to the front page which held my name and photograph. But I did not show him the page where my exit permit was supposed to be. He just glanced at it and let me put it back into my overcoat pocket. So I passed. I suppose he was feeling quite sleepy himself and bored of his routine. So I made it back to London without a German exit permit.

After I got back to London, I was immediately involved in a whirlwind of activities. The Sino-Japanese War had already begun and Chinese students in London were busily doing anti-Japanese propaganda work. I became one of the leading activists. I cannot remember now how many public speeches I made during that period. Meetings were usually organized with the help of English sympathizers of the Chinese cause and there were many English friends who were willing to help. These meetings were either organized by local trade unions, or humanitarian organizations. I made impassioned speeches, the audiences cheered and vowed support, and many kindly old ladies came offering me glasses of milk. It was very moving to share such a feeling of fraternity. I then thought of starting a mimeographed news-sheet to publicize Chinese war news for the Chinese population. Some of my Chinese friends supported my scheme. There were the philologist Lü Shuxiang, now the director of the Institute of Philology of the Chinese Academy, the historian Xiang Da, who is now dead, Professor Wang Lixi, or Shelley Wang, and his wife and several others. I bought a mimeograph machine and every afternoon I would collect items of Chinese war news from the English newspapers, edit them, and Lü and Xiang would do the copying. At that time there were about eight hundred Chinese living in the

East End of London. Mostly they were Chinese workers doing restaurant, laundry, and commercial work. Many seldom read the English newspapers and preferred reading Chinese. So we only put out our paper in Chinese. It was named *Resistance News*, and was a daily evening paper. Every day as soon as our paper rolled off our mimeograph machine, Shelley Wang, his wife, and others would take the printed edition to distribute in the East End. The local Chinese population welcomed it, and we usually could put into people's hands all eight hundred sheets we printed every evening. So we felt it was an effort well-spent. I carried on this work for the rest of the holiday. In October I had to go back to Oxford for the term and let other Chinese carry on my work. During the Christmas and New Year's holidays I went back to London and continued my work on the news-sheet. That small newspaper continued until the winter of 1938.

Besides producing this news-sheet for the East End Chinese population in London, during the winter holidays I went from London to Paris for a brief visit. At that time the Chinese students in Paris, with the support of underground Chinese Communist Party members, were also publishing a news-sheet called the *Salvation News*, and they had an office in Paris. After a discussion with some Chinese friends, I decided to pay them a visit, and since we were fighting for the common cause I took twenty pounds as our meagre contribution to their work. A senior Communist representative came and we had a talk. I do not know his name. He told me his name was something like Wu, but it may not have been his real name. He briefed me on the political situation in China, how the Kuomintang government was only resisting Japan half-heartedly, how they still wanted to exterminate the Chinese Communists, and how we and the Chinese people must work together with the Chinese Communists to resist Japan. He also gave me a simple dinner in a small cafe. I never met him again, so I don't know whether he is still alive or not. He might be somebody important in our government now, but I cannot remember his name or even what he looked like.

So apart from staying in Oxford during the term period, most of the time between late summer in 1937 and early 1938 was spent in London with Chinese friends and students. I spent a lot of time at Shelley Wang's house, no. 50 Upland Park Road, Hampstead, sometimes having heated discussions which lasted to two or three in the morning. I remember that once I did not go to bed for two consecutive days, dashing around or working all day and chatting with friends at night. By the third day I was absolutely exhausted and could not keep my eyes open. I decided to have an afternoon of rest. I drank several cups of strong coffee after lunch, then went to a cinema in Leicester Square to watch a Hollywood film. It was a silly thriller and I fell asleep as soon as the film began, sleeping in my seat so soundly that I did not wake up until the film ended at about four o'clock in the afternoon. After that I felt refreshed and started my work again.

In Oxford during term time, it must have been spring 1938, I also started a small magazine, with an editorial and several articles written by myself, denouncing Japanese aggression and analysing the war situation. My conclusion was that although China was weak, we would ultimately win the war. The magazine was in English, with each issue running to between ten and twenty pages. The magazine was named *Resurgence*. It was mimeographed and each issue had only thirty or forty copies. I did not try to sell them nor ask for subscriptions, but posted them to various friendly organizations in England. I even sent a copy to the Japanese garrison headquarters in Tianjin, just to annoy them. It was a good thing that the Japanese army did not take this diatribe too seriously.

Later, in 1940 when I returned to China via the Pacific, we were stopped near Japan and interrogated by Japanese naval forces. If the Japanese had thought me a dangerous enemy, I might have landed in some very serious trouble over my foolhardy bravado.

In spring that year I also wrote a one-act play in English about the victory of the Chinese over the Japanese aggressors at Pingxing Pass in Shanxi province. This was the first major victory we had had since the war started, and it was reported in detail in most English newspapers. After the Japanese started their aggressive war in July 1937, they quickly occupied major cities in north China, including Tianjin and Beijing. Then they attacked Shanghai and Nanjing further south, in the Yangtze valley, and after some resistance, both cities fell into Japanese hands. There followed a big massacre of Chinese soldiers and civilians in Nanjing. The Kuomintang government retreated from Nanjing to Wuhan in central China, then retreated again to Chongqing in south-west China, in the interior. The Japanese occupied all the main cities and towns near the coast and along the railway lines, but at that time there was no railway west of Wuhan, so the Kuomintang government was safe, and Chongqing was made the temporary capital. The Japanese in north China also tried to penetrate further westwards into Shanxi province, which was partly mountainous country. At a geographically strategic spot called Pingxing Pass, a crack Japanese army division, commanded by General Itagaki, was ambushed by Chinese forces under the command of General Lin Biao of the Chinese Communist Eighth Route Army, and a great part of the Japanese division was wiped out. This was a significant victory for us during the war. It not only temporarily brought the advancing aggressors to a halt, but after that the Japanese never continued their westward thrust. Thus the important city Xi'an was kept intact throughout the war. I do not remember whether I

made mimeographed copies of this one-act play in my magazine *Resurgence*. Anyway later I lost the manuscript, which is of little consequence, since that play was hastily written and must have been very amateurish and inferior. I cannot now remember a single passage from it. My single-handed magazine *Resurgence* only continued for three issues, then I gave up the effort by the end of that year. The war by then was becoming a stalemate. The Japanese had over-stretched their military strength. China was too vast for them to swallow up in one go. They only attempted to make one thrust to the south-west, towards Chongqing from Guizhou, in 1944, after taking Guangzhou (Canton) in the south. In 1945 the Japanese surrendered.

So it was that between late summer 1937 and early spring 1938 I spent most of my time doing anti-Japanese propaganda work. Naturally I had no time to prepare for my Hon. Mods. classics examination. By then I had also lost all interest in doing academic work, knowing that I would have little chance of living a quiet academic life in China. As a Chinese, I knew I had to return to China to serve my country. I would feel very ashamed of myself if I were to abandon my country and live abroad. Anyway I took the Hon. Mods. examination and passed it, getting a Third Class Honours, which was good enough for me. I knew that with my poor foundation in Greek and Latin, I could not get a First Class Honours, and it made no difference whether I got a Second or Third Class. After passing the Hon. Mods. examination in the spring, I had to select another subject to complete my B.A. Hons. course. At that time I was rather interested in anthropology and historical and primitive religions, but at Oxford there was no Honours School in anthropology: I could only take a one year course and get a Diploma, not an Honours School B.A. So many of my friends persuaded me against it and I did not take

anthropology. But I did not want to study philosophy or history because at Oxford at that time it meant studying a lot of Kant and British history, neither of which interested me. So in the Humanities School, I could only take foreign or English literature. I decided to study French literature and studied it for one term before the summer holidays began. However, after studying medieval French literature for a few weeks, reading the *Chanson de Roland* and others, and enjoying them, I went on to study modern French literature and found it difficult. I had never studied French properly, so finally my French tutor told me I had better change to English literature, which I did. It was during this brief period studying medieval French, that I met Gladys, my future wife, who was studying French too. We attended a few lectures together. Later when I changed to English literature, she also decided to give up studying French and took Chinese literature instead. At that time Oxford had just started an Honours School in Chinese literature, and she was the first student to enrol in that school.

11

Gladys

Gladys and I became engaged and we came back to China together in 1940. But before jumping so far ahead, I should explain how all this happened. Gladys, née Tayler, was the youngest daughter of a British missionary. Her father's name was J. B. Tayler. After graduating from university, he decided to become a missionary, so he joined the London Missionary Society and went to China. His wife Selina was a missionary teacher too. Gladys' father had taught Chinese students at the same high school in Tianjin where I studied, the TACC (Tianjin Anglo-Chinese College), but that had been before my time. By the time I went to that school, Gladys' father had left Tianjin to teach at Yenching University (now Peking University) in Beiping (Beijing). Later, before the Sino-Japanese war started, he went to the north-west to work as a teacher in the newly founded Industrial Cooperatives organization, in a town called Sandan in Gansu province. So I never met him earlier, nor did I know Gladys' family then. The Industrial Cooperatives, in Chinese known as Gong He (or Gung Ho), were founded by Gladys' father and a few other younger British idealists of the Fabian Society who believed that for a poor, backward people, the only way to help themselves was to get organized into cooperatives and learn industrial arts to improve their standard of living. China's north-western provinces were, and still are, the economically poorest and most backward areas, apart from Tibet, in all of China. So it was chosen for this Utopian, socialist experiment. They helped educate and train poor orphans in useful technical jobs, and it was good work. A young New Zealander, Rewi Alley, also joined them and later became quite famous in New Zealand and China for this work. The organization has survived until today. J. B. Tayler left China after the Japanese surrender in 1945 and died soon thereafter. Gladys' mother lived on in England into her old age and died during the Cultural Revolution, when Gladys and I were put in jail as spies. Gladys' eldest brother Bernard was captured by the Japanese in Singapore during the Pacific War and was killed on the eve of the Japanese surrender. Gladys' second brother Harold still lives in England, while her third and younger brother John lives in Zimbabwe. Gladys' elder sister Hilda is a retired teacher living in England.

Gladys herself was born in Beijng in 1919, but, accompanied by their mother, she and her sister were sent back to England when she was four or five. Although she had not learnt any Chinese, she had fond memories of her childhood in China. Both she and her sister went to a school in Seven Oaks, Kent, which is fairly close to London. After she finished her high school, she got a scholarship to study at Oxford. Because she had studied French and had been to France in her school days, living for some time with a French family, she decided to take French as her main course at Oxford. She went to Oxford in 1937, a year after me, but because she did not do Greek and Latin, she had a three-year course. Soon after she went to Oxford, she met Bernard Mellor of Merton, my close classmate. Bunny Mellor introduced me to her, and we three spent a lot of time together. Gladys also joined the China Society because of her past association with China, and she worked as secretary of that association when I was chairman. It was quite accidental how we three all tried to study a course in French language and literature. Bunny Mellor and I dropped out and changed to a course in English literature because our French was not good enough. Although I liked French literature very much, my medieval French was better than my modern French. I had never studied French properly and could only read some French poetry. But my French prose was no good at all. Gladys also gave up studying French because at that time an Honours School in Chinese literature had just been set up, and with her family background, she had developed a fondness for studying Chinese literature. Her Chinese language tutor was Reverend E. R. Hughes, formerly a missionary in south China. E. R. Hughes was a kindly, enlightened old gentleman, but his interest was more in humanism and Chinese Confucianism than in literature, and his spoken Chinese was not very good. He taught Gladys to read the Confucian Four Books but little else. After I knew Gladys, I advised her to read more classical Chinese poetry and ancient prose romances, as well as some later classical prose. She learned more modern Chinese language and literature only after she came back with me to China. She got a Second Class Honours in her final examination and was the first student at Oxford to take the Honours School in Chinese. She is now a vice-president of SACU (Society of Anglo-China Understanding), a society of sinologists and friends in England promoting friendship between the English and Chinese.

After summer 1938, when I started my course of English literature, at first I had to learn some Anglo-Saxon literature, Beowulf and all that, then some medieval English literature, then some modern English literature, starting from the Elizabethans to the Romantics. The course did not require studying works after the 1850s, although I read some for my own enjoyment, especially some modern poetry, including T. S. Eliot and Auden. After the first couple of months of reading some Anglo-Saxon, I was lucky enough to have the poet Edmund Blunden as my English tutor. All his pupils liked him and we all called him Teddy Blunden. He was a very civilized, liberal and kindly teacher and liked to take his pupils for drinks in pubs during his tutorial. He had taught for a couple of years in Japan, so he was not unfamiliar with young people from the Orient, and he had several Chinese pupils. I was, as usual, not a very serious student. I only concentrated on things I liked, and I liked poetry, especially early medieval poetry. Blunden was very tolerant of my idiosyncrasies. After Liberation (1949, when the Chinese Communists defeated Chiang Kai-shek and formed the People's Republic of China), Edmund Blunden, by then teaching in the University of Hong Kong, visited the mainland twice and had a good chat with Premier Zhou Enlai. He asked about me and I went to see him once. After his death in the 1970s, Bunny Mellor, who was by then Registrar of the University of Hong Kong, sent me a book of late eighteenth century English sonnets which Edmund Blunden and he had edited together. I still have that book on my bookshelf.

I only have very sketchy memories of Edmund Blunden during those tutorials. He was so mild and modest that he never treated me as a pupil, and we only chatted about books or other things at random. Often he would just take me to a nearby pub to continue our conversation over a pint of beer. I remember that one pub he frequented was called the Blue Bear near Merton. I also remember that once I translated, with Gladys' help, an ancient and famous long Chinese poem called "Li Sao" into English verse and asked him for some comments, but he only made some polite remarks and made no corrections. That poem was supposed to have been written by China's first known poet, Qu Yuan, a legendary individual of the fourth century B.C. during the Warring States period. I have always believed it to be a fake, and that it was really written by Liu An, Prince of Huainan, during the Han dynasty several centuries later. That would make it just like the poems of Ossian, supposedly written by an ancient Gaelic poet, but really fakes done by Macpherson in the eighteenth century. I translated "Li Sao" into English heroic couplets, after the style of Dryden, for fun, and I was very pleased with it. This was the first time I translated works of ancient Chinese literature into English. Later, after Liberation in the early 1950s, I had this translation published in Beijing, at Foreign Languages Press. When the eminent sinologist David Hawkes saw it, he was flabbergasted and made the humorous comment that, in spirit this verse translation of "Li Sao" "bears as much resemblance to the original as a chocolate Easter egg to an omelette". David is a good friend of ours and we both thought his remarks very funny. However I still feel even now that the famous poem "Li Sao" was a fake, and that the mock-heroic style of my translation was justified. But I don't want to discuss here the reasons for my opinion. The incident is worth mentioning because later I became known as a translator of Chinese classical literature, and this translation was one of my first attempts, over half a century ago.

In 1938 I also translated some poems by the late Tang poet Li He, with the help of Bunny Mellor, who had them published in the Oxford student magazine. The magazine was either called the *Cherwell* or the *Isis*, I cannot remember clearly. Bunny Mellor also included some news items about me in the same magazine, a few of my casual remarks. He introduced me as the "Honourable Yang", with a photo taken when I was only a few years old, wearing a Chinese silk jacket. So I became quite notorious among Oxford students. Bunny Mellor, Gladys, and I were together practically every day, at the Oxford student union, punting on the river, or going to a local Indian restaurant, the Taj Mahal, or other places for meals and drinks. There was also a quiet, out-of-the-way place called the Trout Inn which we also frequently visited. Once at the Taj Mahal we got so drunk that upon leaving the place, we rolled down the stairs, with Bunny and myself violently ill and Gladys standing by, looking rather embarrassed.

These days passed by very quickly, but we hardly did any work at all. When I took the final exam, in the spring of 1940, I only just managed to get a pass, receiving Fourth Class Honours, a rather rare beast. Each year there were only one or two Honours students who got a fourth. It was even rarer than getting a first. But since I was returning to China anyway, what class I got made no difference at all. In those days, an Honours student who had studied four years at Oxford could pay an extra twenty pounds for residence fee and get an M.A. degree to boot, without having to take another exam. So I paid my twenty pounds and got my M.A. But I did not wait for the final ceremony, since I was in a hurry to get back to China with Gladys, my fiancée. That period, however, is getting ahead of where I want to be and I shall return to it shortly.

Though Bunny Mellor at that time was chasing Gladys and many of my classmates thought she was Bunny's girl, she was more fond of me than Bunny, and I was in love with her. So one day we declared our feelings to each other and that evening I felt I had to tell Bunny Mellor about it. But he was clearly very sad about it and shunned our company for the rest of that year. Later, when Gladys and I decided to get engaged, I had a breakfast party to announce our engagement in my rooms in the college, with many of my young English friends coming. I invited Bunny too, but he did not turn up and I did not see him again. After the war started, I heard he had become a conscientious objector. He left England soon after graduation and accepted a teaching post at the University of Hong Kong. I heard he did well at the University of Hong Kong and later became the registrar there. He won distinction during the war and after and received the title of O.B.E. (Order of the British Empire). He also married a nice Swiss girl called Mauricette and had several children. He communicated with me again after the Japanese War, when he found some of the books which I had sent to Hong Kong when I left Oxford and which the Japanese had confiscated when they occupied Hong Kong. Bunny managed to send those books to me in Chongqing, but later they were lost again when I left Chongqing for Nanjing in 1946. I saw Bunny again in England in 1983 and 1984, after many, many years. He is now retired, living in Abingdon near Oxford.

Our decision to get married also caused Gladys' mother and my mother a lot of worry. They both doubted that a mixed marriage like ours could last. I heard that my mother in Tianjin wept when she heard the news. Later, when Gladys and she met in China, she was reconciled and treated Gladys very well. Gladys' mother Selina at first did not like Gladys to spend too much time with me during the holidays. She even told Gladys to cut short her holiday in Paris and return to London when she heard that I had gone to Paris too. When she knew Gladys' mind was made up to go back with me to China and get married, she predicted gloomily that the marriage would not last more than four years. Her prediction has proven wrong, though we did have some difficult times during our marriage, since the two cultures were so different and China was, and still is, so poor. It was particularly difficult for Gladys, though, especially during those war years in the interior.

12

Books and Plays

Books and plays, in many varieties, were always an important part of my literary experience, not to mention poetry. I should therefore add a paragraph or two about some of the books I read during this period, which made a strong impression on me, and which were outside my required reading. I read some books written at that time about the Sino-Japanese War, written by English and American writers, and these helped me understand much more about the Chinese political situation. Before I went to England, I was living in the foreign concession areas of Tianjin and knew very little about such things. The Chinese papers I read did not give me any news about the conflict between the Kuomintang Nationalists and the Communists in the south. Among the books I read, I found Freda Utley's book on Japanese aggression, *Japan's Feet of Clay*, very useful. I should also mention two books by an English Oxford graduate, James Bertram, who was a news correspondent in China. He wrote *The Si-an Incident* and *The People's War*. The former was about the capture of Chiang Kai-shek in Xi'an by the north-eastern young Marshal Zhang Xueliang in December 1936. This forced Chiang Kai-shek to bow to the people's demand to stop fighting the Chinese Communists, and resist Japanese aggression instead. The second book was a report

on the people's war of resistance in north China under the leadership of the Chinese Communist Party. Both books made a strong impression on me. Of course I read other books on China's revolution and war, like *Thunder out of China*, and *Red Star over China*. But I liked James Bertram's reports best. Several years later I met him in China. It was 1941, in wartime Chongqing, after Gladys and I were married and back home. He came to our wedding and later we had dinner together, during which he sang the Chinese resistance song "September 18th! September 18th! Ever since that day of sorrow …", composed by the Chinese musician Nie Er in 1931, when the Japanese occupied the Chinese north-eastern provinces. James Bertram also went to Yan'an and had an interview with Chairman Mao during the war. Later he went to New Zealand and became a professor of English literature. We never wrote afterwards and I don't know whether he is still alive.

I read some of Karl Marx and Engels before going up to Oxford. During my Oxford days I read some more but I never read Marx's *Das Kapital*. I was more fond of reading Engels' *Anti-Duhring* and some of Plekhanov's philosophical essays. In those days I also read Trotsky's *History of the Russian Revolution*. It was no accident for a young Chinese to turn to Marxism. Most of the people of my generation went the same way. It was an inevitable historical trend for the Chinese people. In my own case, perhaps my early reading of the Italian patriot and political thinker Mazzini's *The Duty of Man* and the founder of our first republic Dr. Sun Yat-sen's *The Three People's Principles*, and writings by other Chinese and Western pre-Marxist, non-proletarian socialist thinkers, also helped shape my future.

In early spring 1939, an unexpected and amusing incident got me involved with London theatrical circles for a spell. It was sometime just after the New Year's holidays when I received a letter from my old friend and former classmate, Robert Li from Cambridge. He had by then already joined Trinity College, studying history or politics. Robert was never a serious student. After he came with me to England, at first he spent a lot of time playing tennis, then he started chasing young chorus girls in London musicals, squandering a lot of money. In 1938, a new play, written by a poor Chinese professor, Xiong Shiyi, named *Lady Precious Stream*, was staged in London in the Little Theatre. It became an immediate success. I believe I have already mentioned this Professor Xiong earlier. He was staying at Shelley Wang's house in Hampstead. When Robert saw that Professor Xiong's play was a success, he wanted to do the same thing. He was by then already familiar with London theatrical circles. However he had no playscript which he could use, so he wrote to me and asked me to write a Chinese historical drama for him to put on stage. He said I could go to Cambridge during the spring holidays and stay in his place, so that I would not be interrupted by other people, and I could then write a play in a couple of weeks. I agreed and finished the script in about ten days. He then said he must buy the copyright from me but I told him I was only doing it for fun and refused to take any money. However, he insisted that we have a formal business contract, so we drew one up and had a lawyer witness it. I sold the script to him for one pound sterling. This was the cheapest deal he had made during his business career. Robert then sought out an experienced producer and found some actors and actresses for the production. I left all such transactions to him. He must have spent hundreds of pounds on it. It was a rather dull season in London for the theatre, and many professionals were idle. He even managed to get the well-known actress Diana Wynyard interested in this play, and she agreed to take the heroine's part. The professional producer helped with all the preparations and Robert

even got a room in a hotel for him. I do not remember that man's name. All I can remember is the man looked like a charlatan and did not seem to do anything all day but drink like a fish and boast about his past achievements in the theatre. I spent one day with him chatting idly, and together we emptied two bottles of scotch in the afternoon. He must have cost Robert quite a penny. Soon my holiday was over and I left. Later I heard from Robert that they had already done some rehearsals of the play and he was planning to have the premier and was sending out invitations. In summer war broke out and the whole scheme was abandoned. I never asked Robert later how much he spent on his wild scheme.

I should have mentioned earlier what my play was about. It was an historical drama in three acts. The story was the same as a play which my former school principal Huang Zuolin had written during my school days in Tianjin. It was a story of the Warring States period in the fifth century B.C., about the King of Wu, who was defeated and killed by a neighbouring kingdom called Yue. The King of Wu was infatuated with a beautiful woman called Xi Shi, and she was the tragic heroine of the play. I had not read Huang's play, but the story was a familiar one. I had gotten involved with the staging of that play, though, and perhaps this was the reason I chose the same theme. I called my play *Night over the Purple Land*. I cannot now remember any details of it, so it must have been no good at all. I do remember that in Europe there was a sense of impending doom at that time, with the rise of fascism. Probably that must have been the reason why I chose the subject. I do not regret now that the play was lost and never got staged. It must have been very childish and silly. I would feel rather ashamed of it had it succeeded in appearing in a London theatre, although at the time Robert and some people in London seemed to have liked it. I don't know why. Perhaps they thought it quite topical.

13

Heading Home

Heading home was a matter I had to face soon. However, in the summer of 1939 I thought of making a tour of the Soviet Union. There was an Intourist Travel Agency in London which arranged such trips. At their office I booked to travel to Leningrad and Moscow and spend a month there. However the political situation in Europe at the time was getting more and more tense. Hitler had annexed Austria and Czechoslovakia and war was imminent. After I finished my job of helping Robert prepare to put his new play on the London stage, I felt that if I went to Russia and the war broke out, I might not be able to come back to England. So I went again to the Intourist office and cancelled the trip. Since then I have never had another chance to visit what used to be the Soviet Union and is now the Commonwealth of Independent States. England finally declared war on Germany in September, after Hitler attacked and occupied Poland. The general political atmosphere in Western Europe turned very grim, although there was still an illusion that the French Maginot Line was impregnable and that England for the time being was safe. I remember there was a mock air raid in London when I was strolling down Tottenham Court Road, whether towards the end of 1939 or early 1940 I cannot remember. At that time, when we

heard the air raid alarm, people on the street really thought German bombers were coming and all passers-by descended into nearby stations of the underground or subway. I noticed that all the English people were quiet and orderly. There was no sign of disorderliness or panic, although people's faces looked grim and pale, with tightened lips. Later when the all-clear siren came, we all went up to the streets again. Only later did we hear it was just a test, not the real thing. But war was already in the air, and England was completely transformed — no longer the quiet, peaceful place of before. Later, food was rationed, including meat, butter, and sugar. People were issued gas masks, while every day Hitler's Germany and the British traitor Lord Haw-haw were screaming on the wireless that they would bomb England to oblivion. At night the streets were dark and in houses curtains were drawn over windows in fear of the air raids. Everyone's conversations and all the newspaper reports were about the war.

In early summer 1940, however, Gladys decided to go to Paris for a holiday and that was, of course, when the war began in earnest. I waited anxiously for her safe return in London, going to Waterloo Station (or Paddington Station) every day for three or four days. She returned safely just as we heard the news that the French army had been defeated, Hitler's blitzkrieg was advancing towards Paris, and the British army was retreating from Dunkirk. We spent a couple of weeks in Cambridge, having our last idyllic holiday in a place called Granchester, a beautiful quiet village near the university. The English poet Auden once wrote a poem about Granchester, which started with these lines:

> Eith genoimen, would that I were
> in Granchester, in Granchester!

The opening two words are Greek, meaning the same as "would

that I were". It was from the opening line of the Euripides tragedy *Medea*, familiar to all students of Greek literature.

After that short, idyllic holiday I had to return to Oxford to face reality. There was the final graduation examination and packing my luggage to prepare for my return journey to China. Although I had been six years in England and seldom wrote to my mother and sisters in China, I always knew that after Oxford I would return to China. I never had any doubt about it, even though the Sino-Japanese War had changed everything. I knew I could not return to my old home in Tianjin, since it was under Japanese occupation. Still, I had to go back to China. It would have to be to the interior, to places I had never visited, to wait for the day when China was freed from her aggressors. In the spring of 1940 I was invited to go to the United States to continue my study of classics. I received a letter from an American scholar named Barlett from Harvard University. This scholar formerly studied in Merton  College as a graduate scholar and I knew him. He suddenly wrote me a letter, knowing I would graduate that summer, saying that if I wanted to continue my studies, Harvard University could invite me to come and work as an assistant. It was very kind of him, but I wrote back thanking him and saying that I had stayed abroad long enough and felt I had to return to China to work. Actually at about the same time I received another invitation, but this was from a Chinese university. During the Japanese War, most Chinese universities in north China and in the areas near the coast had evacuated to the interior. Three of the best universities in Tianjin and Beijing — Nankai University of Tianjin and Peking University and Tsinghua University of Beijing — had evacuated to Kunming in Yunnan province, in south-western China near the Burma border. These three universities had amalgamated and been renamed as Southwest United University. It had practically all the best scholars in Tianjin and Beijing and was considered the best centre of learning in the interior during the war period. I was recommended to join this university by two famous professors. One was Professor Shen Congwen, well-known novelist and storywriter, and a good Chinese scholar. He was at that time teaching there and my youngest sister Lucy and her fiancé Zhao Ruihong were his students. The other was Professor Wu Mi, a poet and scholar of English literature. I had never met either. Shen Congwen had heard of me through my youngest sister Lucy, and Wu had read some of my early poems, written when I was in high school in Tianjin and was impressed by them. These two kind teachers and friends invited me to join their university because at the time we had no Greek or Latin scholars and they wanted to start a course in ancient Greek and Latin language and literature. I was offered a professorship. I gladly accepted since I had as yet no place to go and that university, well known for its academic standards and liberal atmosphere, seemed the ideal place to settle down. I had received a letter from my mother in Tianjin saying that she had also decided to go to the interior with my younger sister Amy. She would be staying with the Bank of China in Chongqing. Although Chongqing was in a different province, we would not be too far apart and could see each other often. So my mind was made up to go first to Kunming to start my teaching career, then to visit my mother during holidays after term time. I did not know then that things would not work out as planned and that I would not see Kunming until many years later, after the war.

In my mother's brief note, she only said that she and my younger sister Amy had decided to leave Tianjin and go to Chongqing in the interior. She did not know her future address, but said they would be looked after by friends in the Bank of China. She also mentioned that the family was practically bankrupt by then. The old currency we had had on hand had been converted into puppet government money in the bank, and the family had been spending recklessly for years. So she would not be sending more money to me, but hoped that I would go back as soon as I could after graduation. Actually I too had practically used up the last few hundred odd pounds I had in the bank and was hoping that the family would send me more money for travelling expenses. Suddenly I found myself in financial straits, a young spendthrift turned pauper overnight. Fortunately in the past few years I had been buying a lot of books, and since I could not take all those books back with me to China, I sold most of them. The bookshop in Oxford called Blackwell's had a good system. Since many students wanted to dispose of some of their books on leaving Oxford, Blackwell's would accept their books at a discount. Usually one could get two-thirds of the cost back. So I sold most of my books back to Blackwell's and got enough to last me for the last couple of months in England. As for travelling expenses, Gladys' mother gave me a loan which my mother would repay for me after we went back. What books I decided to take back with me were packed into about seven big wooden cases and shipped to Hong Kong, waiting for us to collect them when we got there. Actually we never saw these books again until after the end of the war.

We first planned to go back to China via the Red Sea and Indian Ocean, since I had never been through those parts of the world. However at that time German submarines and battleships were on the rampage and many British ships were being sunk in the eastern Mediterranean. Such a voyage would be too risky, so we still had to return the same way I had come to England — crossing the Atlantic, the North American continent, and then the Pacific. Although there were German submarines in the Atlantic too, at least it was safer having a British convoy of destroyers.

Oxford by this time had changed beyond recognition. All my old college friends had gone. Many had joined up as second lieutenants, no more to be heard from, the first casualties of war. In the front quadrangle of Merton, one young boy went berserk and started shooting at people at random with a pistol from his window. Fortunately he only managed to hit and slightly wound one person. I had finished my final exam and it was certainly time to leave. So I left Oxford without regret, since I had Gladys to go back with me. But when Gladys applied for her visa to go to China, the official in charge was sceptical. He asked why a young girl only twenty-one years old wanted to go to China at that time.

"I shall be going with my Chinese fiancé."

"You'll probably find when you get to China that he has already got a wife at home. Then we'll have to send you back," said the officer.

"My father is in China too. He is teaching at a university there and working for the Industrial Cooperatives Organization," said Gladys.

Hearing that, the officer was assured and Gladys got her visa to wartime China.

14

The Journey Home

The journey home was preceded by a flurry of activity as we prepared to leave. We booked tickets for the trip to Canada and tickets from the west coast of Canada across the Pacific to Hong Kong. From Hong Kong we intended to go Hanoi in Vietnam, then by train to Kunming in the interior. We did not book tickets for the last part of the journey, from Hong Kong to China's interior, because the London travel agency could only arrange as far as Hong Kong. Anyway we felt that as long as we reached Hong Kong, we would be able to contact our parents there and the rest of the journey would be simple. At that time, because of wartime financial restrictions, nobody leaving England could take out more than twenty-five pounds each as pocket money. So we left England with only fifty pounds in our pockets. Since all the travel expenses were already paid for, we felt this was enough for our journey. In Hong Kong, we could ask our parents for more if necessary.

We began our voyage at Southampton on a small passenger boat escorted by a convoy of two destroyers. The Atlantic voyage passed without mishap and we were not harassed by any German submarines. One evening we heard on the wireless on our boat that the German bombing of London had begun. Before we left

England, the Germans had not yet started any serious bombing of England, with only one or two bombs dropped near Cambridge and probably Coventry. But London had been untouched. Our boat took us to Montreal, then by train we journeyed to the Canadian Niagara Falls, then Toronto, the Canadian Rockies, and finally Vancouver. I only have a vague recollection of Montreal. A casual connection I cannot now remember took us on a fleeting tour of that city, which seemed quite beautiful from his car. It resembled more somewhere in France than England. From Montreal we travelled to the Canadian side of Niagara Falls. The waterfall looks less impressive than it does from the American side, but still quite magnificent. We were shown around by a Canadian taxi driver, a university graduate who chatted incessantly. From Niagara Falls we went to Toronto and stayed there one night. Toronto in those days was rather like a frontier town in a Hollywood western — only one busy boulevard with cinemas and large shops, not the busy modern metropolis of today. From Toronto we went on through to the Canadian Rockies and stayed one or two nights in that beautiful tourist spot with forests called Banff. Then we went on to Vancouver, which was already full of Chinese immigrants. There we ate several meals in small Chinese restaurants serving chop suey. The whole trip across Canada was over, a short trip by train across the continent in about ten days or less. It was not like the earlier trip across the United States in 1934, on my way to England, which took about a whole month. This was not because there were less things to see and enjoy in Canada. This time I was not on a sightseeing tour, and we were in a hurry to return to China. Anyway, we had little money to spend. So we ate simple meals all the way and did no shopping and bought no souvenirs.

Because we had little pocket money, we decided in Vancouver

to spend less on our Pacific voyage. Gladys still had to travel second or tourist class because one could not travel third class if one was an English lady. They would not sell a third class ticket to a white person. I travelled third class. It was below, near the engine room, and very hot and stuffy with four or five people to a cabin. But since Gladys was tourist class, I could always go to her deck to see her. We made some friends with the passengers in second and first class and became particularly friendly with a middle-aged plump American who said his name was Brown. We wondered then whether it was his real name as he seemed a mysterious person and did not disclose his profession. We wondered whether he was a CIA agent on some secret mission. Another person we made friends with was an Englishman called Brankston. He was an authority on Chinese Song and Ming dynasty porcelain, a civilized and quiet English gentlemen. We four spent a lot of time together on the first class deck or in the lounge, so the journey was not too boring. I remember that the American Brown, who had travelled a lot and seemed very knowledgeable of political affairs, introduced a new drink to us: half a glass of rum plus half a glass of Coca-Cola, which he called "Cuba Libre". It was very nice with ice cubes. Another foreign passenger we met on the boat was a Russian professor who studied acupuncture, but still our closest friends on the boat were Mr. Brankston and Mr. Brown. We never saw each other again after we arrived in Hong Kong, and only heard that Mr. Brankston caught a sudden disease and died soon after he went to the Far East. We heard this news many years later through some English friends. It was quite a coincidence that the boat we took was also one of the Canadian Empress liners. I cannot remember whether it was called the Empress of Russia or something else.

This time the boat did not stop at Hawaii. There was an incident where the boat went close to Japan. We were stopped by a Japanese naval vessel. It seemed that at that time, although the Pacific War had not yet started, Japan was already the master of the western Pacific. The Japanese naval officers came on board with some guards and all Chinese passengers in third class were told to line up on the deck for interrogation. One Chinese passenger, whose name I cannot remember and who wore thick glasses and looked like a professor, was particularly jittery and frightened. The Japanese officer barked some questions, which he answered in stuttering fashion. Then he was taken off the boat by the guards and was never seen again. I wondered, at the time, what his fate would be. When it was my turn, the Japanese officer asked me coldly what was my profession and I answered "Student". Then he asked me my destination and I answered "Hong Kong". He then asked me what my address would be and I answered "The Bank of China". He seemed satisfied and let me pass. I wondered what would have happened if he had asked me more details, since at that time we had no real address or guarantors in Hong Kong.

Soon afterwards our boat reached Shanghai. Though that part of China was already under Japanese occupation, the Pacific War had not yet begun and an international settlement still existed in Shanghai so we could go ashore. It was in the evening when we disembarked. Suddenly, on the gangway, a big burly fellow turned up and saluted me by genuflecting in a feudal manner. He greeted me, "Young Master!" and I saw it was my old family servant and chief steward Pan Fu. Gladys was quite shocked and impressed by this sudden apparition. Apparently the old family in Tianjin had sent him to meet me in Shanghai. I asked after the "old lady" (my stepmother, or my father's first wife) and my mother, who was called "Second Mistress". He answered that the old lady was well but my mother and my younger sister had gone on to Chongqing in the interior to meet me there. I told him that owing to the situation I would not be going to Tianjin but would go to the interior as well. I also told him that I would only stay in Shanghai for the night and that the next day I would continue my journey to Hong Kong, so he need not wait. Later, when we were in a hotel, he came and told me more about the family situation, but I cannot remember any more of the details.

After Shanghai we went to Hong Kong. Somebody I met on the trip recommended a small family hotel to us in Kowloon, run by some English people. It was quite a nice place, spotlessly clean, in a quiet residential district, and the lodging was good. It was better than most small family hotels in London at that time, and had all the modern facilities. By that time we had spent practically all the money we had on us, though we arrived with a lot of good luggage and looked quite respectable, dressed in English suit and dress. So the hotel management never suspected that we were practically penniless. We decided that we had better stay there for some time, until we had some money sent to us from our two families. I sent telegrams to my home in Tianjin asking for money and to the Bank of China in Chongqing. Gladys also sent a telegram to her father in Lanzhou in China's north-west. We waited about a fortnight in the hotel but no money arrived and no reply. It must have been that our address was inadequate. So we were in a quandary. However, we told the hotel management that we would settle all our accounts when we left so every day we ate all our meals and had all our drinks in the hotel, just signing the bills. When we went out strolling, we never did any shopping or spent any money on restaurants, cafes, or cinemas. So nobody knew how poor we were. We had no friends in Hong Kong or connections from whom we could borrow money. We felt that if the worst

came to the worst, we could sell all our luggage to pay the hotel bills. Still, we had to think about how to continue our journey to the interior. After we arrived in Hong Kong, we discovered that the Japanese had made another push westwards and the railway linking Vietnam and China had been cut. If we wanted to travel by land, we heard some people had gone to the interior walking or riding horses over country roads. But bandits robbed travellers on the way and we did not know how much such a journey would cost. We had no money anyway. The only other way was to travel by air. There was a fairly regular air service between Hong Kong and Chongqing, which operated once or twice a week. The plane would only go at night because during the daytime it could be intercepted by Japanese planes or shot down. That seemed the most reasonable way, but again, we had to have the money to book the tickets.

In our dilemma, Gladys suddenly remembered that her father had said in a letter that he had an old Chinese friend in Hong Kong and that if need be we could go and get help from him. Fortunately, Gladys had his name and address in her notebook. The man was Dr. Chen Hansheng, who was helping Madame Soong Ch'ing-ling (or Song Qingling in modern romanization), the wife of Dr. Sun Yat-sen, in some progressive organization which had an office in Hong Kong. We went to that address and found Dr. Chen. When he heard that Gladys was the daughter of J. B. Tayler and that I was the future son-in-law, he readily gave us a loan to pay our bills at the hotel and he bought us air-tickets to Chongqing. All our troubles were solved. After Liberation, when I met him again at a conference in Beijing, I mentioned the incident of our first meeting and thanked him for his help. But he had completely forgotten the incident and only vaguely remembered that we had met sometime before Liberation. I suppose in those days, when he was in Hong Kong, he had helped many such Chinese friends who were having difficulties in going to the interior.

It was nearing midnight when we got to the airfield and boarded the plane. The plane was very small, taking only about a dozen Chinese passengers. I remember that it was a moonlit night, which the air service people did not like, fearing that the plane might be noticed by Japanese reconnaissance planes. The voyage went without mishap, however, except that after going up to a certain height, the plane had to turn back to see to some trouble in the engine. This delayed us for a couple of hours. When the plane reached Chongqing, it was already after dawn. We hired two bamboo sedan chairs, then two rickshaws, to take us into the city. We found the Bank of China people without much difficulty. The family of the local bank manager had heard that I would be arriving soon and welcomed us with some bowls of soft-boiled eggs and chicken soup as breakfast and told me that my mother would be expecting me at her place. They offered to take us there, so we then went on to my mother's place, not too far away. My mother was staying in a villa outside the city, in the suburbs. It was quite a nice villa, owned by a Mr. Luo, then president of Central University. My mother had rented the downstairs of the villa, while the Luo family had the upstairs. It was in a district called Xiao Longkan ("Little Dragon Ridge") near a road where the bus passed to the city. So we settled down for the time being, and our homeward travel adventures were over.

15

Chongqing

Chongqing is a mountain town in eastern Sichuan, where the Jialing River comes down from the north-west to meet the Yangtze River in the south. The confluence of the two big rivers made it a commercial centre of interior China. When the Sino-Japanese war began, the Kuomintang government decided to make it their temporary capital because of its inaccessibility. At that time there was no railway linking it with Wuhan in central China and even Japanese warplanes going beyond the Yangtze Gorges had to follow the Yangtze River if they wanted to penetrate further west into the mountains towards Chongqing. It was impossible to bomb the city effectively. The Kuomintang government built many air raid shelters in the mountains and all the important government buildings were under the cliffs, impossible to reach. So the Japanese planes would only throw their bombs at certain congested areas within the city itself, which were occupied by the local poor inhabitants. All the top officials had villas and houses in safe places which could not be reached by the Japanese bombs. Their air raid shelters were well furnished, with refrigerators and electricity and carpeting. Chongqing is also a foggy city, so the Japanese planes could only drop their bombs after ten o'clock in the morning, when the fog had dispersed. If they came, the

Japanese planes could only make one or two raids between ten in the morning and five in the evening and their arrivals were noticed before they had even passed the Yangtze Gorges, so there was enough time to head for the shelters. The air raid alarms would start about twenty minutes before the planes arrived at the city. We became quite accustomed to the exercise. Other cities in the interior were not so well situated. The city of Chengdu was on a plain, although it was further west. So were Guizhou and Kunming. Those cities suffered more casualties from the air raids. One day in early summer 1941 I was staying in my mother-in-law's house in Chengdu when an air raid occurred. There were no air raid shelters in Chengdu so I hit the ditch in the courtyard when I heard the bombs come screaming down. I was deafened by the ensuing explosions. After the raid I went out to the nearby street. Most of the houses there were in ruins and many dead bodies were lying around. I heard that several hundred people had been killed that day in a park where people were sitting and drinking tea. In those days China had no air defence system to speak of and the Japanese planes just came in orderly formation and dropped their bombs at will. They seldom bombed the countryside, only bombing the most congested places to frighten the people.

When I went to Chongqing in the autumn of 1940, the city had just been bombed several times, but little real damage was done. However with several houses in ruins, the city was congested with refugees and beggars, and huge rats would come out at night from the sewers, rampaging for food. It was an ugly sight. We heard that Kunming in the south-west had just been badly bombed too and there had been more casualties. My mother heard that we had just accepted the contract from Southwest United University, and as the term had already started, we would be going there within a few days. She was tearful and insisted that we not go. She felt it was safer in Chongqing. Her landlord, Mr. Luo, the president of Central University, also came downstairs and asked us to join his university instead. He said that his university had started another college further up the Jialing River in a village called Baixi ("Cypress Brook"), which was only seven or eight miles away. They needed new professors for their English department, so we could go there if we wished. Although I believed Central University did not have that good a reputation in academic circles, being too connected with the Kuomintang government, there were some good professors there too. And since Kunming did seem a long way away when one considered the lack of communication between provinces in those war days, I felt it was a shame to leave my mother so soon after I had been away for several years. So I was persuaded and accepted the new job at this university. I wrote a letter to Southwest United University in Kunming, apologizing for not going there since I was kept in Chongqing by my mother. Later I heard that Southwest United University had been awaiting my arrival and had kept classes open for a whole year. I felt very sorry about that, especially since my experience with Central University in Chongqing turned out to be not so pleasant. My mother later also blamed herself for persuading us to stay in Chongqing.

The main part of Central University was in a district called Shapingba ("Sandy Bank"), which was on the bank of the Jialing River. The branch college was about seven or eight miles upriver, along the riverbank. Since Gladys and I were used to long walks in the Lake District of England, we would take a rucksack and walk for two or three hours along the riverbank until we reached the village where the branch college was situated. Every weekend we would head back to my mother's place and on Sunday afternoon go back to the college. Since I had no teaching experience, I was only offered an associate professorship for the first year, and Gladys was only offered a lectureship because she did not have a degree in English language and literature, although she knew more English than any other Chinese professor there. We were also their youngest teachers and some of our students were about our age. They did not feel we were distant from them, so we were on very good terms. Our students often came to our place in the evenings, asking us about England or about books or just to gossip. Through them we learned a lot about the political situation in China. At that time, although the Kuomintang and Chinese Communists were supposed to represent a united front to fight Japanese aggression, there was constant friction, with the Kuomintang government still determined to exterminate the Communists. Among our students there were some who had been planted by the Kuomintang government to spy on others or to inform on the more progressive students. From time to time we heard of students who were secretly arrested or murdered. The students told us about one student who had mysteriously disappeared and was found several days later, dead and in a sack in the river, his face smashed in by a blunt instrument. He must have been an underground Communist Party member or suspected of being one. As we had just come from England and often talked without inhibition about anything to our students, we were considered by the university authorities as dangerous liberals. In those days the Chinese Communists had an official representative in the city and there was a Communist newspaper called the *Xinhua* ("New China") *Daily*. Since the official newspaper, called the *Central Daily*, only published news and commentary from the official angle, I decided to subscribe to the Communist newspaper as well. I wanted to see things from both sides. This was considered rather unorthodox by the authorities, although they could not openly admit that I had done wrong. Then one day Gladys said something which was frowned upon by the authorities. Some students asked her what she thought of the student Kuomintang youth league, and she answered that she always disliked such organizations because they reminded her of the Nazi Gestapo. Her words reached the ears of the authorities in no time. Both the Kuomintang and the Chinese Communists had modelled themselves on Soviet or German examples and had their select youth organized into youth leagues, those who would join the Kuomintang or Communist Party later on. Although the Kuomintang and the Chinese Communists were enemies, they both followed the same pattern. Had the students asked her about the Communist youth league, Gladys' answer would probably have been the same. She was against any totalitarian enforcement of discipline. However her remark was taken to mean she was against the Kuomintang government. Soon the rumour was going around  that she was probably a British Communist agent and that no English young lady would want to marry a poor Chinese intellectual unless she was a Communist agent in disguise and acting with a political purpose. The head of the English department, a Professor Zhang, was the brother-in-law of the president of the university, Mr. Luo. As I noted before, he was my mother's landlord. Professor Zhang and President Luo were both Kuomintang bureaucrats. Zhang was a graduate of an American university. He had the look of a weasel or fox and spent most of his time spying on students, always keen to find suspected Communists. President Luo had formerly been a progressive student at Peking University in the early days of the Republic and had been an activist in the students' movement at that time. But by the war years he had turned into a Kuomintang government sympathizer, always eager to climb the ladder to become a Kuomintang official. He had a stumpy and thick figure, with short legs, and looked rather like a bear. This "weasel" and "bear", though outwardly our friends, decided, after finding us too friendly with our students, that we must leave the college by the end of the year. We had signed a one-year contract, so they had to wait for the summer vacation of 1941 before they could terminate our contracts.

My younger sister Amy, who had come to Chongqing with my mother, was then teaching in a high school in Chongqing. Her fiancé was Luo Peilin, whose father was a wealthy businessman in Tianjin and who had been a good friend of my father's. Amy and he had known each other when they were still in high school. Peilin went to Shanghai to study electronics, but after he graduated from university, he secretly went to Yan'an, the revolutionary base of the Chinese Communists. After staying there for several months, because of his family background, his Communist friends told him to come back to the Kuomintang area. At that time the Chinese Communists would not accept a young man with a landlord or capitalist class background as a member of the Party. So he went back to Chongqing, although he still kept his friends in the Communist Party. He earned a living as an engineer for a firm. In late 1940 or early 1941, Peilin took me to call on the Communist Party representative in Chongqing, whose name was Xu Bing and who became later the head of the United Front Department of the Party Central Committee. Xu Bing greeted me warmly and gave me two letters of introduction to two Chinese progressive historians, urging me to work with the revolutionary forces in China for China's liberation. I took these two letters with me to my college, but had not yet gone to see those two historians when the "weasel" discovered them. This further confirmed his suspicions. I had known for some time that whenever we were giving lessons to our classes, either the "weasel" himself or one of his student stooges would search our rooms, which was very annoying. I put these letters into one of my desk drawers and made some marks on the drawer. When I came back I found the marks gone and knew someone had been reading my letters. Sure enough, the following day the "weasel" invited me over for a chat and, trying to look kind and solicitous like an elder brother, said that things were complicated, that I was newly back from England and should be very careful about the friends we made. He threw in some dark hints and a threat about the serious trouble we could get into. After that, there were more veiled threats and warnings. But when summer vacation arrived and new contracts for the next academic year were issued, the university still renewed my contract. Gladys, however, got no word of a new contract. When I asked the department head why, he just hedged and said that he had heard some students did not like her teaching. Actually the students all liked us and Gladys was a very conscientious teacher, much better than I. Clearly we were being pushed out. One of our neighbours, an old teacher nearing seventy, whose name was Zhang as well, told me that a new college had just been set up in the adjacent provincial capital of Guiyang. It was called Guiyang Normal College and they needed a head for their English Department. He had been invited to go but felt he was too old to travel any more. So he asked me to take up the position in his stead. I felt rather ashamed of going back to Southwest United University in Kunming, after having broken my contract the year before, leaving them with a vacancy and much inconvenience. In any case, Guiyang was closer to Chongqing than Kunming, so I accepted his offer and Gladys and I went to the other province after teaching only one year in Chongqing. This was in the summer of 1941.

<h1 style="text-align:center">16</h1>

<h1 style="text-align:center">Marriage</h1>

Marriage between Gladys and myself took place in Chongqing before we left that city. In early spring my mother decided that we should be formally married. Gladys' father was in Lanzhou in the north-west, doing his Industrial Cooperatives work and teaching. Gladys' mother had also returned to China to join her husband. But life in China's north-west was too austere for her, so she took a teaching post at a university in Chengdu, also in Sichuan but west of Chongqing. Chengdu was the provincial capital, a very nice city with many foreign teachers and a good climate. So Gladys' parents could also come to the wedding. My sister Amy and her fiancé Luo Peilin determined to get married at the same time, so my mother decided on a double wedding, with the ceremony to be held in Chongqing in early March. It was to be in a hotel, and over a hundred friends of both families were invited. My mother also designed a wedding dress for Gladys. It was a Chinese style satin gown with short sleeves and embroidered all over with dragons and phoenixes, rather tight-fitting and not very practical. Early March in Chongqing can be quite chilly, and the wedding gown was rather thin and uncomfortable. I do not think Gladys enjoyed wearing it at all, but she obeyed my mother's wishes. It was neither a traditional

Chinese wedding nor a Western Christian wedding. There were two sponsors of the wedding, chosen from the family's elder connections. One was Dr. Zhang Boling, President of Tianjin Nankai University. The other was Luo Jialun, President of Central University, my mother's landlord, and the "bear" I spoke about earlier and disliked. The president of Nankai University was chosen because my sister was a teacher in that university's high school in Chongqing. The two brides and two bridegrooms were made to stand in a row while the sponsors gave speeches in turn and congratulated us. We bowed to thank them and the whole ceremony was over. There was a banquet with about a dozen round tables, and we were plied with drinks from all the family and friends. I drank an awful lot on that occasion without enjoying it.

Some time after we were married, we were invited to dinner by Dr. Hang Liwu, then Vice-Minister of Education in the Kuomintang government. Dr. Hang had been a student in the London School of Economics, but he was there a few years before my time. He boasted to have been a student of Professor Laski, but whether he had got a Ph.D. or not, I am not sure. Whatever the case, he was always called Dr. Hang and his spoken English was not too bad. He was also chairman of the Sino-British Cultural Society and a trustee of the Boxer Indemnity Fund. In this last capacity he was a colleague of my father-in-law J. B. Tayler. Because of his connection with my father-in-law, he was very good to Gladys and me, and at that time he wanted me to help him in Sino-British Cultural Society work. As a Kuomintang high official, he was of course ambitious and trying hard to climb the political ladder. But he was a civilized person and always wore well-tailored Western suits. He looked rather timid and on the defensive, like the rabbit in *Alice in Wonderland,* and there was always a nervous twitch on his cheek. The other guests that evening included Dr. Kong, Kuomintang

Finance Minister; General He, Kuomintang War Minister; Dr. Kong's wife, who was the elder sister of Madame Song Meiling and Chiang Kai-shek's sister-in-law; and the American Ambassador and the American Embassy's First Secretary. We were the only couple that held no official posts. During dinner the Americans plied me with questions about Tang poetry and such things and we talked a lot of nonsense. After dinner Dr. Hang and his wife asked if we would like to stay the night since my mother's place, where we were staying at the time, was outside the city and a good distance away. In those days there were no taxis in Chongqing. We thanked them and said we had other places to visit in the city and left this distinguished party. We found a small middle-class hotel in the city and proceeded to embark on an amusing adventure in the night.

We did not realize in those days that, although outwardly calm, the Kuomintang government was very vigilant against Communist agents. They would search all the hotels in the middle of the night for suspicious guests. We were fast asleep in our bed after midnight when suddenly I was awoken by people banging on the door. Without getting out of bed I told them to come in, since the door was not locked. Two armed policemen came in, looked at me in bed suspiciously, and asked me what my name and profession were, and where did I come from. I told them I was a professor at Central University. Then they looked at Gladys and became even more suspicious.

"And who is this foreign woman?" they barked.

"She is my wife." I answered sleepily.

Then they demanded to know when and where we were married. Unfortunately at that moment I could not remember the name of the hotel where the wedding ceremony took place nor the exact date of our wedding. This made them really suspicious, so I nudged

Gladys and woke her up to ask the name of that hotel and the date of our wedding. But in her sleepy state, she too could remember neither. Obviously to the policemen, we must have been making it all up. One of them started addressing me as "comrade" and said:

"Comrade! I am afraid we will have to ask you to come to the police station with us, so that we can clarify this matter."

As soon as he started addressing me as "comrade" I realized the situation was getting rather serious. In those days to call somebody "comrade" meant that you were considered an underground Communist agent. If I had to go with them to the police station for interrogation, I might never come out alive, like so many other young Chinese citizens who were secretly taken away, never to reappear. So I decided to bluff. I looked at him sternly and said I knew Dr. Hang, Vice-Minister of Education, very well, and had just come from his house. He could, if he like, ring him up and ask about me. I also mentioned the names of other Kuomintang high officials. The policeman was taken aback. He hesitated, looked at the other policeman, and suddenly changed his attitude. He clipped his heels smartly, like a German soldier and saluted:

"All right, sir. You did not say so clearly before. Please excuse me," and they beat a hasty retreat. We then continued our sleep, but I decided never to stay in a small hotel again in China. It was not, after all, London.

When the summer vacation was nearly over, my neighbour in Baixi, old Professor Zhang, told me he had heard from that college in Guiyang welcoming me to go to there as head of the English department. Gladys was to be invited as a full professor as well. So we made preparations to go to our new college. In those days there was no regular public transport between different provinces in the interior. Government officials had their own cars, various organizations had their own trucks, but ordinary citizens had to rely on their own resources for transport or they could try hitch-hiking on one official truck or another. The Chinese postal service always had regular trucks carrying sacks full of letters and people often asked for rides in these trucks, if they had the connections. So the Bank of China made arrangements for us, and we went by postal truck to Guiyang, which took less than two days. Such hitch-hiking back then was called *huangyu* ("yellow fish"). I never found out the etymology of this term.

I forgot to mention that before we set off for our new post in Guiyang, we went to Chengdu in the summer of 1941. We made that journey too by hitchhiking in a postal truck. Gladys' mother, who was teaching at a missionary university in Chengdu, invited us during the vacation, so we went for a short holiday. The journey to Chengdu went smoothly and without mishap. In Chengdu we stayed in the house owned by some missionaries where Gladys' mother was staying. It was on a street called "Three Saints Street", but who the three saints were I never knew. Perhaps they were meant to be Confucius, Buddha, and Christ (or Laozi). It was in this house that I witnessed the bombing mentioned earlier. We stayed there for nearly a month. When it was time to return to Chongqing, we also used our connections and went by postal truck. There were two other Chinese passengers. One was the president of Tsinghua University, Dr. Mei, and the other was a professor of linguistics, Luo Changpei. Both Dr. Mei and Professor Luo were well known in Chinese academic circles. Western Sichuan that summer had had much rain, so after a day's journey we found the road flooded out. Ahead we could see nothing but turbulent water. The truck could neither turn back nor go forward. Fortunately there was good company and Dr. Mei and Professor Luo humorously produced two bottles of Maotai, that famous and potent Chinese liquor, and we passed one evening pleasantly, with

humorous anecdotes and jokes in scholarly fashion in a peasant's hut by the roadside. When the truck could go on again, it was only a short while before we had to stop again. At some point we had to abandon the truck and continue our journey by boat. After struggling for three or four days we finally reached Chongqing. Since none of us was in any great hurry, we rather enjoyed this eventful journey, and Professor Luo even wrote a travel essay about the hazards encountered on a Sichuan road, which was later published in a magazine.

After we got back to Chongqing, Gladys received a notice from the British Embassy. It had black margins, as if it were an obituary notice. It stated that since the European War had started and Japan had joined the Axis, China and the Western powers had become allies. Now China had been at war with Japan for several years, during which time the British government had never lifted a finger to help us, but had, in fact, continued to sell scrap iron to Japan (although I must say that the British people had shown much sympathy to our cause). It was amusing to a Chinese that now, suddenly, the West had become our allies. The notice stated that owing to these new circumstances, if Gladys had married an "enemy alien", she could keep her passport, but since she had married a "friendly alien", she must give up her British passport and take up Chinese nationality papers instead. Gladys had to comply with the official rule and give up her passport. The next thing to do was to apply for Chinese nationality. However in those days, and even now, it was quite complicated for a foreigner to apply for Chinese citizenship unless there were official connections. So Gladys got no reply from the Chinese authorities, and since we were going to Guiyang right away, she had to go as a stateless person. Her stateless position continued throughout the war and she never bothered to apply again. Only quite some time after the war ended did the

British government change the rule, and Gladys got her passport back. After Liberation in 1949 she never applied for Chinese citizenship again and has remained a British citizen until now. It is more convenient for her to travel abroad with a British passport, and to have Chinese papers means nothing, since in China she would still be considered a foreigner, whatever her documents.

17

Guiyang

Guiyang gave us quite a favourable impression when we first arrived. It was then still a backward provincial town, but had the minimum of modern facilities like electricity and running water. It too had been bombed by Japanese planes the year before, but with little damage. Some houses lay in ruins, destroyed by fires which followed the bombing, but the new college grounds were intact. In the branch college of Central University, located in that small village of Baixi, we had been lodged in a house built with mud walls. At one point, one side of the wall near the bed where we were sleeping simply collapsed during a storm at night. There, too, every day we had to walk through muddy rice paddies to get to our classes. After teaching for a year under such conditions, we were glad to stay in the city instead of the countryside. Even more important was that we now had more congenial and better-qualified colleagues. There were some good teachers in Baixi, but there were no good scholars. At Guiyang Normal College there was Professor Yin, a scholar in his sixties, who was quite erudite and had a sense of humour: Professor Yin was the head of the Chinese department. With him was an assistant professor named Li, who was very young but quite civilized. He was the son of a well-known scholar of the late Qing dynasty. The head of the mathematics department was also called Li. He had studied abroad and was quite knowledgeable. Near our newly established college, there was Daxia ("Cathay") University, a missionary university evacuated from Shanghai. That university also had some good professors, among whom was Professor Li Qingyan, who taught French literature and had done a lot of translation of Maupassant. So in the company of these professors, we felt there was a bit of an academic atmosphere. However, the president of our college, a man named Wang, was a stupid and ignorant Kuomintang bureaucrat. Every morning at ten o'clock he would summon all the teachers and students to the college grounds, and he would take the lead in singing first the Kuomintang national anthem, and then reading out loud Dr. Sun Yat-sen's last will. The whole ceremony took about fifteen minutes and was totally ludicrous. He must have copied the pattern from a Christian service. Fortunately he did not mix with the teachers and students in his daily life, and we did not have anything to do with him. He only invited the professors to a meal at the end of each term and had little to talk about.

The first day we arrived at the college we had one small but unpleasant incident. We had just put down our luggage in our room, unpacked some of the suitcases and thrown some things onto our beds, and then decided to go to the canteen for lunch. After lunch and meeting some of our new colleagues, we went back to our room. We had never thought of locking the door since we were within the confines of the college. However to our dismay we discovered that many of our belongings had been stolen. We lost, among other things, a typewriter, a couple of woollen rugs, some of my better London-made suits, and a little money. Apparently the thief was someone inside the college who knew that we had gone out. We reported it to the college. They expressed regret but could do nothing. They said it was probably one or more students, but there was no way of finding the culprits. In those days most of the teachers and students were refugees fleeing to the interior from Japanese aggression along the coastal cities. Most of these young students were penniless. They had to rely on their university or college for board and lodging, and could not pay for their education. All the things we had brought from abroad must have given them the feeling that we were very rich. So how could we blame them? Anyway the thief had no interest in our books and manuscripts, so no great damage was done. Ever since we had gone to the interior, I never wore a Western suit, feeling it rather odd and ostentatious. I much preferred to wear a long, blue cloth gown. Gladys never bothered to dress up either, choosing a long cloth gown and trousers too. So many people must have thought us a rather eccentric couple. In those days I never liked to wear a Western suit because it made me feel too colonialist. But I did not wear a Sun Yat-sen type of suit either, because I did not want to look like a bureaucrat. So I was reduced to wearing my shabby long gown.

We became friends with our colleagues in no time. Old Professor Yin, the Chinese scholar, was particularly fond of me. When we first met, he thought that since I had just come from abroad, I must be very fond of Shakespeare. So he told me a story about his friend, Professor Liang Shiqiu. He said he liked Professor Liang very much and that Professor Liang had translated some of Shakespeare's plays into Chinese. Once he had asked Professor Liang:

"I've heard you mentioning the English poet Shakespeare a lot and that you like Shakespeare's poetry very much. What is the date of Shakespeare?"

"He was born in 1564 and died in 1616," Liang answered.

"Then he was only a Wanli Period man. How can he be compared to our Tang dynasty poets?"

Old Professor Yin laughed at his own joke. He did not know English, but he was erudite in classical Chinese literature. I had heard of Professor Liang. He was quite a well-known literary figure, had studied in the United States, and was one of the founders of the Crescent Society, a literary society at that time. The Wanli Period was one of the dynastic year names of the Ming dynasty, roughly coinciding with the time of Shakespeare. Later on I met Professor Liang in Chongqing and was his colleague for several years. I mentioned the story which Professor Yin had told me, and he remembered this old man's joke. Knowing that Yin was fond of classical Chinese poetry, I wrote a narrative poem in the *fu* style of "Li Sao" about my wanderings abroad, and showed it to him. He was very impressed. Professor Yin used to see a few of the local Guiyang scholars regularly. They would from time to time hold a poetry session and have a feast at somebody's expense, drinking wine and composing classical poems together. So Old Yin introduced me to his poetic friends and I would contribute a poem or two on such occasions. So from Chongqing to Guiyang I seemed to have gone to a different world and a different age: no more political intrigues and disinformation, just Chinese classical literature and poetry writing. I found it quite relaxing. During some of these poetry sessions with the old local scholars I also came across one amusing man. He was called Lu Qian, or Lu Jiye. He was a member of the Kuomintang Consultative Council, which was an advisory body with no real power, consisting of certain men of senior status in society. He was not then very elderly, still in his forties, but he was quite a scholar, had some literary fame, and was a poet. He thought highly of me because I could often dash off verses faster than the more elderly poets. A year or two later he sought me out in Chongqing and had me join the National Institute of Translation and Compilation. I shall speak of that again later.

Old Professor Yin was asked by the local newspaper, the *Guiyang Daily*, to edit a newspaper supplement. He began a literary supplement to be printed every fortnight. This literary supplement was called *Xiaoya*, meaning "little culture" or "little elegance" (that is, "a little bit of culture" or "a little bit of elegance"). It is the title of one section of the *Book of Songs*, a Confucian classic. He had me and his assistant teacher Professor Li be his co-editors. The supplement only went on for a few issues and I contributed some of my doggerels. During that year in Guiyang, I remember I also wrote a short essay denouncing those men in power who tried to emulate certain Western autocrats like Hitler, Mussolini, and Franco and said such people who were against the people would not come to a good end. I aimed this against Chiang Kai-shek without mentioning his name and it got published. I wrote it under a pseudonym. I remember I also published some translations of Western poems, like the seventeenth-century poet Herrick's "To His Coy Mistress". It was published in a Chongqing newspaper supplement under a pseudonym. What other things I wrote and published I cannot now remember, since I never kept any of my early writings.

I also remember during that year I usually joined the other teachers to dine in a restaurant once or twice every month because we found our canteen meals tedious. During that time inflation was not too bad. With our two professorial rank salaries and without children, Gladys and I could easily afford to eat outside. Nowadays university professors can hardly afford to eat in restaurants, especially if they have children, unless they are invited or have official connections in Beijing. In Guiyang we used to frequent one small restaurant with a quaint name. It was called Peiyang Zhengqi, meaning "fortifying the spirit", and it specialized in well-cooked chicken. The soup was especially delicious. Another local speciality was the well-known Guiyang liquor called Maotai. The liquor was made from spring water near the city and very potent. Once we two, Gladys and I, together with Old Yin and young Professor Li, went to a friend's house in a suburb called Huaxi, or "Flowering Brook". That friend brought out a big pot of this choice brew, which he had kept for dozens of years. We finished up the whole pot of at least six or seven pints. Young Professor Li was so drunk that he had to stay the night and only came back the next morning.

In Guiyang, Gladys consulted a doctor and discovered she was pregnant. She wrote to her mother in Chengdu, and her mother wrote back suggesting that she ought to have her baby in Chengdu because she could get better medical attention there. In those days Guiyang had no good hospital, while Chengdu was a city with many foreigners, especially missionary teachers in the various missionary universities which had been evacuated to the interior. She also suggested that after this year we should both move to Chengdu. Qilu University, a missionary college, had been evacuated there from Shandong near the coast, and she knew the president of that college and could have us invited there as professors. So it was decided that Gladys should go to Chengdu in January 1942. I would stay on till the summer because we had already signed a one-year contract. I would take over Gladys' classes, which meant four or five hours of teaching every day. Although it was exhausting, I did not find it difficult because the Guiyang college was new and we were only teaching freshmen English. It needed no preparation to speak of, but was time consuming. We hoped that life in Chengdu would be more comfortable, but as things turned out, it was not to be so and we found ourselves leaving Chengdu again after only half a year.

18

Back and Forth

To move constantly back and forth between the various cities of south-west China during the war years had certainly not been part of our plans. It seems, however, it was to be our lot.

In Guiyang there was a young foreign community as well, and we got to know those people quite well. Because it was wartime and there was a lot of sympathy in the West for the Chinese people's plight, a group had been set up called the Friends Ambulance Unit (F.A.U.) to send medical supplies to China. In Guiyang there was a F.A.U. centre consisting of mainly young volunteers from all walks of life, not necessarily medical workers. We got to know very well an American couple, John and Irene Vincent, and a young English Cambridge graduate, Michael Sullivan, and his Chinese fiancée Khoan. John Vincent was a young anthropologist, I believe, and Michael Sullivan was an art historian. We spent quite a lot of time together. We have been good friends to the present. John Vincent is now retired and Michael is now an authority on Chinese art, living in Oxford. By the summer of 1942 Gladys had already gone to Chengdu and was about to have her first baby. When I had to leave Guiyang, I asked the local F.A.U. to help with my transport. They had a truck going to Chongqing, but unfortunately there were already two other of their people going in the truck and it was fully loaded with medical supplies. They suggested I ride on the hood of the truck, in the front. The young foreign drivers drove rather recklessly and there was a sudden storm on the road. I was battered by the pelting rain, which came down like bullets. I was wet through and through but fortunately did not fall off the truck. When we reached the next roadside inn, the rain had stopped and I drank a full bowl of strong Chinese liquor, which brought back some warmth to my body. In Chongqing I paid my mother a brief visit and then negotiated another postal truck to Chengdu. I had bad luck again. This truck too was full, so I had to climb up onto the sacks full of letters in the back and there I perched atop all that mail. I had to fasten myself with the ropes to the bags so I would not fall off. This time I sat facing backwards, learning from my experience of the last time, so that when the truck set off I would not be facing the wind. That night we stopped again at a wayside inn. In those days the truck drivers had friends and temporary "wives" all along the Sichuan roads, so our driver went as usual to his temporary "family" to play mahjong and drink all night. The next day we had to start on our journey early, before dawn, in order to reach our destination, Chengdu, before dark. The driver, still half drunk, warned me to be careful and hold fast to the ropes. He said that only a couple of days earlier someone perched on those bags in the back had rolled off the truck and got his face all smashed up. He then started off cheerfully. As the truck passed swiftly around a bend, although I could not see clearly in the morning mist, there were apparently many soldiers resting in the middle of the road. Then they began jumping up and shouting. As we passed I felt a jolt and then I heard some soldiers shouting: "Stop the truck! You've killed our comrade!" Apparently some press-ganged new soldiers had been

sleeping in the middle of the road when our truck came down on them and one unfortunate soldier had gone under the wheels. Our driver knowing that something unfortunate had happened did not stop but went on at a terrific speed. The soldiers then started chasing us shouting, "Stop! Or we'll fire!" Several of them had already raised their rifles and were aiming at me. Since I was perched on top of those postal bags and facing them, I was the natural target. They might not succeed in stopping the truck, but they could certainly get me. Fortunately the driver realized that he could not escape and stopped the truck before they fired. We climbed down and were immediately surrounded by a mob of very angry soldiers. Then an officer came out and he and the driver had a heated discussion. Finally the officer calmed down. He agreed that it was an unfortunate accident. The soldier who got run over was a new conscript and he should not have been sleeping in the middle of the road. But they had never expected a truck to come by so early in the morning and our truck should not have been driving so fast and come without warning.

In those days the Kuomintang government always went to the countryside and press-ganged poor peasants' sons into the military, taking them away by force as new conscripts. They would not touch the sons of rich landlords, but the officers had their quotas to fill and this officer had to take so many conscripts back. If one was missing, he had to get a new one in his place. The officer explained that for him to "buy" a new one would cost him two hundred silver dollars, so the driver must pay him that exact sum as compensation. Our driver agreed but said that he did not have that much money with him. He had to drive back to the house of his "mistress" to get the money. That journey would take him several hours and would be impossible to do on foot. The officer agreed this might be the case but said, "If I let you and the truck

go, how can I be sure that you will come back with the money?"
Finally they hit upon a solution. The driver suggested, "How about
I leave this gentleman, a university professor, with you as deposit?
Then you can be certain I will come back." Both the officer and
myself agreed and the matter was settled. The officer and I, together
with his soldiers, waited in a wayside inn for about five or six
hours while the driver and the truck went off. We drank tea while
waiting, and the atmosphere was tense, without much conversation.
God knows what would have happened if the driver had never
come back. I suppose the officer and his soldiers would have just
taken me away as substitute for the dead conscript. However the
driver did keep his promise and finally came back soon after noon.
He handed the exact amount of silver dollars to the officer, who
beamed with delight. He probably never thought he would finally
get so much and doubtless ended up with a handsome profit at the
expense of his poor conscript's misfortune. The officer and his
soldiers were suddenly all smiles. They apologized to me for giving
me such a bad fright. The officer then insisted on playing the host
and invited us to a good meal. We lunched and drank wine and
parted as friends. We resumed our journey again and reached
Chengdu without further mishap. I did not offer to help the driver
with the money he lost. I did not have that much money with me
anyway. But he did not seem to care. In those days, just like now,
in China a truck driver can be much richer than a university
professor.

I forgot to mention earlier that before I left Guiyang for Chengdu
in the summer of 1942, I received a letter from Chengdu saying
that Gladys' mother had gone to India to teach there, and that
there had been some trouble at Qilu University, the university which
had invited us to come and teach. The president of the university,
whose name I forget, had had some trouble with his staff and

students and he had been dismissed. The new president refused to honour any of the former president's commitments, so our appointment vanished into thin air. In the meantime another university in Chengdu, Guanghua University, heard of this and invited us to join them. Guanghua University had also been evacuated from Shanghai and had only a small staff and few teachers. Under the circumstances, we had to accept their invitation since Gladys was already in Chengdu. After Gladys gave birth to our first child, in the beginning of August, we moved into the university compound. It was in a western suburb of the city. Our living quarters were adequate, but a professor's salary there was rather low, less than in the missionary universities. It was difficult to get a maid in the suburbs and we could not manage without some domestic help. So we hired a male servant. The man was more expensive than a maid, but even though his wage was higher, he would only cook our meals and did nothing else. So we had to spend a lot of time looking after our first baby and washing diapers ourselves. Our first child was a son. I gave him the Chinese name Ye, but Gladys liked to call him "Skunko" because she thought he had such a strong smell, like a skunk. We had no difficulties with the university authorities. They treated us cordially, but offered no help with our domestic problems. We also had no good friends among the teachers, so life was rather boring and hectic. After a few months we decided we would only teach there for one term and then go somewhere else. There were several possibilities. One was to go on to Kunming and join Southwest United University. But although I had heard it was the best university at the time and knew of many good professors there, I still felt too ashamed to write them after breaking my contract with them just after we arrived in the interior. Another possibility was to go to Sichuan University in Leshan, where their English department head had written to me asking me to go there to take over his job as department head. However, it meant that we had to go further into the interior and I was by then feeling rather disillusioned about Chinese universities. There was too much Kuomintang politics, and teaching English to students who knew so little about the West was very tasteless and boring. One day I received a letter from Chongqing, from a friend named Zhu Yanfeng. He had been at Oxford doing a B. Litt. thesis during my time. He was a Tsinghua University graduate studying ancient history. He wrote a thesis on the Western Turks during the Tang dynasty. I knew he was not a brilliant scholar and did no real original research. His study of the Western Turks was all based on research done by the French sinologist Chavannes. However, he had been to Oxford and I knew him. His offer sounded rather attractive to me: he wrote that since India was about to declare its independence soon and China was interested in relations with India, the government wanted to set up an institute of Indian studies. He had been appointed director of that institute. The institute's building was under construction in Chongqing and would be ready before the end of that year. He wanted me to join the institute and become its first and only research fellow. I could help him in his work. His spoken English was not very good and he felt I could help him when dealing with foreigners. He would offer me the highest professor's salary and he could introduce Gladys to the Kuomintang National Central Library in Chongqing as a researcher. So we decided to accept his offer, and in January 1943 we left Chengdu to head back to Chongqing.

19

Beibei

Beibei or the "North Promontory" is a small scenic spot near Chongqing. In our travels back and forth, I had no idea we would end up there. By the time we got back to Chongqing in early spring 1943, my mother and my sister Amy had moved from President Luo's house in Xiao Longkan ("Little Dragon Ridge") to the Nankai high school not far away. Amy was a teacher there. The Institute of Indian Studies, my job before heading to Beibei, was in a district called Lianglukou ("Crossroads"), which was nearer the city and not very far from the high school. So we stayed with my mother and my sister at their new place, and I went twice or three times a week to the institute. Gladys too did not have far to go to her work at the library, which was also on the same road to the city. This institute of Indian students had just been built. We had no staff except a young assistant and no books and few pieces of furniture. Professor Zhu had no plans for the institute. He just spent his time running to see various Kuomintang high officials asking for more funds. He was an inefficient and timid man and often got scolded by his wife, who was an awful shrew. As one would expect with a hen-pecked husband, there were constant quarrels in his family. Once as I was entering his office, a bowl came sailing over my head. It was aimed at her husband's face but it did not get to him, nearly hitting my head instead. After that I kept away from them when I heard them quarrelling.

During that summer there was a representative of India in Chongqing. I think his name was Richardson and he had an office there. I called on him at his office. He was quite a nice fellow and when he learned that I was an Oxford man, he beamed and said that he had also done Hon. Mods. and Greats at Oxford too. We talked about translating Aristophanes and other things and parted as friends. He gave me a bundle of their publications, including books and pamphlets on Indian culture, among which was a small book introducing Indian music. I translated it from English into Chinese in my spare time at the office. That little book never got published. I left the manuscript in the office when I left the institute at the end of the year. It was probably my only real contribution to the institute. I don't think that institute lasted very long, for I never heard it mentioned by anybody after I left. As for Professor Zhu, I heard from some friends that he began teaching in a university in Shanghai after the Japanese surrender. I don't think he could have ever been a successful Kuomintang official, however hard he tried. We never communicated later. I have always been a very poor correspondent and hate writing letters.

Some time in autumn that year, I got a call from someone I knew in Guiyang. It was the fat poet Lu Qian, or Lu Jiye, whom I mentioned earlier. He said that he had been asking a lot of people about me and had gone to a lot of trouble to find me. He said that there was an Institute of Translation and Compilation in a town not far from Chongqing. In fact it was still within the Chongqing municipality. His friend, Professor Liang Shiqiu, was there as head of the Translation Committee. He had been recommending me to Professor Liang very strongly, so now the latter wanted me to join their institute. They offered me and Gladys the highest professor's salaries, making me a senior research fellow like himself. The institute's translation committee so far only had people translating Western classics into Chinese and they wanted us to head a section translating Chinese classics into English. They suggested that since Chinese history classics were unknown to the West, I should translate *Zizhi tongjian* (An Historical Guide to Assist in the Governance of the Empire). This was a Song dynasty classic compiled by the scholar Sima Guang. Since I was rather disappointed with the Institute of Indian Studies and Gladys was also happy to leave the Central Library, we gladly agreed. We had never liked the general atmosphere in Chongqing, and for Gladys to live under her mother-in-law's roof all the time was not particularly comfortable. Her health since the birth of our son had not been very good. She had had an attack of malaria, with constant fevers and diarrhoea, and during this period I had to spend a lot of time in town. We heard that this suburban town near Chongqing, called Beibei, was on the northern bank of the Jialing River. It had some hot springs nearby and the air was fresh, unlike murky Chongqing. It was also a scenic spot near a mountain, with a monastery and plenty of forestation. The town was fairly modern, with electricity and water, not like the village called Baixi where we had taught before. On top of all those advantages, we liked this fat poet Lu Qian and we had heard many favourable accounts of his friend Professor Liang, a well-known scholar. We felt we would be doing well with such company. In fact, it did prove to be a good choice. We stayed on with this Institute of Translation and Compilation until after Liberation in 1951, when the new Communist government decided to abolish it. I still have fond memories of that institute.

So before the end of 1943 we moved again from Chongqing to

this suburb town of Beibei (I should mention here that the town is often pronounced "Beibei", commonly so in the north of China). The Institute of Translation and Compilation was divided into several departments. One department compiled and edited books in the social sciences or the humanities; one department compiled and edited books in the natural sciences; one department compiled and edited school textbooks; one department compiled and edited popular reading books; and one department, called the Translation Committee, published translations of Western classics into Chinese. I belonged to the Translation Committee as a senior fellow or editor, the same as Professor Liang, who headed this committee. After Gladys and I joined this department, we started a new section translating Chinese classics into English. This institute had first been set up in Nanjing and was evacuated to Chongqing after the war began. It had more than a hundred editors and translators, mostly former professors and lecturers from various colleges. Professor Liang, for instance, had taught in one of the universities in Shanghai. In Beibei he lived in a small villa owned by the wife of a Beijing university professor. When Gladys and I went there he and the fat poet Lu Qian put us in the dormitory of a neighbouring institute called the Institute of Ceremony and Music where Lu Qian worked in an advisory capacity. That institute, with its bizarre name, was smaller than our institute. Its work was to institute proper ceremony and music for certain official occasions of the Kuomintang government. Actually this Confucian-sounding institute had little real work to do. It was just one of many such organizations the real purpose of which was to provide a refuge for intellectuals who had fled inland from Japanese aggression. We shared our dormitory with two senior musicologists, both of surnamed Yang. So this house became known as the House of the Three Yangs (Sanyanglou). It was a two-storey building with some

modern facilities and a neglected garden in the back. The well-known writer Lao She, author of the novel *The Rickshaw Boy*, lived just a couple of hundred yards away. So our living quarters were quite adequate and with such congenial company we enjoyed our stay for the next three or four years.

I became good friends with my two neighbours in no time. They were both excellent people and much older than myself. One of them, Yang Yinliu, was in his late fifties. He was a professor at the Central Institute of Music and was good, not only in music theory, but also in Chinese and Western musical instruments. At that time he was compiling a history of Chinese music. I used to chat with him about ancient Chinese music, although I was quite ignorant about that subject. His enthusiasm about the history of ancient Chinese music inspired me to learn more about the subject, so between 1943 and 1945 I managed to write some half-dozen short research monographs on Tang dynasty music, and he encouraged me a great deal. After the Japanese war he went back to rejoin his former institute of music. Although we still saw each other from time to time, I gradually lost interest in the history of Chinese music. But I shall always remember him as a good teacher and friend in those war days. I still remember him crouching near his bed and playing the game of *go* all day with a colleague, forgetting his lunch and supper. *Go* is Japanese for what we call in Chinese *weiqi*. It is an ancient Chinese chess game with black and white pieces, more like draughts than chess. I used to watch him play one game after another. I would often bring him his meals, which he took without taking his eyes away from the board. He asked me in his later days to translate a history of Chinese music into English for him. Unfortunately my life later became too hectic and I never found the time for it after Liberation.

The other Yang in our dormitory was an old scholar, in his

early sixties, named Yang Zhongzi. He was also a professor of music and had a Swiss or Belgian wife. He was also a cultured gentleman, quiet and modest, and I liked him too. He died before the Cultural Revolution in his eighties in Nanjing.

My colleague, Professor Liang Shiqiu, had studied English literature in the United States. When I knew him in Beibei, he was translating some of Shakespeare's plays into Chinese. He was a brilliant man and very quick-witted. At the same time he did not take academic work seriously. He would do a translation of one of Shakespeare's plays within ten days and never bother to read his manuscript again. When I knew him, we never talked about literature. He did not like to talk politics or current affairs either, because once he had had some arguments with Lu Xun, the famous Chinese writer, and was very much criticized by the latter for his laissez-faire attitude towards life. He wasted a lot of time fooling around with Kuomintang officials, playing mahjong most of his evenings, or feasting and drinking. Though the house he stayed in was always full of visitors and friends, I did not go there very often because I did not like some of his friends, and you could never have any serious talks with him. However, he was always very good to me, and always very courteous and considerate. He introduced me to the president of the Central College of Drama in Beibei. I taught English there, as well, in 1944 for a year as a part-time professor. After the Japanese surrender in 1945, he left the interior and went back to Beijing, leaving me to head the Translation Committee in the institute. Later I heard he went to Taiwan and we subsequently never communicated. I was glad to hear that he had translated all of Shakespeare's plays into Chinese before he died.

Another close friend during those days in Beibei was Professor Liang Zongdai of Fudan University. Fudan University was originally in Shanghai. During the war it was evacuated to Chongqing. At the time it was on the south bank of the Jialing River. Our institute in Beibei was on the north bank, so we were separated by the same river. When we went to Beibei, Fudan University wanted us to teach for them too. Since I had already agreed to teach as a part-time professor in the Central College of Drama, it was decided that Gladys should teach part-time at Fudan. However Gladys' health was not very good and she had to look after her baby. So I usually went by ferry across the river to take over her classes. So in a way both of us became connected with Fudan University.

Fudan University at that time had a good and enlightened president and quite a few good professors. Among them I liked Professor Liang Zongdai best. He was educated in Paris and knew quite a few French writers and poets quite well, like Verlaine and Paul Valéry, being a poet himself. In his younger days he had translated Paul Valéry's poem on the Greek god Narcissus, and I had read his translation when I was still in high school in Tianjin and liked it very much. So we became good friends as soon as we met. On weekdays he used to come to our dormitory every other evening after supper, and we chatted about our student days in Oxford and Paris and about French poetry and literature while drinking strong local liquor. I remember one amusing incident about him in the winter of 1943. When he turned up one evening, I had one whole earthenware pot full of strong liquor with preserved dragon-eye fruit in it. I had put that pot under my bed. As it happened, I had put another pot of the same size but full of kerosene under the bed. In those days the supply of electricity was erratic and in the evening we usually lighted a kerosene lamp on the desk. The colour of the kerosene was light yellow, just like the colour of the liquor I had prepared, and the two pots looked the same when placed side by side. So by mistake I took the wrong pot

out and poured him a full bowl. He tasted it and remarked that my liquor seemed quite strong and had an unusual taste, but he emptied the bowl without flinching. After he left, I discovered that it was the wrong pot, but by then it was too late and he had already left by ferry for his university. I feared that I had poisoned him, but he turned up the next day unharmed and we had a good laugh over it. In those days he was very healthy, very fond of drinking and chasing young good-looking women. He had quite a few affairs with the wives of his colleagues and later he had a serious fight with his dean, who had a young and pretty wife. Because of this scandal he had to leave Fudan and go back to his hometown in Guangxi. Later I heard that he went into business, and soon after Liberation this good scholar and poet was jailed as a local despot landlord, having connections with local brigands, and he was sentenced for life. Later he was released and went to teach Shakespeare and Elizabethan poetry in Guangzhou (Canton). I met him during a conference on English literature in Guangzhou in the late seventies. He was by then an old man, but still healthy and cheerful. He told me that he had done a translation of Shakespeare's sonnets and Goethe's *Faust* from German. He was interested in Chinese medicine, and he gave me a bottle of his special brew, a liquor supposed to have aphrodisiac properties. A year later I heard that he had died. I don't know whether he was poisoned by his own brew. He was a man after my own heart. It is a pity that there are now few scholars and poets like him.

20

During the War Years

During the war years, Beibei, like Kunming in Yunnan, Chengdu and Leshan in western Sichuan, and Guilin in Guangxi (now a national minority autonomous region), became temporarily a centre of culture, full of university professors, scientists, writers and artists taking refuge from the war. I met and made friends with many Chinese intellectuals during those years of 1943 to 1946, but it would be too confusing for my readers to list all those Chinese names, so I have mentioned only a very few friends directly connected with my life there. I turn now to my work at the institute and my writings during that period.

My main work at the institute was translating that massive historical classic, *Zizhi tongjian*, into English. Apart from that I remember translating a short history of Chinese drama, written by a young scholar. I finished that work within a couple of months, but for some reason the manuscript never got published. This was the fate of many translations. The publication of books was difficult in the war days. There was a scarcity of both paper and printing facilities in the interior. At any rate, the Kuomintang government was not interested in publishing those kinds of manuscripts. They were only interested in printing books such as the Chinese translation of Hitler's *Mein Kampf*. Their principal aim was to keep intellectuals like myself in institutes so as to keep them quiet.

One good thing in the institute was that it had a good library. There were not many good foreign books, only a few classics like Gibbons' *Decline and Fall of the Roman Empire*, but there was quite a good collection of Chinese books, and I spent much of my time in that old library reading and making notes. So between 1944 and 1946 I jotted down copious notes and wrote a couple of hundred short articles on ancient Chinese history, on the history of Chinese literature, on ancient legends and myths, on ancient Chinese relations with foreign countries, on the early history of China's minority nationalities, and so on. At that time I had some  university friends who had gone back to Shanghai, even though it was still under Japanese occupation. The Japanese army had stopped advancing towards the interior, much too occupied with the war in the Pacific. In Shanghai things were returning to normal, so many publishing houses there were publishing books and magazines again. Some friends asked me to send some of my articles to a magazine called *New China* (*Xin Zhonghua*), published by Zhonghua Bookstore in Shanghai. They were published and later collected in a volume called *Random Notes* (*Lingmo xinjian*). After Liberation, much later in the 1970s, it was republished in one volume, with many short articles added. During those years I was rather prolific, turning out many articles and translations. If that period of my life had lasted longer, I might have become an historian, an authority on various subjects related to ancient Chinese history. But later events turned me away from such academic research.

I also did some translations from English to Chinese and from Chinese to English. I remember translating a couple of essays from Lamb's *Essays of Elia*, some one-act plays of Synge, some poems of Herrick, and other literary pieces. Whether they ever got published in Shanghai or not, I am not sure. My friend from Oxford, the scholar Qian Zhongshu, was in Shanghai then and edited a magazine called the *Philobiblion* for the local library. He asked me to contribute several articles in English, so I wrote a number of articles on China's relations with the Byzantine Empire during the Tang dynasty. With the help of Gladys I also translated a late Qing dynasty novel, *Laocan youji*, which became *The Travels of Mr. Decadent* in English. The manuscript was taken by a friend to England and published by an English publisher. I forget whether it was Allen and Unwin or Collins. Anyway I don't think it ever had a second printing. After Liberation it was printed again as the *Travels of Lao Can* in the Panda Books series of Chinese Literature Press, Beijing. I also translated into English, among others, the poems of Tao Qian (Tao Yuanming), the lyrics of Wen Tingyun, the poems of Li He, some Tang dynasty chante-fables, including "The Swallow" (which is like the English "The Owl and the Nightingale"), and one called "The Saint and the Devil" (which is about an Indian saint), some debates during the fifth dynasty about the immortality of the spirit, and a Miao nationality creation poem. Many of these translations were published after Liberation in the 1970s and early 1980s, but some manuscripts were lost. I also translated some modern Chinese literature, including poems by Ai Qing and Tian Jian, a play by Guo Moruo and one by Yang Hansheng. The latter two plays were done either for the American Fulbright Foundation or the American scholar John Fairbank. In those days they set up a fund in Chongqing to help Chinese writers because inflation was beginning to set in and Chinese intellectuals were feeling the pinch. I myself had to take a number of extra teaching jobs to make ends meet.

After the Japanese had pushed their way to Wuhan in central China and taken Guangzhou in the south, there was a lull on the war front. They set up puppet governments in Nanjing and north China and stopped advancing so as to consolidate their gains. They also turned their interests elsewhere, being harassed by Chinese guerrilla activities in the occupied territories. In the autumn of 1941 when we had been teaching in Guiyang, the Pacific War had started. I remember every day we read the local daily newspaper with great interest — how the Japanese bombed Pearl Harbour, sank British warships, and rampaged all over South-east Asia, from Hong Kong to Singapore. Gladys read the news with anger and concern, worrying about her eldest brother Bernard who had been captured by the Japanese when they took Singapore. As for my feelings in those days, frankly I felt an outsider, watching with interest one fascist power beating up other, older imperialist powers. The war seemed to be receding from the Chinese mainland.

When I came back to China in 1940, I was full of enthusiasm, hoping to serve in some way in our patriotic anti-Japanese war. But very soon in Kuomintang China I became frustrated and disillusioned, and resigned myself to live in the interior in a meaningless way, just managing to keep afloat. My escape to Beibei or "North Promontory" was just to stay in the library with my books, or to joke and drink strong liquor with my friends. The war seemed very far away. In the spring of 1944, however, I was temporarily shaken out of my lethargy. The Japanese army made another push towards the south-west, captured Guilin in Guangxi, and had advanced into Guizhou province, adjacent to Sichuan — where Chongqing was. The people of Chongqing were rather alarmed. My friend, the fat poet Lu Qian, talked about joining the Nanjing puppet government if Chongqing fell. He said he had old Kuomintang friends there. I was thinking that if that happened I would go to Yan'an, the Communist resistance base in the north-west. I actually wrote a letter to the Xinhua News Agency in

Chongqing and asked if they could give me transport to go to Yan'an. They immediately wrote me a reply, saying that although they would welcome me and my family, the travel was difficult, so they advised me to stay on in Chongqing and work for the revolutionary cause. So I gave up the idea. But the Japanese did not advance further and soon retreated from Guizhou. I suppose they were fighting on too many fronts.

The year after that, in autumn 1945, the war ended. The United States dropped their atom bombs and the Soviet Union defeated the Japanese army in China's north-eastern provinces known as Manchuria, and Japan surrendered. We received the news that the war had ended one evening when I was chatting with our neighbours, the two other Yangs of our dwelling, while enjoying the rising moon on the verandah. It must have been around Chinese Moon Festival. First we heard the sound of firecrackers and people cheering and banging gongs in the distance. Then people were running in the streets, selling newspaper extras printed with big red characters announcing the joyful news. Although after reading the newspapers those last few days we all knew that the war was ending, it still came as a great surprise. After eight long, weary years of war, it seemed that a new chapter in life had begun. The war immediately seemed something of the past and we talked excitedly about the future. The other two Yangs talked about going down the Yangtze to their old homes and colleges. Gladys and I had no plans for our future. We did not want to return to Tianjin to the old family and felt we might as well go back to the institute to Nanjing. At that time everybody who had come to the interior was a refugee from down river and was considered a "down-river person". So everybody wanted to go down the Yangtze to Nanjing and Shanghai. Others wanted to go to north China to see their families and former organizations. Since there was such a rush, transportation was a problem. Those with official connections managed to travel back in no time. My colleague, Professor Liang Shiqiu, went back immediately to Beijing and left the institute. He left me to head the Translation Committee. We ourselves did not manage to get transport to Nanjing until one year later, and that was by travelling in a very cramped, uncomfortable wooden junk down the Yangtze River in autumn 1946. When we arrived in Nanjing, it was again the autumn Moon Festival. My fate seemed to be linked to the Chinese autumn Moon Festival. It was Moon Festival when I first arrived in London, it was Moon Festival when I came back to China, it was again Moon Festival when the Japanese war ended and when I returned from Chongqing to Nanjing.

Before I go on with the story of my life after the war and after my journey to Nanjing in 1946, I must mention some of my foreign friends and contacts during our stay in Beibei between 1944 and 1946. Beibei, being close to the wartime capital Chongqing, and a scenic spot with well-forested hills and hot springs, was often frequented by the foreign community in Chongqing during weekends. So many foreigners, both embassy people and tourists, came to call on us from time to time. Here I can only mention a very few who played some part in my later life. In 1944 a distinguished British photographer, Sir Cecil Beaton, came to visit us. He took some photos of my family and friends. I still have a photo he took of the fat poet Lu Qian and me in a cave in a hill near Beibei. He also photographed my son Yang Ye when he was little more than one year old. We put the baby on a table, but the baby looked rather uncomfortable. We did not know why at that time. After our visitor left, we found that Yang Ye had had a bowel movement. Alas he had made the table dirty, so Sir Cecil never gave us that photograph — probably because he had noticed it too. Later he sent me an album of his photos, including his photo of me and Lu Qian in the cave. It is probably the only photo I still have of that period. We never communicated again and he probably died long ago.

Another distinguished visitor we met at that time was India's first ambassador to China, K. P. S. Menon. He probably heard of me from that Indian agent, Mr. Richardson, who had been representing India before India's independence and whom I had met in Chongqing the year before when I was working in the Institute of Indian Studies. Menon and I became good friends. Since I was very interested in ancient Indian history and relations between ancient India and China, Mr. Menon lent me many books on ancient Indian and Central Asian history from his personal library, including a Cambridge History of Ancient India, Aurel Stein's books on ancient Central Asia, and others. These helped me a good deal in writing notes about King Asoka, Kanishka, Mihiragula, and other topics. At that time my old friend Xiang Da, who had studied the Dunhuang manuscripts kept in London and who was then at the Chinese Academia Sinica in Leshan in western Sichuan, often wrote to me and we exchanged ideas on such subjects. Professor Xiang Da knew a bit of Sanskrit. His other name was Jue Ming, so he would translate his name as Bodhi-yasa, and I would reply to him signing my name Xianyi as Dharmavardana. People who happened to read our letters would wonder who those two Indian monks called Bodhiyasa and Dharmavardana were. Actually my knowledge of Sanskrit was negligible. We had just picked these names for fun, out of old Chinese Buddhist books. Mr. Menon later went back to India via Central Asia and wrote a book about his travels. His son, young Mr. Menon, in the 1980s too became ambassador to China and he presented me with a copy of K. P. S. Menon's book.

21

Down River

Down river was, as I mentioned earlier, the place everyone was going back to after the Japanese surrender. Ultimately we were headed that way too. In 1944 Gladys became pregnant again. During that time an old acquaintance, an Austrian Jewish young woman named Ruth Weiss, came to visit us in Beibei. We had known her since 1942, when we went to Chengdu to stay with Gladys' mother. She had been staying in the same house where Gladys' mother lived. When Ruth was leaving our place, Gladys offered to carry her suitcase and this caused Gladys to have a miscarriage and she lost the baby. So Gladys was quite ill for a couple of months. She recovered soon, though, and in 1945 we had another baby, our first daughter Yang Ying. Ruth Weiss had also married a Chinese man, but he later left her and went to the United States. After Liberation Ruth came to the Foreign Languages Press in Beijing and became our colleague. There she too became a foreign expert like Gladys. She is now over eighty, still hale and hearty. She has taken Chinese citizenship and is a member of the Chinese People's Political Consultative Conference.

Between 1944 and 1946, whenever I went from Beibei to Chongqing to see my mother and friends, I used to stay with some English friends who were members of the British Embassy. One of them, John Blofeld, who was then Second Secretary, had been a student at Cambridge. He was quite an odd character, an ardent Buddhist. In his younger days he had gone to Wutai Mountain and had become a monk there for some time. When I went to stay with him on occasional weekends in Chongqing, he used to tell me all sorts of weird stories about opium smoking and prostitutes in Vietnam, about yogi experts, about his early Buddhist experiences, and other fabulous tales. We used to drink a lot of Chinese liquor together and when he got drunk, he would lie on the floor and sing doleful Russian songs and weep. I think this was because his mother was Russian and he had some of the Russian character. I got on very well with him and we enjoyed each other's company. Later, when he was still Second Secretary in the British Embassy, he decided to marry a Chinese girl. He invited the British Ambassador to the ceremony but then got cold feet and disappeared before the wedding took place. This caused a scandal and he left the embassy. Later he became an English professor in a college in Bangkok. He produced many books about popular Buddhism, but in the early 1980s he got skin cancer and came to China for treatment and stayed with us in Beijing. He presented me with one of his recent books on Chinese tea. He died soon after he went back to Bangkok.

Through John Blofeld we became friends with several other members of the British Embassy in Chongqing. The one I liked most was Henry MacAleavy, another Cambridge man. He studied first Greek and Latin, then some of the European languages including Russian, then went to Paris and studied under Pelliot and became a brilliant sinologist. He used to drink copious amounts together with me and John Blofeld in those days. After the Japanese surrender, he married a Japanese woman called Ayako in Chongqing. He left the embassy and I introduced him to work as my colleague in the Institute of Translation and Compilation. After a year he went to Shanghai and worked with the British Ministry of Information until Liberation. Then he went back to England and became a professor of Chinese history and literature at the London School of Oriental and African Studies (SOAS), and produced a couple of books on the late Qing dynasty and the Empress Dowager. Unfortunately he died too young, in the 1950s or early 1960s. He was a brilliant scholar who dissipated his life away. I was very fond of him. Of my other friends at the British embassy, I could say much about friends like Joe Ford and Pat Coates. But I will remain brief and only mention one person, a British military attaché at the embassy, named Adrian Conway Evans. He too came to visit us in Beibei after the Japanese surrender, and even offered to take us to Nanjing in his jeep, although we declined. I shall talk about him later, because after we arrived in Nanjing in the autumn of 1946, we used to see him a lot and that had a great deal to do with the later events of our lives.

In early 1944 — some time before Gladys had her miscarriage and subsequently gave birth to another baby girl in 1945 — Gladys' father J. B. Tayler came to Beibei to visit. In those days he spent most of his time in the north-west, in Lanzhou, doing his Industrial Cooperatives work. But from time to time he would come to Chongqing because the Kuomintang government had become interested in that Industrial Cooperatives experiment started by foreigners. They felt it could be made into a showpiece to get contributions from abroad. So they began to take control of the organization. My father-in-law periodically had to consult the Kuomintang government about his organization's future develop- ments. He was a good but naive person. He only wanted to do good, working for the Chinese people, and never suspected that he was being manipulated by the Kuomintang government in their bid to get money contributions from abroad. When he visited us this time, he was in quite high spirits. We went to the hot springs and climbed Jingyun Mountain nearby. He was quite old but still vigorous, and I remember when he reached the mountain top, he was quite elated and cried out, "Excelsior!" After he left, he wrote Gladys a letter saying that when he was leaving he had hesitated and was about to say "God bless you" but didn't because he felt we did not share the same Christian faith. It would have been, he thought, presumptuous to say "God" to us, thus forcing his religion upon us. That was what J. B. was like — a modest, kindly old gentleman, who never wanted to force his own views on other people.

After the Japanese surrender in autumn 1945, we received the sad news from England that Gladys' eldest brother Bernard had been forced onto the "death march" in Borneo or thereabouts before the Japanese surrender, and had died. We were asked to break this sad news to his father. Since Gladys was still recovering after the birth of our daughter Ying, I had to go to Chongqing to see J. B. Tayler. When I broke this sad news to him, he did not burst into tears but retired to another room. After a while he came back quite composed and said goodbye to me, although I knew he was heart-broken. He was very fond of his eldest son Bernard, who for some years had been a good chemist and engineer in Southeast Asia. My father-in-law left China soon after that and died not long after returning to England. Gladys' mother, who had gone to teach in India, also went back to England after the surrender of the Japanese. She lived on for many more years, but died when we were put in jail in the late sixties during the Cultural Revolution. She never saw Gladys' release from jail in 1972. I felt very sorry for my parents-in-law, who lived and worked for China during those unhappy times.

So in the summer of 1946 we finally managed to get ourselves, our two very young children, and our belongings onto a wooden junk hired by the institute. Together with many of our colleagues we sailed down the Yangtze from Chongqing. Thus started a new chapter of our lives. As an academic organization, our institute was not rated very high in the Kuomintang government, so we could not get better transport. All the proper ships and boats, airplanes, and trucks had been commandeered to take Kuomintang officials and people with official connections to Nanjing. All that the institute could get for hire after one year of negotiations was two or three wooden junks to negotiate passage down the Yangtze River for us and our colleagues. The journey took several days. There were so many of us on the junks that each person only had a tiny bit of space, less than eight feet long and three feet wide. We could only lie down and hardly moved at all. There was no toilet or washing facilities. Our youngest child, our daughter Ying, developed boils all over her body because of the poor sanitary conditions. In those days people talked about bandits coming down from the mountains to rob passing boats near the Gorges at night. Fortunately we were spared such a misadventure. Once, when passing through the Gorges, there was alarm on the junk that it might overturn, with considerable panic ensuing. Finally everyone just lay down flat and nothing happened. So we passed through those beautiful Yangtze Gorges and reached our destination Nanjing unscathed. After we reached Nanjing, we heard that the junk behind us, the one carrying many of our books and other belongs, had caught fire and sunk, with some casualties on board. The junk was carrying several tanks of gasoline, so when it caught fire, there was no question about saving it. Before we left Beibei, a lot of books in big wooden boxes had just arrived from Hong Kong. Those were part of my books which I sent to Hong Kong by sea

from Oxford, about seven or eight big wooden boxes, in the summer of 1940. Apparently when those cases arrived in Hong Kong, the Pacific War had started and the Japanese militarists took them. They were very methodical. They put a stamp on each of these books with the mark "Yang's Library" in Japanese. When my old friend Bernard (Bunny) Mellor went after the war to be the Registrar of the University of Hong Kong, he recognized these were my old books, and he sent them to Chongqing. I only opened one or two of these wooden boxes and took a few books out; the rest I sent unopened to the junk to go to Nanjing. Of course all these were destroyed in the disaster, together with some clothes and old family photographs. It was a pity to lose all these books and photos, but we were lucky not to have been in that junk. We arrived in Nanjing with just the few books which I carried with me. I still have on my bookshelves today a few books with the Japanese stamp as souvenir.

22

Nanjing

anjing immediately provided us with our next big challenge: finding a place to stay. I remember there was a full moon that evening. It was the Chinese Autumn Moon Festival. Because most lodgings were full, we had to sleep on the wooden floor in our office building. In the middle of the night, after I was sound asleep, I suddenly jumped up with a premonition of danger. When we arrived I had not switched off the lamp because I was dead tired. In the light I saw a huge, dark-red centipede on the floor, poised with its mandibles aimed at my forehead. It immediately ran off and I could not catch it. I could not sleep after that, although Gladys and the two children went on sleeping soundly through the night. The next day we started to look for lodgings. One of the workers in the institute introduced us to a family living behind a coal shop and we moved into that house. We had the downstairs rooms, while the landlord and landlady stayed upstairs. The rooms and facilities were adequate but the landlady was a very troublesome woman. She was greedy, trying all the time to squeeze money out of us, and she always quarrelled with her henpecked husband, creating pandemonium in the house. We couldn't find a moment of peace in the evenings. After half a year we decided it was too much, so we moved to other lodgings near our institute. It was a better house and much quieter. We had half of the house there too, but this time it was the front rooms while our landlady's family lived in back and had the backyard. However, the rooms proved rather expensive for us, so after less than a year we left again. We decided it was no good to try to rent rooms without official help. The Vice Minister of Education of the Kuomintang government, Dr. Hang Liwu, whom I mentioned earlier and who was very good to us when we first arrived in Chongqing, came and asked me whether I would take up the part-time job as Secretary-General for the Sino-British Cultural Association. He was the current Secretary-General of the association but was too busy with his ministerial duties and wanted me, a fellow Britain-returned student, to take his place. The Sino-British Cultural Association in Nanjing had a good building with a garden in the back and a large meeting room and offices upstairs.

I hoped to be able to move into that house, so I agreed to take up this part-time job while still working at the Institute of Compilation and Translation. However Dr. Hang did not want my family living in that office building. He promised to find us rooms elsewhere, but they never materialized. I worked for that cultural association until Liberation. The duties were simple. I just had to organize various lectures and cocktail parties for Chinese professors and some English-speaking officials and foreign friends, mostly foreign embassy people, about once a month. There was only a skeleton staff of one administrative secretary, who also looked after finances, and another young accountant. These two and a gardener looked after the maintenance of the building and other needs. They came to work during office hours and the rest of the time the building was empty. I went in once every few days. In 1947 and 1948 I organized several lectures, one of which I gave myself, on China's relations with the Byzantine Empire during the Tang dynasty.

Another was given by Professor George Ye, later the Kuomintang foreign minister in Taiwan, on the role of Chinese intellectuals during the time of Confucius. I also organized several cocktail parties and an auction of Chinese curios, mostly fake antiques, and Chinese paintings and calligraphy. I remember the Soviet sinologue, Fedorenko, came several times to these lectures.

After trying unsuccessfully twice, from the winter of 1946 to the end of 1947, to rent suitable lodgings in town, and failing to get lodgings through Kuomintang official connections, early in 1948 I decided to stand as a part-time professor in a new college called the Jianguo College of Law and Commerce. This new college had first and second year English courses and needed an English teacher. They offered me a bungalow on the college grounds and I accepted. By this time the Kuomintang government's economy was in a sorry state. Inflation was getting out of control, and most intellectuals found it hard to live on one salary. So many of us took to moon-lighting, holding several part-time jobs at the same time. I remember during 1948 and the beginning of 1949, when the Kuomintang government was collapsing, my professor's salary per month was equivalent to about eight U.S. dollars or two sacks full of flour. Even six or seven jobs at these rates was barely enough to support a family. We were however in a more fortunate situation. An American friend of Gladys, Ruth Lieban, was working in an American relief organization called the E. C. A. (Economic Cooperation Administration). She got Gladys to work with her as the administrative secretary to that organization. Gladys thereafter had a salary of something like two hundred U.S. dollars a month. With that income we were much better off than most other university professors. However, I still kept my various other jobs during that period: senior fellow and section head of the Institute of Translation and Compilation, Secretary-General of the Sino-

British Cultural Association, professor of English in the College of Law and Commerce, and later the post of professor of Byzantine history in the history department of Central University (which became Nanjing University after Liberation). I decided to start a course in Byzantine history then because I was making a parallel between Byzantine and Chinese history. The decline and fall of the Eastern Roman empire reminded me of the current situation in China, with its feudal bureaucracy, nepotism and corruption, and military autocracy. Many students came to my lectures. The more intelligent ones hoped that I would draw more parallels and expose the moribund Kuomintang regime. Later the students at Central University began to go to the streets, their slogan being "We oppose starvation! We oppose Civil War!" Gladys and I supported these patriotic demonstrations, and we helped translate the student slogans and declarations into English. By the end of 1948 the students of Central University stopped attending classes, so I too gave up my Byzantine history course.

I should now turn to the part I played in the anti-Kuomintang patriotic front, which came to a head during the years after the Sino-Japanese War down to the collapse of the Kuomintang government in Nanjing in April 1949. Actually I first made the decision to join the anti-Kuomintang forces when I was in Beibei, towards the end of the war in 1945 and 1946. Ever since I had arrived in China in 1940, changing from one job to another, from Chongqing to Guiyang to Chengdu and then back again to Chongqing, I had been in a state of political lethargy, disgusted with what I saw and experienced in Kuomintang China. The Pacific War did not shake me out of this state of lethargy and the Sino-Japanese War had seemed very remote from my life. So I just buried myself in books. The end of the Sino-Japanese War made me aware of realities. The Kuomintang government had decided to resume their war to exterminate the Chinese Communists, although the majority of the Chinese people were against starting another civil war. Many things I witnessed at that time made my blood boil. During the war, in one of the bombing raids in Chongqing, one air raid shelter was locked up for one whole day, with hundreds of people inside. Hundreds suffocated to death. Many of the dead and dying were thrown onto trucks for burial by Kuomintang soldiers. This was witnessed by many Chinese and foreign reporters. I myself saw a dying Kuomintang conscript on the road, a man with malaria and suffering from diarrhoea. He was simply abandoned, covered with flies. Nobody dared to help for fear of being suspected a Communist agent. There were too many such inhuman and barbarous things in those days in Kuomintang China. Soon after the Japanese surrender, I received a letter from my friend, Professor Xiang Da, saying that a friend of his, a professor and talented translator, had just died of poverty, leaving his family no money for even a simple burial. In his indignation, Xiang Da was writing to friends appealing for help. I sent him a letter and some money. In my letter I said that since the reactionary Kuomintang government had no use for intellectuals, we must join together with the Communists to topple this hateful regime. This was the spring of 1946. Soon afterwards, together with two of my younger colleagues at the Institute of Translation and Compilation, I decided to join one of the anti-Kuomintang underground parties which were organized within various universities and government organizations at that time.

23

Underground Activity

Underground activity during those post-war years in Nanjing easily became part of my life. In our institute I had a good friend, Xiao Yiwu, who was a disabled soldier. Xiao lost one of his legs during a bombing raid and had been abandoned by his regiment. He was not an intellectual, having only a primary school education. He had been press-ganged to join the Kuomintang army. He had a natural talent for telling stories, so after he lost his leg and lived on the streets of Wuhan as a beggar, the famous novelist Lao She came across him and recognizing this young man's talent took pity on him. He introduced him to our institute, where he was given work in the department which published books and pamphlets for popular reading. I knew Lao She and through him became Xiao's friend. Xiao, who was my age, had led an interesting life and would often tell Gladys and me many tales of army life. Through him I came to know a lot about the corruption in the Kuomintang army. I told him I would like to join an anti-Kuomintang underground party to help topple the government. He said he had the same idea. He had a young colleague named Shao Hengqiu who had participated in a peasant movement in north China and wanted to join us. Through Shao we got to know a man named Sun who worked as a clerk in the Ministry of Finance, but who was actually an underground Communist Party member. Comrade Sun introduced us to join an underground political organization called at that time Minlian ("Comrades of Dr. Sun's 'Three People's Principles'"). Although its affiliation with Dr. Sun Yat-sen's "Three People's Principles" made it sound like a Kuomintang party organization, it was really a secret party connected to the underground of the Chinese Communist Party. Its members consisted of former Kuomintang party officials and patriotic generals who opposed the Chiang Kai-shek regime. Later, in 1948, it was incorporated into the Kuomintang Revolutionary Committee, which had its base in Hong Kong. Xiao, Shao, and I joined this organization, though we were not Kuomintang party members. Shao's job was to organize an underground political force in Nanjing. Xiao's job was to find connections with his former army comrades and get some regiments in the Kuomintang army to defect to the Communist side. My job was to get political and military information of use to the Chinese Communists in the north through my connections with foreign embassies and the Kuomintang upper class, including university professors. This was in the winter of 1946, soon after we arrived in Nanjing. From that time on, though I had not yet become a Chinese Communist Party member, I was working for the same cause and could call myself "comrade". Later I did ask our friend Sun to let me become a real Communist party member, but he had to leave Nanjing in a hurry when Nanjing was liberated. So my wish was not realized. From 1947 to early 1949 we three, Shao, Xiao and I, often met, either in the Sino-British Cultural Association or in a small antique shop we rented in Nanjing, to discuss affairs, pass on information, or read secret Communist documents of the Chinese Communist Party, such as Mao Zedong's "On New Democracy", sent to us from Yan'an, the revolutionary base of the Chinese Communists in north-west China.

The Institute of Translation and Compilation at that time was an empty shell and very little work was being done. We just went in from time to time for appearance sake. I, for all practical purposes, stopped translating my history classic. That history began with the Warring States period of the fifth century B.C. and ended with the last years of the Tang dynasty in the tenth century A.D. I only translated the early part, down to the end of the Western Han dynasty of the first century A.D. During the three-year Civil War between the Kuomintang and the Communists, few government workers and university intellectuals did any work. Inflation was rampant and none of us intellectuals felt any hope for the future. Many younger intellectuals fled to other countries, to Hong Kong, India, the United States, and elsewhere. Some of my friends asked me to go and teach abroad, in an Indian university or at the University of Hong Kong. However, at the time I had faith in the Chinese Communist Party and felt that liberation would ultimately come. So I stayed with my family in Nanjing and refused to leave. At the same time, with Gladys' salary from her work in the American relief organization, we were comparatively better off than most academics, so we persisted until the liberation of Nanjing in April 1949.

Though by the time I settled in Nanjing I was doing little translation work for the institute, I spent a lot of time with my part-time teaching and political work. I still managed to write a few short articles and research notes from time to time, mainly on the ancient history of China's minority nationalities in the north, such as the Mongols, the Manchus, the Turkish tribes, the Koreans, and others. In 1947, an old friend from Oxford, Professor Yang Renbian, whose thesis work, if you remember, was on Saint-Just and who was a good scholar of the French Revolution, came to see me. He said he had been in contact with Huang Shaogu, who had formerly studied political economy in London and was Vice-Minister of War in the Kuomintang government at this time. He and Huang were old comrades from the time when the Kuomintang and the Chinese Communists had started their Northward Expedition against the northern warlords before 1927. He said Huang was the editor of a newspaper which belonged to the War Ministry, formerly called *Campaign Daily* but now changed to *Peace Daily*. Huang wanted Yang Renbian to edit a literary supplement for that paper but Yang recommended me and another old friend, Professor Lü Shuxiang instead, to do the job. This was because Lü and I had done such newspaper work before, in London, when we edited that mimeograph sheet in support of the Chinese Resistance. Both Lü and I accepted the work, but I said my interest was ancient Chinese history and I would not do anything on contemporary affairs. So we decided to do two supplements instead: Lü would edit a supplement on contemporary literature, while I would edit the supplement on ancient Chinese history. I published most of my research notes in that supplement. There were very few other contributors — a few short articles from my younger colleagues — so I published my notes on ancient literature and history under different pen names. The supplement was published once every two weeks, and I continued it until the beginning of 1949, when the Kuomintang government was nearing collapse. In this way I got most of my notes on ancient history published. Later, after Liberation, I had them published as a second volume to my *Random Notes*.

At this point, I must return to that Englishman I mentioned earlier and whom I got to know very well in Nanjing. My relationship with him had much to do with our family's history after Liberation, with my being suspected as a spy in the fifties and early sixties. This landed both Gladys and me in jail for four years during the Cultural Revolution, between 1968 and 1972. The Englishman was Adrian Conway Evans, a military attaché at the British Embassy. As I said, we had first met in Beibei, through our mutual friendship with John Blofeld and others. He was a young bachelor, fond of driving a German Volkswagen and visiting scenic spots. Both Gladys and I liked him a lot. After we went to Nanjing, he used to call on us very often, and we went with him in his car to several cities along the Yangtze river valley near Nanjing — to Yangzhou, Suzhou, Yixing, Wuxi, Zhenjiang, and elsewhere. His company was always a pleasure. Adrian was a naive, likable fellow but not very competent in his job. He always worried about what to write in his official reports every month and we often made jokes of it. Through him I managed to get some odd bits of information about the civil war, and once he even showed me a map of the disposition of the Communist troops in the north and told me about his contacts with Kuomintang generals. This information I passed on to my Communist contacts. In April 1949 the Chinese Communist armies crossed the Yangtze River and captured Nanjing. All the Kuomintang government officials fled south or to Taiwan, and Nanjing no longer was the capital. The British government was thinking of recognizing the new Communist government in Beijing in the north, but they also wanted to keep a consulate in Taiwan. So Adrian Conway Evans was sent to Taiwan. We never communicated after that, although years later I heard from some foreign friends that he died in Taiwan, in a mountain-climbing accident. In the 1950s, when there was a government-organized movement to root out hidden counter-revolutionaries, they investigated my past connections with foreign embassies and thought this a suspicious case. From then on, I became a political suspect, with my case only being cleared up twenty years later, in the 1970s.

24

Liberation

Liberation came upon the heels of the increasing collapse of the Kuomintang government in Nanjing. By the beginning of 1949, it was already in a shambles. The Chinese Communists, after the Japanese surrender, had built up a strong military force in China's north-eastern provinces. After the Soviet army had destroyed the main bulk of the Japanese army stationed there, they withdrew, leaving a lot of army equipment to the Chinese Communist forces. The Chinese Communists, well-equipped with Japanese tanks and guns, were able to defeat the Kuomintang forces in the north-east by the winter of 1948. In another major campaign, they took Tianjin and Beijing and made Beijing their new capital. In spring 1949 there was another major campaign in the Huai river valley south of the lower reaches of the Yellow River. Practically all of the hand-picked divisions of Chiang Kai-shek's army were wiped out. After these three major campaigns, one in the north-east, one around Tianjin and Beijing, and one in the Huai River valley, the Chinese Communists controlled north China down to the banks of the Yangtze River.

At that time the United States government was equipping and helping the Kuomintang government. The Soviet Union, while recognizing the Kuomintang government in Nanjing, was secretly helping the Chinese Communists in the north. Stalin suggested to the Chinese Communists that they should stop at the banks of the Yangtze, leaving central and south China to the Kuomintang and the United States. Thus China would have been divided in two. Mao Zedong and the Chinese Communists felt that the Kuomintang regime was crumbling and had lost the support of the majority of the people, so they decided to advance to the south and drive the Kuomintang out of the mainland. They rejected the Soviet advice. In April 1949 the Chinese Communist army crossed the Yangtze and Nanjing fell. The Kuomintang army in the south offered little resistance and within a year the whole of the Chinese mainland, including Hainan Island in the south, was in Communist hands. The remnant of the Kuomintang fled to Taiwan and the War of Liberation, as it has come to be known, was complete.

During the liberation of Nanjing in April 1949, I was just moving to a new bungalow. After the Kuomintang government had moved back from the interior to Nanjing, there was a sudden increase in the population and it was very difficult to find suitable lodgings. So between 1946 and the end of 1948 we had to move house several times, finally living in a bungalow within the compounds of the college where I taught part-time. By the beginning of 1949, however, the college, like many other organizations, closed down. Students no longer went to classes, and many minor government workers went to the streets to do illegal transactions, trading in American dollars or Chinese silver dollars in exchange for Chinese bank notes. A thousand yuan note during that period could be worth half its value within the space of two to three hours. Because of Gladys' additional income from her work at the American relief organization and my various sideline jobs, we were better off than most other professors. At this point, although lodgings were still scarce, there were many empty plots of land within the city, so a few of my colleagues and I at the institute were able to rent some land and built our own bungalows. In the spring of 1949, I left the college bungalow and moved into our own simple three-room bungalow near the Institute of Compilation and Translation. Our family lived there for about a year. Then in 1950 we moved to another, better bungalow nearby, with a small courtyard. By then, Nanjing was no longer the capital, and since most Kuomintang officials had fled, we were able to buy a better house with only a few hundred U.S. dollars. We lived in this new place until the end of 1952. We left the house with some regret upon being invited to work as translators in the Foreign Languages Press in Beijing.

During the winter of 1948 and early spring 1949, workers at the Institute of Compilation and Translation, including translators and editors, formed themselves into a Workers' Welfare Committee, which was a sort of trade union to protect their own rights. I was  elected Chairman because of my popularity with the people. In early spring 1949 the president of the institute, Doctor Zhao, who had studied chemistry in Germany and was a Kuomintang Party member, suddenly went to Shanghai to teach in a university there and refused to come back. He knew that the Kuomintang government was about to fall and did not want to face the poor and angry people in his institute when the Communists arrived. A popular meeting was held to elect a temporary new president and I got a great majority of the vote. The president of the institute had always been appointed by the Kuomintang government and had to be a Kuomintang Party member. I became the only president of the institute not appointed by the government and not a Kuomintang Party member.

The institute was under the Kuomintang Ministry of Education. Its minister was Dr. Hang Liwu, whom I mentioned earlier, and who had been very good to me when we lived in the interior. He ignored the fact that the president of the institute had disappeared and that I had been elected by popular vote. He never made any comment, so even now I still do not know whether I was the legal president or not. By the end of March 1949, most high officials were fleeing Nanjing for Guangzhou and then on to Taiwan. This minister of education Dr. Hang was leaving for Taiwan too. Some colleagues at the institute heard of this and asked me to go and see him before he left, to ask him to leave some money for the staff. Since we got our monthly wages from the ministry, if it suddenly stopped functioning, the staff of the institute would simply starve. Government personnel in those days lived from hand to mouth. When I went to his office and explained to him the dire straits of the staff, he immediately issued a cheque sufficient to cover three months wages for the whole institute. Then he said to me in earnest:

"Are you planning to leave Nanjing soon?"

I answered that I had no such plan and that I would probably stay on for a while to see how things were after the Communists took over.

"But you should know that the Communists will not tolerate intellectuals. We have already heard of struggle meetings against intellectuals at Peking University the other day."

I did not argue with him but just smiled and said that I was not a Kuomintang Party member. Probably I would not be considered a class enemy. Gladys was British, so she too would not be in any trouble. Then he told me that he would be leaving by plane for Taiwan with his family the following day, and he offered to take me and my family on the same plane.

"If you decide to leave, come with me on my plane, with Gladys and the children, but don't take too much luggage."

I thanked him for the offer and for the cheque and left. Later I heard that he had become the president of an international anti-

Communist league in Taiwan. I never communicated with him again. He might still be alive. When I went back and handed the cheque to my staff, they were very pleased. The institute at that time had over a hundred editors and translators and some administrative staff. Without this sum, they would have all left. As it was, the great majority stayed on into the beginning of the following year. Then the new central government in Beijing decided to discontinue the institute, and the editors and translators were sent to other government organizations.

On April 22nd, the eve of the liberation of Nanjing, the Chinese Communists were on the north bank of the Yangtze River, facing Nanjing and other cities on the south bank, poised for the final attack. In Nanjing, all the major Kuomintang officials and generals had already fled, leaving only a skeleton force to guard the city. The city seemed dead, most shops having closed early, fearing robbing and looting. But nothing happened and most people stayed at home in the evening. We retired early too, before eight o'clock. When night fell, one could hear the dull and heavy rumbling of guns on the north bank, at Pukou Harbour. I slept soundly, feeling elated about what was to come, although I had no idea what the future Communist government would be like. But I was so disgusted with what I had seen and experienced under the Kuomintang regime, I thought that living under any other government would be better. The next morning when I got up, the city outside was very quiet. Then around nine o'clock I heard that the Communist army was entering the city. I went to the nearby main street by the drum tower in the northern part of the city. There were already crowds of people, mostly university students along the road, with hot water and biscuits or cakes, to welcome the coming army, or idle onlookers come out of curiosity. There was no panic or wild cheering. All was rather quiet. Then we heard that the People's

Liberation Army (PLA) was coming from the north of the city, through Xiaguan ("Lower Pass"), the gateway into Nanjing from the north via the riverbank. Several contingents of troops ran past, all young soldiers in rather shabby uniforms, looking dusty and tired, but very disciplined. They accepted some hot water from the students and smiled at us, but did not stop. They were on a quick march to the centre of the city, then would turn east towards the Sun Yat-sen Gate, where Chiang Kai-shek's presidential residence was. They occupied that place and continued east through the East Gate in pursuit of the remnant Kuomintang troops. Those remnants offered no resistance at all. They were completely demoralized. Some stragglers who fell behind were captured or surrendered. Others abandoned their uniforms and disappeared into the countryside to live as peasants. Within a day all was quiet again and the shops reopened. Thus Nanjing fell to the Communists without a single battle. It was different in Shanghai, where nearly a month later it fell to the Communists after a short but fierce battle.

25

The Transition

The transition to the new regime did not occur over night, but it was not a slow process either. Before the Communists came to Nanjing and took control, Xiao, Shao, and I organized a group to act as night watchmen to guard the institute property. We armed ourselves with clubs and patrolled the institute grounds at night, in case looters or thieves ventured in. But nothing happened. I did my turn two or three times. It was very eerie to prowl around the empty grounds among the trees after midnight. The city was absolutely quiet and nobody wandered the streets after dark, so after a week or so we gave up, having caught no thieves. However, the institute used to have eight or nine big tanks full of kerosene in its storeroom. Later we discovered that half of the tanks were filled with pure water. We never discovered when or how the theft was done. Besides that, thanks to our vigilance, the institute had lost no property when we turned it over to the new Communist authorities. A couple of days after the PLA entered the city, I was summoned by the city's new Communist cultural commissar, together with the heads of other cultural organizations, such as the Nanjing libraries, museums, universities and colleges, to listen to and carry out his instructions. This newly appointed cultural commissar was a man named Zhao. He wore a shabby

and none-too-clean PLA uniform and straw sandals on his bare
feet. When he sat and gave us his instructions, like "Guard your
property well", "Keep everything intact and wait for further
orders", and so on, he told us to take our pens and write these
instructions down. His manner was abrupt and somewhat
superficial and not too polite. As he gave his dictation, he kept
scratching his dirty bare feet. His rather uncouth manners suggested
that he was a veteran Communist "cadre" of peasant origin from
Yan'an in the north-west. Actually we discovered later that he was
nothing of the sort. Rather he was a former university intellectual
who had joined the underground Communist Party and gone north,
only to return south of the Yangtze with the army. Many progressive
Chinese intellectuals in those days were like that. They liked to
wear baggy and shabby PLA uniforms and assumed an uncouth
peasant manner in order to pose as old revolutionaries. Later we
hardly had any direct dealings with him. He assigned a young
university student named Zeng as his liaison officer to our institute.
I got on very well with young Zeng. He was the great grandson of
a well-known Qing dynasty official, Zeng Guofan, who had
suppressed the Taiping Revolution in the 1850s. Zhao the
commissar kept our staff busy by instructing us to go through all
the institute's old files and dossiers and to throw out all useless
documents. Later he was rebuked by the central government in
Beijing for this move, and all remaining files had to be preserved
intact and sent to Beijing. I heard that Zhao the commissar died
soon afterwards, probably of tuberculosis. Zeng stayed on in
Nanjing until 1957, when he was branded a "rightist". He
committed suicide during that so-called mass movement.

Within a week after Nanjing's liberation on April 23rd, 1949,
the new Communist authority was established and things returned
to normal. Rampant inflation suddenly stopped and people no

longer rushed to the streets to buy U.S. dollars with their Chinese currency. All the former government workers and teachers in schools and universities went on with their work and were paid the same wages. There was no more uncertainty and chaos. The former Kuomintang daily newspaper was replaced by the new *Xinhua Daily* of the new Communist government. Every day we read news of victory as the PLA pushed further south to liberate the rest of the mainland. There was little resistance, except when the Communist armies reached Hunan in central China and Guangzhou in south China. By the end of the year the liberation of the entire mainland was complete, and the Kuomintang remnants had fled to the islands around Taiwan. A few days after Liberation, a new Communist mayor was appointed in Nanjing. He was a middle-aged veteran named Ke Qingshi. He invited me to lunch and for a chat several times. In those days Communist Party officials were very frugal and did not spend time or money on lavish banquets like nowadays. We would eat only four small simple dishes and a soup each time. Mayor Ke was very friendly and we got on well, without ceremony. He was originally from Anhui province, so he considered me a fellow provincial — Anhui being my ancestral home. This new mayor did not have a car, but went about riding a bicycle or on foot, as did all the other city officials. Such things made a very good impression on me. Later I also had dinner with Dong Biwu, who was elected Vice-President of the People's Republic, Marshal Chen Yi, who was in command of the Fourth Army, and several other leading Communist comrades. I liked and respected them all. None of these veteran Communist leaders assumed any official air, but behaved like ordinary citizens. It is a pity that later Chinese Communist officials did not keep up the good tradition.

My underground group was incorporated into the Kuomintang

Revolutionary Committee, one of the several so-called democratic parties working together with the Communist Party of China (CPC). The idea was to have a united front consisting of many parties working together to form the new Chinese government, with the CPC in the lead. There was a People's Congress, a People's Consultative Council, which included all the parties, and a State Council, which was the executive body of the government and other government organs. My colleague Xiao, the disabled soldier, decided not to join the Kuomintang Revolutionary Committee. He wanted to join the CPC, so only myself and Shao joined the new party. I headed the secretariat and Shao looked after the organization of the party. I made all the declarations and speeches representing the Nanjing group in voicing our support of the CPC. These were published by the local Party paper, the *Xinhua Daily*. I also wrote a number of articles explaining the CPC's policy on the national economy, education, culture, and other topics. These were published in the daily paper between 1950 and 1951. Later I happened to write an article on freedom of religion in China and mentioned the positive role the early Jesuits had played in introducing Western science to China. I was in a conference discussing the local situation with the Communist leaders. The head of the *Xinhua Daily*, who was also a leading comrade in charge of propaganda, quietly handed this article back to me. He had underlined in red pencil certain statements and had added exclamation marks. He said he would like to discuss this article with me later and hoped I would make certain changes in my text. At that time I had read in the paper that they were denouncing some local Catholic priests, charging them with being imperialist spies. It was clear that they did not approve of some of the statements I had made. I just took the article back and smiled, saying nothing. We never discussed the matter again, but I realized that not all my ideas coincided

with the Communist line. So I stopped contributing articles to the paper. During that period in Nanjing, my relationship with the local Communist government was very good, and the new mayor and others always treated me very cordially and with respect, and we never argued over any issue. However there were instances, like this case, which made me realize that I had to reserve certain of my opinions. This was the only reason why, during those early years after Liberation, I did not again ask to join the CPC, choosing to remain outside, as a "fellow-traveller".

By the end of 1949, it was decided in Beijing that the Institute of Translation and Compilation should be abolished and incorporated into the Publication Bureau. Since at that time I was already doing full time "United Front" work, I was appointed Vice-Secretary-General of the Nanjing PPCC (People's Political Consultative Council), something like the British Upper House of Parliament. My time was divided between the local Kuomintang Revolutionary Committee and the local Communist Party's United Front Department. I stayed on in that position until the end of 1952, when I was transferred to Beijing to work as a translator in the Foreign Languages Press. My daily work mainly consisted of organizing meetings and presiding over meetings with all sorts of people in Nanjing. Quite often we had to work from morning until after midnight, since after each meeting I had to discuss the meeting with my Communist comrades and our next move. The rest of my time I spent with comrades of the local Kuomintang Revolutionary Committee. Since the liberation of Nanjing I had had very little time to spend with my family. Gladys had the third baby, our second daughter, Yang Zhi. She was born in November 1949, not too long after Liberation. During the period Gladys was in hospital, I seldom went to look after her. But she was well taken care of by her friends at that hospital. This was because she had

done a lot of work with hospitals as a member of the American relief agency, the ECA, where she had been employed earlier. After she had the baby, she was invited by Nanjing University (originally Central University) to become a professor in the English Department. Her former organization, the ECA, stopped functioning immediately after Liberation because the United States, which backed the Kuomintang government, never recognized the new Communist government. Then in 1950 the Korean War began. There was a bit of xenophobic hysteria among the young people against the American and British imperialists, and this feeling spread to the Chinese universities and colleges too. Gladys felt it more in her university than I did, since I was working with the Communists. However, the hysteria soon passed without causing any trouble, other than making British citizens feel like second-class citizens. We were, however, quite enthusiastic and supportive of the Chinese war effort and contributed quite a bit of money to the funds collected by the masses to buy planes for the front. As a leading comrade in the city government, I went several times to the railway station to comfort wounded soldiers on their way to hospitals as they returned from the Korean front. When China first entered the Korean War, there were quite a lot of casualties. Later the war entered a stalemate and China was able to stop the other side's advance.

26

Elder Brother

Soon after Liberation elder brother became our cherished ally. In spring 1950 China and the Soviet Union signed a friendship, mutual-aid treaty and we formally entered the Soviet bloc. In Nanjing there were organized celebrations, the Soviet Union became the "elder brother" noted above, and there was a lot of propaganda about Soviet achievements and articles and books about the infamous role of the U.S. in helping the Kuomintang and its cultural aggression against the Chinese people. Russian became the favourite foreign language instead of English and many teachers who taught English before had to switch to learning and teaching Russian. As a leading comrade in the city government, I too was invited by the Soviet consulate to a party celebrating the event. I drank many toasts of vodka and amidst a flurry of red flags we watched a show of waist-drum dancers from Yan'an, the old Communist revolutionary base in north-west China. I wrote an impromptu poem comparing this event with the beginning of the Tang dynasty, when the Turkish empire was still strong on China's northern and north-western border and China had to consider the Turks as elder brother. Later the Tang succeeded in driving the Turks into central Asia. Watching the drum dance amidst red flags made me think of the time when the first Tang emperor was celebrating his victory. Later, when I recalled this poem, I was struck by its strong nationalist sentiment. It was certainly not the correct sentiment for a Chinese Communist. A proper Chinese Marxist-Leninist at that time would have considered Moscow as the centre of world revolution and would not have compared our situation to the beginning of the Tang dynasty. Some of my Chinese Communist comrades saw the poem but thought nothing of it. They did not understand its historical implication.

At about the same period, I was discussing with some comrades the Soviet Union's industrial achievements and in a thoughtless way suddenly asked my friend:

"How long will it take to achieve and surpass the Soviet Union's achievement?"

My Communist friend at the Communist Party's United Front Department was very shocked and remarked sternly:

"Why should we think of surpassing the Soviet achievement? Isn't Moscow the centre of world revolution?"

I realized then that I had raised an improper question. However my friend did not criticize me after that. I was mildly criticized, however, over two other issues by the Communist Party's United Front Department during that period. Soon after the liberation of Nanjing, I read in the Chinese newspaper that there had been an "Amethyst Incident". A British warship named the Amethyst was crossing the Yangtze River while a Chinese boat was crossing over from the north bank. According to the Chinese Xinhua news version, the British warship opened fire and caused some casualties. I thought at that time that it was very odd for the British boat to do such a provocative act, since the British government did not have the same policy towards China as the Americans. The Americans were supporting the Kuomintang government, but the British, knowing that the Kuomintang government was collapsing, would not behave in the same way. A couple of days later I read an English newspaper in which they said that it was the Chinese boat that opened fire first and they returned fire. This made better sense to me. I showed the paper to my Communist colleagues and told them what I thought.

"But why should you believe what a foreign imperialist newspaper says and distrust our own account?" they retorted. I was politely criticized for my wrong political stand. However they could not convince me I was wrong. Last year there was an account in the Chinese *People's Daily*, written by a Chinese naval officer, about that incident over forty years ago. He said that he had been the captain of that Chinese boat and had given the order to open fire on the Amethyst first. Afterwards he dared not speak the truth to reporters, so the blame was put on the Amethyst. I felt vindicated after so many years.

I remember another incident in those early days after the liberation of Nanjing. It had something to do with the Canadian Embassy. Before Liberation I had made many friends in foreign embassies, especially the British, American, Australian, and Canadian. After liberation the British recognized our new government first and moved their embassy to Beijing. The American embassy in Nanjing closed and stopped functioning. The Canadians could not make up their minds whether to follow the British or American pattern. So their chargé d'affaires, Chester Ronning, stayed on in Nanjing for a couple of months. I knew Chester quite well. He used to invite me to supper often and would discuss his collection of Chinese antiques bought from local antique dealers, mostly fakes. The new Chinese government did not recognize the Canadian embassy, which was still set up in Nanjing, so Chester Ronning was only counted as a private foreign citizen. One evening he invited Gladys and myself to supper and after supper mentioned that he would be leaving China very soon, since the Canadian government had decided to follow the American line. While going through the embassy's property and packing and storing things, he found a lot of bone fragments in an old cupboard, left there by an old Canadian missionary named Menzies, who had long since died. Since nobody claimed those bones, he was free to throw them away or do whatever he liked with them. He thought they looked like Shang dynasty oracle bone fragments and seemed to have characters inscribed on them. He asked me to examine them and wondered whether some local antique dealer would like to have them. After casual examination, I told him they were certainly Shang dynasty oracle bones, but whether they were genuine or not, I was not an expert to decide. I told him if they were genuine, they should be sent to a museum. It would be a great pity to let antique dealers have them. He said he would be glad to present them to the Nanjing Museum, but he had no contact with the local authorities. He suggested that if I really thought they were valuable, he would let me keep the whole lot and do whatever I thought was fitting. I agreed. The next morning the bones were delivered to my place, together with the old cupboard, by a rickshaw boy. There were altogether over four thousand pieces. I immediately telephoned the Nanjing Museum. The woman director was an old friend of mine, a returned student from England who had studied Egyptology at London University. She immediately had those bones taken to the museum. After examination, she rang up and told me excitedly that this was the famous Menzies collection of Shang oracles bones which was thought to have been spirited out of the country long ago. Apart from a few fakes, the main bulk were genuine and the recovery of the collection was a great contribution to the study of ancient Shang dynasty history and language. She would send an immediate report to Beijing and

the central government would thank me for its recovery. I was having this telephone conversation in my office and one of my young Communist colleagues overheard it and felt the way this had all come about was not quite correct. He said in a worried voice:

"Excuse me for overhearing your telephone conversation, but don't you think you should have consulted the government first before making this transaction with the museum, since it involved a former foreign embassy?"

I told him I did not think it mattered very much, especially under such circumstances. If I had not accepted those Shang bones, they might have been sold or given to some antique dealers and we would have lost this precious collection. But my young colleague argued and said that I should have informed the government first. Then they could demand that this former foreign embassy hand over the "stolen property" and be duly punished if they refused. Anyway the transaction was done, and my young colleague reported it to the Party's United Front Department. They mildly criticized me, saying I was letting the "foreign imperialist agents drive a wedge between our Communist government and the democratic parties." I could not see the logic of the argument, and the matter was closed. Years later, during a Geneva conference, Chester Ronning became the good friend of Premier Zhou Enlai, and in the early 1970s he managed to revisit China. In 1975 he wrote his memoirs about his China experience and mentioned the oracle bones episode. He did not mention my name because at that time I had been in jail during the Cultural Revolution and he had not wanted to get me into more trouble. I still have an inscribed copy of his book.

Despite such minor differences, my relationship with my Communist colleagues remained good during those early days. I was fairly well trusted and took part in local government discussions and helped make decisions. I was on the presidium when the first mass meeting was held to suppress local counter-revolutionaries. When a former secretary of the Institute of Translation and Compilation was about to be sentenced to life imprisonment for destroying documents, I pleaded on his behalf and they respected my opinion. The sentence was shortened to four years. I did not go down to the countryside to take part in the Land Reform Movement of 1950 because my presence was needed in the Nanjing government. In 1951 I took part in the mass movement against capitalist profiteers and presided over a struggle meeting against several comprador merchants who had worked for an American oil company. I was also asked to draft a report about the achievements of that movement, but it was not used because the tone was too mild.

27

An Invitation

An invitation to work in Beijing as a translator arrived in the early spring of 1951. Many of my earlier academic friends were already there, like Xiang Da, who had studied the Dunhuang manuscripts in the British Museum, and Professor Qian Zhongshu, who together with his wife Yang Jiang, had been for some time in Oxford during the Japanese War days. Xiang Da was teaching history at Peking University and Qian Zhongshu was heading a committee to translate the works of Mao Zedong. Xiang suggested to Qian that he get Gladys and myself working on this translation committee. It was considered to be a most prestigious job for a Chinese intellectual to translate the works of Chairman Mao and we would get the highest salary a Chinese university professor could get. When the official invitation came to the Party's United Front Department, they told me that they valued my work in Nanjing very much and were reluctant to let me go to Beijing. However since this was a decision of the Central Government, they could not stop me from going. I was left with the option to continue on in Nanjing if I wished. After doing United Front work for nearly two years, I felt like switching to academic work. However, I did not want to translate Chairman Mao's political and philosophical writings either, much preferring to translate classical Chinese literature instead. So the matter was dropped. I was also rather reluctant to leave Nanjing. I had just bought a nice little bungalow, and the two magnolias in my courtyard were just about to bloom. Some years later my refusal to help translate Chairman Mao's works into English was brought out, in one of those repeated political movements in China, as evidence of my lack of respect for Chairman Mao. I had to make a great criticism of myself for this unpardonable crime.

I did not wish, however, to continue wasting my time with all those United Front meetings and the democratic party work in Nanjing. During the two years after Nanjing's liberation, I had written or translated practically nothing and had done little reading — except a lot of Marxism, including works by Marx, Engels, Lenin, and Stalin, and of course the works of Chairman Mao Zedong. I had also read some English translations of research done by Soviet historians on central Asian ancient history and archaeology, and I remember translating into Chinese an English translation of a book on Kiev by the Soviet historian Grekov, and some other short articles. I lost these manuscripts later, so they never got published. Anyway, I was beginning to feel rather bored with so many political meetings and was wanting to change to another job when a number of incidents occurred which further convinced me that I had better leave Nanjing and start a new career.

In 1951 it was decided that the democratic party I belonged to, the Kuomintang Revolutionary Committee, should hold elections to re-elect its leading comrades. A former veteran Kuomintang party member named Li had just joined and some of our members wanted him to head the committee. I wanted my former colleague Shao, who had been doing organizational work, to be the leader. There was some contention and I was criticized for my sectarian attitude. I was rather disgusted with all the political bickering and wanted to quit. About this time, the Communist Party in east China decided to set up a new college in Suzhou to reform old intellectuals, including university teachers and senior members of former Kuomintang organizations. The training course was to be about two to three months long, during which the members would review their past histories, make self-criticisms in front of other members, and the others would "help" them with "criticisms". It was a kind of "brain-washing". After this period of training, the intellectuals would be assigned new jobs. Since I was already a leading comrade in the new Nanjing government, I did not need to take part in this reform course, but I chose to go because I wanted to be assigned a new teaching job at a university. I took part in this training course and was made a group leader. After two months I came back to Nanjing and was told that I could give up my administrative job and join Fudan University in Shanghai. Gladys was then teaching in Nanjing University, but she and the children could go and join me in Shanghai when the term ended. I wanted to join the history department teaching Chinese or Western ancient history, but the university said they needed me more in the English department teaching English literature. I went to Shanghai for a brief visit to see the head of the Bureau of Education and the matter was decided. This was in the early summer of 1952.

Just at this moment something happened to completely change my plan to go to Shanghai. A peace conference for the Asian and Pacific region was to be held in Beijing in early autumn, and they needed many translators for that. My name was among those considered talented translators, so I was summoned to Beijing, together with Gladys, to work for that conference. In the meantime we had to leave our young children with a good and reliable maid. When we arrived in Beijing, we were lodged in a quiet courtyard adjacent to the Palace Museum in the centre of the city. Then we were told that Madame Song Qingling (Soong Ch'ing-ling, wife of Dr. Sun Yat-sen), who was vice-president of the new republic, wanted to have a collection of her past addresses and articles edited and published in one volume and have them distributed to delegates of the conference. She wanted Gladys and me to edit this volume so we were spared the job of working at the conference. We stayed in our lodging and edited these manuscripts for about a fortnight, after which the work was finished and published in English, ready for the delegates. Madame Soong presented us two of these volumes with her name inscribed on the front page to thank us for our help. We left Beijing soon after that, never attending the conference ourselves. During our stay in Beijing, we met a lot of old and new friends, mainly professors from Beijing universities and heads of different publishing houses. Among them were the head of the Foreign Languages Institute and the head of the Foreign Languages Press. Both organizations had just been formed, and both heads urged us to come to Beijing to join them instead of going to Shanghai. The Foreign Languages Institute was a new college set up to teach different Western languages. We already knew many of their professors and they were all good scholars. We were rather tempted to join them but dreaded teaching English again, owing to our experiences at the universities in the interior.

So we decided to join the Foreign Languages Press. The head of the Foreign Languages Press was a veteran Chinese Communist comrade named Liu Zunqi. He used to edit various magazines in Shanghai before Liberation and had the idea of systematically translating all the important works of Chinese literature into English. He wanted me to head up this scheme. I was to be the "expert" to decide the books to be translated and published, and I could choose some to translate myself with the help of Gladys and other younger editors and translators. I rather liked the idea of spending many years doing this sort of work, so we decided to immediately go back to Nanjing, give our apologies to Fudan University in Shanghai, and then pack up our belongings and move to Beijing with our children. When I returned to Nanjing and reported our decision to the United Front Department, they had no objections, only expressing some regret to see us head north. We sold our little bungalow which we had bought for a few hundred U.S. dollars during liberation and started on our journey to Beijing. Before we left Nanjing, I asked permission to break our journey in Tianjin to see my mother, and it was granted. We stayed in Tianjin for a few days at my mother's house. This was not the old house where I had lived during my childhood. It had been sold long ago. Rather my mother had rented a much smaller house in the former British concession. My mother and my younger sister then decided to move to Beijing to be near me. After breaking our journey in Tianjin for a short spell, we continued on to Beijing. The Foreign Languages Press put us in a small house in the centre of the city, which we shared with several other foreign workers, including a French woman Denise and her Chinese husband Li, and two Japanese couples by the names of Suganuma and Ikeda. They were all very nice people and we lived in this house until 1954 when the new building for the press was built. Then we moved to a western suburb of Beijing, to a district called Baiwanzhuang, near the zoo. We lived there for nearly forty years.

28

Beijing

Beijing after Liberation made a very good impression on us. Although my birthplace, Tianjin, was not far from there, in my childhood I had only visited Beijing two or three times. I had liked old Beijing but it was dusty and not too clean. But just after Liberation the old city had been cleaned up and still retained most of its former beauty, with quiet lanes called *hutong* and curio shops and old bookshops, and the old city walls had not yet been destroyed. In 1952 there was a health and cleanliness campaign and the whole city was spotlessly clean. People were pleased with the new regime and the young people were especially enthusiastic about the future. There was the beginning of a mass movement against corruption and profiteering. Though a few innocent people got into trouble and were criticized, it only affected a few officials and some merchants. At that time the majority of people supported such movements organized by the new government. It was nothing like all the later mass movements which caused such widespread damage and complaints.

We were satisfied with our new work at the Foreign Languages Press. Quite a number of my earlier translations of Chinese literature were published, including "Li Sao" and other poems supposedly written by China's first poet Qu Yuan in the fourth century

B.C. I also translated a classical novel, *The Scholars*, written during the Qing dynasty, a historical drama about Qu Yuan, written by the well-known modern scholar and poet Guo Moruo, and other modern works of literature. Probably the most important piece of translation was the four-volume edition of the selected works of Lu Xun, the most significant writer and thinker of modern China. In 1954 I was introduced to the Communist writer Feng Xuefeng, who had been a good friend of Lu Xun's. Together with him, a selection of Lu Xun's writings was chosen and translated. Feng and I selected and Gladys and I translated. Feng was a veteran Communist who had been imprisoned by the Kuomintang in a concentration camp for many years before Liberation. I liked him very much. He was a very gentle man and a man of great passion and moral integrity. In many ways he was rather like his friend Hu Yaobang, who was to be the CPC's General-Secretary in the 1980s. Feng introduced me to Hu once when we were in the seaside town of Beidaihe in the summer of 1954. Another book Gladys and I liked a lot and translated into English was the folk poem called "Ashma", which was illustrated by the young artist Huang Yongyu. Huang at that time was not yet famous, but later became a well-known artist. We have remained good friends to today. As for all the translations of classical and modern Chinese literary works we did during that period and subsequently, it would take too long to mention them here. Suffice it to say that since 1953 Gladys and I became fairly well-known as translators of Chinese literary writings, and still enjoy this reputation until now.

In 1953 I was invited to attend the national PPCC (People's Political Consultative Council) conference as a non-voting delegate. I was also chosen to join the Chinese Writers' Union and the National Association of Writers and Artists. Later I was elected a member of the standing committee of these associations, a position

I held until the 1980s. In 1953 or early 1954 I was invited to go with about twenty other intellectuals, including scientists and writers and artists, to meet Chairman Mao. This interview took place in Zhongnanhai, a large park with lake in central Beijing where all the leading Party leaders lived. By that time China's leader, Chairman Mao Zedong, who used to meet and chat with intellectuals freely in the Yan'an days, had already been elevated to a deified, august position and was seldom seen by the average individual. Following in the footsteps of China's long feudal history, Chairman Mao had become like an emperor, and to have an audience with him was considered a great honour. I still remember that scene quite vividly. We were all ushered into a hall and waited there with bated breath for the great man to arrive. First Premier Zhou Enlai came out and chatted freely with us. Zhou Enlai was always like that, behaving like an ordinary citizen and never putting on airs. It was a quality which the Chinese people, and especially intellectuals, loved in him. Then it was announced that Mao Zedong was coming. We all stood in a row waiting for the audience. Chairman Mao entered from a door to the front of us. He walked slowly towards us, smiling and looking rather shy. He was already rather plump but looked very healthy. He came and shook hands with us in turn, with Zhou Enlai by his side introducing us one by one. When he came to me, Premier Zhou introduced me as the translator who had translated "Li Sao" into English. Chairman Mao loved Chinese classical poetry and "Li Sao", an ancient poem from the south of China, was one of his favourite poems. He shook my hand warmly, with a sweaty palm, and said:

"So you think 'Li Sao' can be translated, eh?"

"Chairman, surely all works of literature can be translated?" I replied, without thinking.

He halted as if he wanted to discuss this matter further. But

after a short hesitation he just beamed and shook hands with me again, then went on to greet the others. Later I thought that obviously he doubted that great poetry like "Li Sao" could be translated into another language, and he certainly had reasons for his doubts. I myself wonder whether one can ever do justice when translating poetry — despite my own efforts with "Li Sao". Chairman Mao himself wrote poetry and he was no fool. It was a pity that he did not elaborate on his idea further on that occasion. After he had shaken hands with all of us, he left and I did not have a chance to discuss the matter with him. Later I saw Chairman Mao two or three more times on different occasions. Once he invited a number of writers and others to a meal. We were all sitting at different tables and he was at a small table with Premier Zhou Enlai, Marshal Zhu De, commander of the armed forces, and Vice-President Dong Biwu. I was sitting with the group of writers. During dinner, after drinking several cups of Chinese liquor with my colleagues at the table, I asked the writer sitting next to me, a novelist named Du Pengcheng, who had written a novel about the defence of Yan'an, whether he would join me in going to Chairman Mao's table to offer him a toast. He agreed and we went over. Chairman Mao looked a little surprised, since so far nobody from the other tables had ventured to ask him to drink. Premier Zhou Enlai, always the suave and astute diplomat, immediately stood up with cup in hand and said:

"The Chairman nowadays doesn't drink liquor. I'll drink a cup with you two."

We drank up and left without saying another word to Chairman Mao. He just sat there and smiled and nodded to us. On another occasion Chairman Mao invited a small group of writers and stage artists to an evening gathering. I was included among them. It was in the Ziguangge ("Purple Light Pavilion") at Zhongnanhai.

Chairman Mao asked a cross-talk artist named Hou to tell some jokes. Mao was very fond of traditional comic cross-talk and he laughed a lot on this occasion. Then he asked a Uighur woman dancer to sing and dance. There were several other items of song and dance on the programme and I just listened to these performances and joined in with the clapping. But there were too many of us there that evening so I did not have a chance to talk to Chairman Mao. I was invited one other time to listen to Chairman Mao discuss the contradictions and ideological problems in our society. That was just before the Anti-Rightist Movement in 1957, when many Chinese intellectuals were labelled "rightists" and sent into exile. After that occasion I never saw Chairman Mao again in the context of a meeting. After Liberation, for many years there were military parades at Tiananmen Square on National Day, that is October 1st, and Chairman Mao would appear on the rostrum and wave to the people at the end of the celebrations. I was in the stands many times and could see Chairman Mao from a great distance. I cannot remember the last time he appeared on the reviewing stand. It was sometime before the Cultural Revolution, before 1966.

So much for my meetings with Chairman Mao.

29

Translating

Translating and writing took up much of my time during the 1950s. But I should mention other things I did besides my Chinese to English translations while at Foreign Languages Press in the early years after Liberation. After I was elected to be a member of the Association of Chinese Writers and Artists, I made many friends in the literary and art circles. During those years, I also did some translations of foreign literature into Chinese. Among them I remember translating Vergil's *Eclogues* from Latin, Aristophanes' *The Birds* and *Peace* from Greek, Plautus' *Mostellaria*, a Roman comedy in Latin, George Bernard Shaw's *Pygmalion, Caesar and Cleopatra*, and others. In those years China followed the Soviet Union in celebrating a world "cultural giant" every year. So the publishing houses asked me to translate Aristophanes and George Bernard Shaw during the years in the early 1950s when they were chosen as "cultural giants". I was also asked to write several articles for magazines and newspapers introducing Walt Whitman, Ovid, and others for the same reason. It was not because I particularly liked these writers. At about the same time one publishing house specializing in children's and young people's literature asked me to write something for young readers. So I wrote a short historical novel called *The Red Eyebrows*, about a famous peasant revolt at the end of the Former Han dynasty. I intended to write a whole series of historical novels on Chinese peasant revolts through the centuries. The view of Chinese historians, based on the ideas of Chairman Mao, was that peasant revolts were the moving force propelling Chinese history. I finished another manuscript, *The Yellow Turbans*, about the peasant revolt at the end of the Later Han dynasty, but the editors felt I had not depicted the peasants as heroic enough. I could not agree with them, so I threw the manuscript away and gave up the scheme of writing historical novels for children. In 1955 and 1956 there was a popular magazine called the *New Observer*. Its editors came and asked me to write some historical anecdotes on various popular subjects. So I wrote quite a number of articles on subjects like the Chinese stamp-seal, Chinese chrysanthemum, Chinese goldfish, Chinese bamboo, Chinese water-lily, and Chinese plum blossom. They proved very popular. The editors showed me a lot of letters from their readers, who wished I would write more. Such articles were easy to write and I was willing. However, in 1957 the Anti-Rightist Movement descended upon China and the young editor of the *New Observer*, a talented young man named Huang Sha, was made a "rightist" and sent into exile. I stopped writing for the magazine. I think it had to stop publication too, not because of the articles I wrote, which were harmless, but because it published certain items expressing views which were too liberal.

Before the Anti-Rightist Movement in 1957, there was also a news agency which sent articles to overseas periodicals on various subjects, and they solicited articles on Chinese flowers. Just before the movement, Chairman Mao and the Chinese Communist Party wanted to encourage Chinese intellectuals to exert their creative efforts to bring about the flourishing of art and literature and science in new China. So the new slogan, "Let a hundred flowers flourish and hundred schools of thought contend", came into vogue. The poet Guo Moruo immediately wrote a hundred short poems on a hundred Chinese flowers. This news agency caught on to the idea and asked me for some articles. However, the period of euphoria did not last long and the Anti-Rightist Movement set in and I stopped contributing. I think I probably wrote less than a dozen articles. I never kept a copy of them and I don't know how many articles on Chinese flowers were published at that time.

In those years apart from translating works of Chinese literature for the Foreign Languages Press, I was also involved with a magazine published in English called *Chinese Literature*. This magazine first appeared in October 1950. It was the brain-child of the Chinese dramatist Hong Shen, who headed a bureau fostering cultural relations with foreign countries. Hong Shen asked a friend named Ye Junjian, who had returned from England as a British Council scholar, to help him with the magazine. Ye knew me and wrote to me in Nanjing asking me to contribute translations. In this way Gladys and I became connected with the magazine from its beginning. Apart from Gladys and myself, a young American, Sidney Shapiro, who had married a Chinese wife in Shanghai, also worked on the magazine. We three were the only translators for the magazine in 1950 as well as the next few years. Only a few issues were published before 1954. In 1954, when Gladys and I and Sidney Shapiro were transferred to Beijing, we decided to make the magazine a quarterly. The magazine only published some pre-Liberation literature from the northern liberated areas and some works of classical Chinese literature. The choice of material was very haphazard. For works of modern Chinese literature, Ye asked the opinion of the Chinese Writers' Union, which had just been set up. The design and format of the magazine were modelled on Soviet literature. In 1956 *Chinese Literature* was incorporated into

the Foreign Languages Press, when the government decided to have all foreign language publications put under one organization. We then joined the office of *Chinese Literature* as a separate department, though we continued to translate books for the English section of Foreign Languages Press.

I think I should mention some of the friends we made, especially foreign friends, in the early 1950s. I shall leave out most of my Chinese friends and acquaintances because their names in English transliteration would be too confusing and difficult to remember for my readers. In the early fifties, because of the Korean War, Communist China was isolated by Western countries. As a result, we had no contact with foreign embassies, and very few of our former foreign friends had remained in China. However, during this period we made a new group of foreign friends, the foreign "experts" sent by Western Communist parties and employed by the Chinese government. Some of them had come to China during the war years as doctors or newspaper correspondents, but the great majority came after Liberation. Many were Jewish or people without nationality papers or Communist Party members sent by Western Communist Party organizations. Many of them were not highly trained academically, but there were exceptions, and there were some very fine, intelligent people whom I came to respect and like very much. I can only mention a few names here. There was Alan Willington, a veteran English Communist Party member and a newspaper man who had come to China before Liberation and knew Chairman Mao. During the Korean War he denounced the United States for its use of germ warfare. In the late 1950s, when there was a split between the Soviet and Chinese Communist parties, he took the side of the Soviet Union and soon left China. Several other good friends of mine, all English Communist Party members, like Nan Green, Ted Brake, Janet Springhall, and Tony

Durrell, took the same line. They all defended Khrushchev's Twentieth Congress line and left China by the end of the 1950s. There were some from other European countries too, like the newspaper correspondents Harry Sikrovsky from Austria and Harry Thurk from East Germany. These were among my best friends and we all held the same political line at the time. Most of these friends have since died. Most were later disillusioned by the Soviet Union over issues like the invasions of Hungary and Czechoslovakia, but they kept their Communist ideals. We used to see each other very often in the evenings. Some cafes in east Beijing were our favourite haunts, and we would go there to drink beer or liquor and sing songs like "Los Quadros Generales" of the International Brigade of the Spanish Civil War. Although at that time I had not yet joined the Communist Party, I felt a strong sense of comradeship with our Communist friends. I still have fond memories of that era and those friends.

30

Mass Movements

Mass movements were to become a part of Chinese life beginning in the late 1950s. The state of euphoria I had shared with my foreign Communist friends did not last long. By 1955 there was another Party-organized mass movement to root out "hidden counter-revolutionaries". In literary circles, one veteran writer, Hu Feng, who had quarrelled with powerful writers like Zhou Yang, was accused of "counter-revolutionary activities." Then other intellectuals were suspected of similar crimes and a witch-hunt began. That summer I was heading to the seaside town of Beidaihe with Gladys for a holiday rest when suddenly I was notified that I could not go because there was something "unclear" in my past which had to be investigated. After a week the office informed me that I could go on my holiday out of consideration for Gladys because she was a foreign "expert". She had become a "foreign expert" in 1954, when the government set up a bureau to look after foreign experts. The salaries of foreign experts were three or four times what Chinese professors made. Subsequently, thanks to Gladys, our combined monthly income was several times what two professors could earn in China. I suppose this was when New China began to have its privileged classes. Government high officials above the ministerial rank and foreign employees enjoyed certain material privileges beyond what ordinary people could attain. They became a special class apart, even with special shops catering to their privilege. The Soviet Union was the same. In reality, this was just a return to the old feudal mentality. It was probably the same in Ming and Qing dynasty China or in Czarist Russia.

Anyway nothing much happened to me during the movement to root out hidden counter-revolutionaries. There were a few investigation meetings, mostly about my past connections with foreign embassies and other foreign friends before Liberation, but no conclusions were drawn. However, from that time onwards, I could sense a subtle change in my status. I was no longer considered a Chinese expert, just an ordinary translator, and I was barred from some of the Communist Party meetings. When I asked to join the CPC, the matter was politely waved aside. So from 1955 until I was released from jail in 1972, I was politically under a cloud. No longer was I a trusted friend of the CPC.

The 1955 movement did not affect many intellectuals, only several suspected of something in their past careers. I saw people dragged away to prison or exiled to the countryside, but they were mostly people I did not know very well. After the counter-revolutionary movement, there was a short lull and a feeling of relaxation was in the air. The Party again emphasized its "Let a hundred flowers flourish, and a hundred schools of thought contend" slogan, and the CPC encouraged the so-called democratic parties to "criticize and help" Communist government cadres to mend their ways. Many meetings were held towards the end of 1956 and the beginning of 1957, with responsible Communist Party members and members of democratic parties and leading intellectuals in different organizations participating. As a veteran member of the Kuomintang Revolutionary Committee and a leading member in literary and art circles, I had to attend many of these meetings. We were encouraged to speak openly and criticize the faults of the CPC. I spoke very little during these meetings, not because I was afraid to talk but because I was still very enthusiastic about our socialist revolution and firmly believed in the leadership of the CPC. Some other intellectuals in those meetings criticized the Communist Party sharply. Then in June 1957 the axe fell. Chairman Mao denounced several members of the democratic parties and other older or younger intellectuals, saying that they were bourgeois "rightist" elements trying to overthrow the Communist Party leadership. Organizations were given quotas on how many people to punish and many branded as many as ten percent of their intellectuals as "rightists". Such people were either dismissed or sent into exile. Even their families had to sever their relations with them, and they became social outcasts. Only after the Cultural Revolution, more than twenty years later, was this social stigma removed and their social status restored. Although I was not labelled a "rightist", in later movements I was called a "rightist who had escaped the net". After that period I lost many of my best friends within literary and art circles, and China lost many of its best intellectuals. My old friend, the historian Xiang Da, was labelled a "rightist". So was the director of the Foreign Languages Press, Liu Zunqi, who had invited me to Beijing. With his dismissal, the press lost its only able director. Comrade Feng Xuefeng, who had helped me produce the selected works of Lu Xun, was also made a "rightist", although he had been a veteran Communist. After 1957, although I still had faith in the leadership of the Party, I was very disillusioned and my admiration for Chairman Mao diminished.

Despite all the political movements, the 1950s were my most

prolific years in translating material from Chinese into English. After the publication of *Li Sao and Other Poems*, the four-volume set of Lu Xun's writings, and the Qing dynasty novel *The Scholars*, I also translated, among other things, a collection of tales from the third to sixth centuries, a collection of Tang dynasty prose romances, a collection of Chinese stories of the Song and Ming dynasties, an early Qing dynasty poetic drama called *The Palace of Eternal Youth*, an abridged version of the Ming dynasty poetic drama called *Peony Pavilion*, a collection of plays by the Yuan dynasty dramatist Guan Hanqing, a number of local opera scripts, including a *kunqu* opera called *Fifteen Strings of Cash*, a Peking opera called *The Fisherman's Revenge*, and a Peking opera called *The White Snake*. For the magazine *Chinese Literature* I also translated selected poems by Tang and Song dynasty poets, including Li Bai, Du Fu, Wang Wei, Wen Tingyun, Li He, Su Shi (Su Dongpo), Lu You, and Fan Chengda, and some Tang prose writings, including material by Han Yu, Liu Zongyuan, and others. All these translations, and many more, were done with the help of my wife Gladys. Without her, I could not have rendered them into good English.

Gladys in fact worked more diligently than myself and translated many volumes of modern and contemporary Chinese literature by herself, especially modern Chinese novels and short stories. Unfortunately, since we were in essence employed merely as hired hands and since the selections were made by young Chinese editors whose knowledge of Chinese literature was rather limited or because selections had to suit the political tastes of the period, many such translations done by us were not worth the time spent on them. I only translated classical Chinese literature, so I was often lucky with my choices. However sometimes even classical poems were chosen for their "ideological" or political content, and we often argued with the editors about their choices, reaching a compromise only after lengthy discussion.

When I was translating Song and Ming stories, because the popular Chinese editions were expurgated, we had to go to Beijing Library to make copies from an early Ming edition. There was a very nice story called "The Pearl Vest". The original edition contained some exquisitely written erotic passages. Though we were using the original unexpurgated edition, our English edition was censored and these passages were deleted. Another story from the same collection mentioned Japanese pirates during the Ming dynasty. We had to cut that reference because our editors were afraid to annoy Japanese friends. Another story was a good Song dynasty ghost story called "Ghosts of the Western Hills". The story was nicely written, full of humour, and translated well by Gladys, but because Chairman Mao had just made his famous dictum, "We should not be afraid of ghosts" (meaning foreign imperialists), this ghost story was purged from the collection. These are only a few examples of the trouble we encountered during our translation work in those days.

Many friends abroad, who did not understand our situation, thought that since we seemed to churn out millions of words in translation during that period, we were making pots of money. Actually we were never paid for all of our translations of Chinese classics, nor did we have any copyright. The only exception was our translation of the Chinese classical novel *Hongloumeng*, which we translated as *A Dream of Red Mansions*. Because the *Chinese Literature* magazine was separating from the Foreign Languages Press to become an independent organization and we were considered staff of *Chinese Literature*, our work was considered to have been done for an outside organization, so the Party secretary of *Chinese Literature* asked Foreign Languages Press to give us money for our translation. This was the only instance we were paid for our translation, outside of our wages.

During the Great Leap Forward movement of 1958, we translated books like mad, churning them out day and night and producing them very fast. Naturally the quality of our translations was affected. One book, Lu Xun's *Brief History of Chinese Fiction*, a very good book, was finished in ten days. I have always regretted we did not have longer to produce a better translation. Such was the fate of a Chinese hack translator in those days!

After Liberation the emphasis was always that Chinese intellectuals should serve the workers, peasants, and soldiers and reform themselves through physical labour. By the mid-1950s, especially after the Anti-Rightist Movement of 1957, this was further emphasized. This was also the period of transforming agriculture, industry, and commerce throughout China. Private industry and shops were replaced with government-owned industry and shops. In the countryside villages became cooperatives and then amalgamated into bigger cooperatives and in 1958 became people's communes. The socialist revolution was being speeded up. The Great Leap Forward began, and widespread damage and misery was wrought on the countryside. In those days I took part in some "voluntary" physical labour too. For instance, every year during the early summer wheat harvest, all government workers had to spend from one to three days in the countryside to help with the harvest. I rather enjoyed this break from desk work, although it was a waste of time. In 1958 I joined other government workers at the Ming Tombs Reservoir for about ten days. We worked very hard digging and transporting sand with wheelbarrows. There was quite a bit of enthusiasm for the work, but we got so exhausted by evening, that we could hardly raise our rice bowls to eat. In 1959 I also joined other workers at the building site of the Great Hall of the People. I also spent a lot of time visiting peasants in the suburban villages and learned more about the poverty and ignorance of the peasants in the countryside. All this activity was for our re-education. However, the thinking of an intellectual is very hard to change. When the Party encouraged government workers to speak frankly about the countryside being transformed into people's communes and the peasants having their own factories and no longer being dependent on the cities for industrial goods, I expressed my doubts and said, "Wouldn't the peasants stop farming and stop supplying cities with agricultural products? Wouldn't the cities cease to exist and wither away?" My question was considered outrageous, but for the time being I was not criticized. As for the Great Leap Forward, the Party claimed that China would surpass Britain in steel production within three years and the United States within five. I was sceptical and thought it impractical, but did not argue because I admired the spirit of movement. However when they said we could double yields on the land infinitely, provided we had the spirit, that one *mu* of land could yield one thousand catties of wheat, then two thousand catties, then four thousand catties and so on, I thought this sounded like superstition. I noted that one could not possibly produce an infinite amount of wheat with a limited amount of land; it was against the laws of physics. The Party authorities felt I had such doubts because of my bourgeois background and deep-rooted bourgeois ideology. Still, they did not criticize me. Later, when we were discussing the international situation during our section's political study group, and the situation in Cambodia, I defended Prince Sihanouk against the Khmer Rouge's radical line, saying that the majority of the people of Cambodia would support the Prince. The rest of my group supported Pol Pot's radical line and wished Cambodia would soon turn Communist. This argument went on for a couple of weeks

but I was firm in my convictions and they could not persuade me to change my views. Then the Press authorities decided to get six or seven of our best young editors from other departments to argue against me. Still I could not be convinced. Then one day the Party secretary of Foreign Languages Press came and told me very politely that they would hold a meeting of the whole Press to debate my bourgeois way of thinking and help me change my erroneous views. They hoped I would understand it was for my own good, and not be resentful. I agreed. Then a meeting of the whole Press, including editors, translators, and functionaries, was called. It went on for two days. People would go in turn to the platform to denounce me for my reactionary bourgeois views; my bourgeois ways had led to my reactionary remarks. I was told to sit in the back and listen to the denunciations. Many people were asked to come forward voluntarily and express their views. Actually the whole thing was staged. Many speakers worked themselves into a frenzy in their denunciations, spouting a lot of nonsense, exaggerations, and untruths. Even one maid, who worked for another family, was called to speak. They had hoped that our own maid would come forward, but she was too honest and could not see why I should be denounced, so she refused. The other poor maid, who had never known me or my family, had to speak in general terms about how she had always been badly treated in the past by landlord families. She got so worked up in her denunciation that she was weeping and cursing at the same time. Although I had not taken part in the Land Reform Movement soon after Liberation, I had been quite moved by it. Now I was being put in the position of a reactionary landlord to be struggled against. After three denunciation sessions, I had to speak briefly to thank my colleagues for their ideological help. At heart I felt the whole set-up to be a senseless farce. All their efforts were in vain anyway, since I still held to my original opinions. However, after this ludicrous show, I decided to speak less at our meetings and to stop arguing against my comrades.

31

Madness

Madness and the so-called Cultural Revolution seem synonymous to many people outside China who do not know much about China's history in the past few decades. They think that that period between the late 1960s and the early 1970s was the only time when China went mad. Actually this madness had started already ten years earlier. Either the sense of absolute power had befuddled the brain of Chairman Mao and other veteran revolutionaries, or Chairman Mao felt he was growing old and wanted to see the socialist revolution speeded up so that he could see the victory of world communism before he died. Anyway from the time when the witch-hunt to uproot all hidden counter-revolutionaries started in 1955, to the Anti-Rightist Movement of 1957, then on to the Great Leap Forward Movement of 1959, there was a continuous political movement without respite, and the whole country turned more and more radical. The social position of Chinese intellectuals sank lower and lower. I am not saying that in those forty odd years China, under the leadership of the Chinese Communist Party, did not make some great achievements, especially in industrialization and military strength. But, oh what a price we paid! But I must stop digressing and return to my personal history.

It was sometime in 1958, not long after the turmoil caused by the Anti-Rightist Movement, when I had a strange visit from a young comrade whom I did not know. He said he came from the Party's United Front Department, but I sensed that this was not the truth. He must belong to some secret service organization, probably the Ministry of Public Security or something like that. He said that his organization knew of my work for the underground Party in pre-Liberation days, collecting information from my foreign contacts, especially foreign diplomats, about the Kuomintang government. He said that the Party had found my work useful and would like me to pick up such contacts again and supply the Party with news and views collected from similar sources. Since by that time most foreign legations and embassies had moved to the eastern suburbs of the city, he could supply a house for us to live in the eastern part of Beijing so that we would be nearer to the foreign diplomats' quarters. He said he had a friend who owned a house in north-eastern Beijing but the friend had gone abroad and the house was empty. We could move over there. I said that before Liberation I had kept my underground contacts a secret from my wife Gladys, because I had not wanted to have her involved in danger. But now things were different, so I must consult her about this proposal. So I told Gladys and we both agreed to have a try. We were pleased to live in an old fashioned house with a courtyard in the city, much better than living in a flat outside the city in the western suburbs. In no time we told the office that a friend had offered us a house in the city and we had decided to move there. The house was in an alley called Babaokeng ("Eight-treasure Ditch") on the north-east side of the city. It had a spacious courtyard with some jujube and pepper trees. We enjoyed living there very much and stayed for about three years, from 1958 to 1960. But afterwards we decided to have nothing to do with those mysterious comrades and moved back to live in the office compound. Here is why.

During those three years when we lived inside the city, I was told that they would like me to pick up contacts with foreign embassies and make friends with foreign diplomats and report to them any conversations we had on such occasions. After Liberation, because of the Korean War, China was isolated from the Western world and I had no more contacts with foreign diplomats. After 1956 the situation eased and China re-established relations with Western countries. Thus we could resume relations with foreign embassies again. We at that time already had some good friends in the Pakistani and Indian embassies. With this encouragement, we began to make friends with some diplomats in the British and other embassies and spent many of our evenings with them. However in our conversations we mainly talked about cultural matters and the evening's entertainment, so that I had little to report afterwards. I only remember that once a British friend discussed with me the resurgence of nationalistic feelings in Asia and the friction between China and India over the border issue. This was the period when Sino-Indian relations were still very good and our quarrel over the border issue had not come into the open. I learned a lot myself about the McMahon Line and Aksai Chin and all that, but I could not report much on that issue except that the British were concerned about it and were closely watching developments. There was also the Tibetan situation, but nothing special about it in our evening socializing. Though I faithfully reported all conversations to my mysterious contact, they did not show much interest in my reports and must have been rather disappointed. Then in 1960 the storm finally broke. I was politely invited to have a meal and chat with them. We had a sumptuous dinner and the atmosphere was most cordial. But after dinner my host, a young man whom I

met seldom but who was obviously the head of the group, suddenly asked me what I thought of the historical individual Cao Cao. Now, Cao Cao was the founder of the Kingdom of Wei during the Three Kingdoms period in the second century A.D. He was an able warlord, a brilliant strategist as well as a man of letters. Later he was very much maligned in Chinese popular prose romances and popular dramas because he had been so ruthless in his dealings with people and had massacred many. I was rather taken aback by this sudden unwarranted question, but I answered saying that I felt he was a great man and I liked his character because he was fond of poetry, women and wine, and he was versatile and gifted. My host answered cryptically that he had thought I would like him because he was very crafty and treacherous. Then he added:

"I think you have something of his character in you."

Then he abruptly turned to another subject and said:

"I hear, Mr. Yang, that before Liberation you mentioned to friends that you were rather fond of an ancient Chinese proverb: 'A cunning rabbit has three holes for safety's sake.' Is that true?"

I replied that I had said something like that because at the time I had to take several jobs, working at the institute and teaching in various colleges at the same time, because lodging was difficult.

"Quite so," he interrupted. "But there is another meaning, no? The three holes could be the Kuomintang, foreign imperialists, and the Chinese Communist Party. Aren't you working with them all at the same time?"

I was dumbfounded. So all the time they were suspecting that I might be a double agent, pretending to be loyal to the Chinese Communist Party but actually working for some British secret service as a foreign agent. I was very hurt and angry. Then he said coldly that it was time for me to make a full confession of my doings. I left in a huff and they sent me back with a car. The following morning they sent a messenger with a whole wad of writing paper for me to write a full confession. In anger I just wrote ten characters on the front page and sent it back. The words were:

"Only after a long distance can one test the horse's strength (*lu yao zhi ma li*);

"Only after a long period of time can one know the heart of the other (*ri jiu jian ren xin*)."

These too were words from an ancient Chinese proverb. After that I decided to have no more to do with that mysterious group. After a week of silence, the young comrade who first came to ask me to stay at that house sheepishly turned up again and said something like, "It's been nice knowing you, but now my other friend who owns this house has come back from abroad, so we would like to have the house back at your convenience." I answered that we would be glad to move back to the Press compound in about a week's time. So we moved back to the Press compound soon thereafter, and the Press did not ask me the reason. Doubtless the Party leadership of the Press knew all about the affair.

For a time I was in a state of gloom, knowing now that I was definitely considered a political suspect. However in the Press everything went on as usual and my colleagues were as good to me as ever. Gradually I got used to the situation.

32

A Great Leap

A great leap took shape in the early 1960s. In 1960 the Chinese Academy of Social Sciences, having heard that I had studied ancient Greek and Latin at Oxford and done some translations of Greek and Latin classics, wanted me to translate Homer's epics. Since this would take some time, they wanted the Foreign Languages Press to release me for a spell so that I could devote all my time to translating Homer. I was at the same time holding a position as senior research fellow in the Institute of Foreign Literature at the academy, so the Press could not refuse the request. I finished the translation of the *Odyssey* in a year, but then the Foreign Languages Press felt I should go back to translate a Chinese classical novel into English. They decided that I should translate *Hongloumeng* (*A Dream of Red Mansions*), a Qing dynasty novel, which was very popular in China. I started to translate it and finished a rough draft of about a hundred chapters by 1964 but then was told to stop. The work only resumed in 1972, after I was released from jail, with the whole translation finished in 1974. During the time I was translating Homer in 1960, I also translated the French classic *Chanson de Roland* into Chinese, a work I always enjoyed when I was studying medieval French in those Oxford days more than twenty years earlier.

It was about the same time that the Foreign Languages Press was made into a bureau with a separate printing press and a separate office for distribution of books and magazines abroad. Since then its name was changed to the Foreign Languages Bureau, and it became a more unwieldy, incompetent and bureaucratic organization. Its staff expanded from a few hundred to two or three thousand with more printing workers and a huge administration staff. The new bureau chief had some strange ideas. He felt the former editors and translators were all bourgeois-minded intellectuals from the old society and therefore unreliable. So he put in a few hundred young demobilized soldiers and wanted to give them a quick training as editors and translators within a year to take over their jobs. Those young soldiers were semi-illiterates with only primary school education, or at the most some middle school education, and they had practically no foreign language education. But he felt with a quick short-term training course, he could turn them into new translators. I and other older translators were given two or more such pupils to teach English or other Western languages. I had two young ex-soldier pupils and I gave them a few lessons every week. They were fairly bright young men but of course it was quite hopeless to expect such young men to turn into translators in a year or two. When the Cultural Revolution came in 1966, these young men became the main bulk of those young "rebels" in the revolution in the Foreign Languages Bureau, and they played havoc and did a lot of damage to our work. In 1960 or 1961, the new bureau head decided that there must have been a lot of bad books published in the Press in the past. So he started a movement to examine all past publications. Many people were mobilized to this task. They discovered a book of Chinese stamps printed after Liberation with a stamp of Lenin half cut off for lack of space on the page. This was supposed to be sabotage, and the young editor responsible for that album was immediately dismissed and sent to the countryside. There was a short history of Chinese classical literature which I translated. The book was written by a professor from Shandong province who had modelled the book on the official version of the history of the Communist Party of the USSR by quoting Chairman Mao at the end of each chapter in great detail to prove that Chinese literature had always been progressing according to Chairman Mao's ideas, just as the Soviet textbook was based on Stalin's dictums. I thought this kind of writing ridiculous and unsuitable for foreign consumption so I consulted the editor and had all those sacred edicts cut out. The result was that the book was reduced to less than half the original length. When they discovered this during the examination, they were flabbergasted. The new bureau chief barked out during a mass meeting:

"How dare this man Yang Xianyi do such a thing. This is outrageous! Isn't the translator's job just to translate. Why should he do any editing work?"

Anyway, they finally decided it was the editor's responsibility. He should not have agreed to my request to have Chairman's Mao's words cut out. Because he was a scholar with a landlord class background, he was considered a counter-revolutionary and sent to the countryside. I was spared, but the translation of that book was destroyed. It was only reprinted in the eighties. That editor also returned to the bureau after the Cultural Revolution, with his name cleared, but it was after more than twenty years. He retired soon thereafter. The other day I heard he had died of heart failure; he was a year younger than I. He was a good man and a good scholar.

It was also during the Great Leap Forward that Gladys decided to ask permission to visit her family in England with our young

daughter Zhi. She had not seen England since she came to China in 1940, about twenty years earlier, so her request was quite justified. However the *Chinese Literature* office was reluctant and made a lot of excuses. Finally Gladys had to write a letter to Premier Zhou Enlai about it and then it was quickly granted. Gladys went to England for about three months and Zhi stayed a few months longer. I did not ask to go with them because of all the troubles I had. I felt that the bureau would raise more objections if I did. This was the time when China was in great economic difficulties. All the empty boasts about a super bumper harvest and a great industrial revolution came to nothing, and China was in a state of bankruptcy. This was also the time when China and the Soviet Union quarrelled and the Soviet Union withdrew all their experts from China and stopped supplying China with oil. Later China blamed the Soviet Union for those three years of difficulty. Actually the real cause for China's economic difficulty was the Great Leap Forward. Anyway when Gladys was away, the economic situation in Beijing was at its bleakest period. All commodities were scarce, especially foodstuffs, and people were starving. Government officials were given ration coupons to buy food. I was rated second-class among the privileged group, and I could buy two pounds of pork, four pounds of eggs and some sugar and vegetable oil every month, so my situation was not too bad. Between 1960 and 1962, because of the economic difficulty, there was a lull in the political movements and one felt on the whole more relaxed. So although at the same time I had my own special troubles, my relations with my colleagues were good, and nobody made further troubles for me. In 1963 and 1964, economic conditions were improving, but the Party was not yet ready to start a big fresh political movement. There was however a movement to start socialist re-education among the village cadres, and some government functionaries, mainly Chinese Communist Party members, were sent to the countryside to "re-educate" the village functionaries. I, being considered already a bourgeois, backward sort, was spared such duties, and so avoided further trouble.

However in early spring 1961 I had written some poems defending Khrushchev's new line against Stalin and criticizing the Chinese Communist Party's line and their support of Albania's Enver Hoxja. Those poems brought fresh trouble on myself. This was the time after the Soviet Union's Twentieth Congress, when Khrushchev denounced Stalin for his crimes and proposed a new line for the Soviet Party. The Chinese Communist Party considered Khrushchev a revisionist and by that time there was an open split between the two parties. This was about the time when I had just quarrelled with those mysterious comrades and I was in a bad mood. So one evening I just dashed off these poems and the next morning when I went to my office I made a copy of them and left them on my desk. I did it half-intentionally for my colleagues to see — as a kind of protest. Some of my young colleagues saw them and thought nothing of it, but the Party secretary of *Chinese Literature*, who used to be very good to me, happened to see them. She was very shocked and told one of the editors to copy the poems. Nothing happened at that time, but later when the Cultural Revolution began in 1966, these poems were copied onto big posters and this was made a very serious issue. I shall go back to it later. Anyway in 1961 although I was not criticized in the Foreign Languages Bureau, I could feel I was "under a cloud". About the same time the Chinese writers held their Third National Congress, and I, as a member of the standing committee, was invited to attend. But just as the congress was about to be convened, I was told that this time I need not attend, and they asked me to hand back my admittance card. No explanation was given. This incident put me

into a state of deep gloom, knowing that I was definitely suspect. However nothing happened during the next few years and I nearly forgot that I was in for trouble. Then the Cultural Revolution arrived.

33

The Cultural Revolution

The Cultural Revolution need not be dwelled upon in detail. It was simply the culmination of a whole series of events, not something accidental caused by a handful of ambitious conspirators wanting to usurp power. Though it started in force in the summer of 1966, one or two years earlier, one could already sense that a terrific storm was brewing. Actually the Party's tendency towards a more radical development had already started with the Anti-Rightist Movement and the socialist transformation of industry and agriculture in the mid-1950s ten years earlier with its nationwide witch-hunt, struggle meetings, big-character posters and the like. The ingredients were already there. The whole country, especially the younger people, were being trained for the crazy experiment. It only needed Chairman Mao's stirring call at Tiananmen Square (Gate of Heavenly Peace) to set the whole plain ablaze. In my own case, I knew that something was coming to me long before 1966. I had started on a translation of Sima Qian's history before 1960. This book was a very well-known Chinese history classic, compared to Herodotus, and its author Sima Qian is considered the father of Chinese historical writing. The Foreign Languages Press agreed to let me make selections from this monumental work, and I finished the translation by 1961 or 1962.

After I submitted my manuscript, I waited a long time but the book was never published. In 1964 after making various inquiries about it, I was told that it was long since sent to the printers, but there was an order from above that the book was not to be printed, not because they felt the quality of the translation was faulty, but that they had decided no books bearing my name as translator should be printed for the time being. No more was heard about the manuscript until the Cultural Revolution. After I came out of jail with my name cleared in 1972, I was told I could resume my translation work again, but when I asked about this manuscript, they told me that it must have been lost and there was no record of it. Then someone from Hong Kong told me that the book was printed in Hong Kong, with my name on it. I managed to get a copy, then found out that an editor before the Cultural Revolution had given or sold that manuscript to Hong Kong. After the Cultural Revolution a new Beijing edition was reprinted by the Foreign Languages Press. Even now I do not know who has the copyright to that book. It is certainly high time for China to have a copyright law!

By 1965 I was told that I was to stop translating the novel *A Dream of Red Mansions* or do any other translations, but no reasons were given. I knew then that the axe was about to fall, but it had to wait until the summer of 1966 when Chairman Mao issued the call to mobilize all the Red Guards to start the Cultural Revolution.

In 1965, the year before the Cultural Revolution began in full force, there were articles already appearing in newspapers denouncing certain "reactionary" films and plays, as well as certain "reactionary" writers and scholars in order to prepare the minds of the masses. In the schools and universities and government offices there were big-character posters stuck up on walls written by young hotheads. Then the President of the Republic Liu Shaoqi and the Party General Secretary Deng Xiaoping were singled out as arch-revisionists within the Party, together with other government and Party leaders, especially those on the ideological front. By July 1966 an all-China mass movement was organized, with Chairman Mao as the spiritual leader leading a revolution to clean up the government and Party. He was the chief wizard, waving his magic wand on the platform overlooking Tiananmen Square. He waved his hand and all the young Red Guards swarmed to his call. The whole city was covered with big-character posters and all the walls were painted red. Within a few days the whole city was transformed into a "red ocean". Young people went mad; innocent old men and women, even school servants, were dragged out onto the streets and cruelly beaten and kicked at the orders of the street committees. Thousands or tens of thousands were killed. Many bad people used this occasion to take out their private vendettas. Even now there is no accurate account of how many innocent people were killed in the month of August. The people of Beijing called the month of August "Red August". All over China the mad movement spread. There were many deaths in other cities too. During August the Beijing crematorium was so choked with corpses that they could not all be burnt. But even in this month of terror I heard an amusing incident. One jobless young man was working temporarily in the crematorium carrying corpses to be cremated. He noticed the corpse of a young girl with a gold watch on her wrist. He decided to take off the gold watch because it was too good to be burnt. When he touched the corpse he noticed that the body was still warm and the girl was not quite dead. He took pity on her and revived her. Then the girl was grateful to him for saving her life and fell in love with him and they got married. There were many such stories told by eyewitnesses at that time. Of course the ending

of these stories were not all so happy. My old friend, the well-known writer Lao She, was beaten up during a struggle meeting during this time and later drowned himself in a lake.

During the month of August I never dared venture out on the street lest I become involved in some trouble. The street committee of Babaokeng in the east city, where we had stayed in that house lent to us during the Great Leap Forward between 1959 and 1961, came to the Foreign Languages Bureau to demand that I be handed over to them for a struggle meeting, saying that during those years I had mysterious foreign connections and my lifestyle showed that I was a bourgeois and bad character. During those years Gladys often went to the special Friendship Store to buy bread, cheese and tinned goods, and our neighbours were very jealous of our wealth and special privileges. Now they felt this was the time to settle old grievances. The Bureau, however, did not hand me over, so I escaped a beating. Otherwise I might have been killed. This was one good thing my Bureau did for me — giving me protection during that month of terror.

Within the Foreign Languages Bureau itself, however, the movement soon spread. Young hotheads of the administration, including editors, translators and other office workers, especially those young demobilized soldiers recruited by the Bureau chief, began to put on red armbands and styled themselves "revolutionary rebels". They organized struggle meetings against their superiors, department and section heads, and bureau chiefs. Soon all the low-ranking workers became "rebels". This suddenly started one afternoon. We heard sounds of gongs and people cheering, and then we saw in the bureau compound gangs of rebels pushing the two section leaders of one of the magazine offices in a parade in front. Both men had tall white paper hats on their heads. Then they were forced to a struggle meeting in their office. It was just like what happened throughout the country in the Land Reform Movement just before and after Liberation. There were big-character posters everywhere. The chief crime of those two section leaders was apparently that they were fond of eating good food. So the posters were full of accounts of the good meals they had eaten in earlier times. It was as if the bureau had suddenly become a big restaurant, with menus of food written in big characters everywhere. The following day other bureau leaders were denounced on big-character posters. The woman Party secretary of our magazine *Chinese Literature* was spared because she was ill and was absent from the office. Then the whole bureau was full of a new lot of big-character posters denouncing me. There must have been several tens of thousands of those posters stuck up on the different buildings in the bureau compound. The most out-standing poster had my poems supporting Krushchev's new line copied out in bold characters with red headlines, denouncing me as a reactionary revisionist, Krushchev's grandson, and other nonsense. Then somebody pointed out that since I was not yet a member of the Communist Party, I could not be labelled a revisionist; then they changed the label to "counter-revolutionary". Some of my colleagues who were sympathetic towards me suggested that this was a ruse engineered by the Party secretary, so that the masses' anger could be turned towards me instead of her, since at that time the other people being denounced were all section leaders and Party secretaries, and I, not being a section head, was the only exception. They called it "sacrificing the Castle to protect the King" (in Chinese chess there is no Queen and the Castle is the important piece protecting the King). Whether this was true or not, I was not in a position to say. Anyway after that I became the worst criminal in the whole bureau, with all sorts of labels thrown at me. One afternoon when I was translating or checking a manuscript in my

office, there came a telephone call from downstairs saying a visitor was waiting downstairs for me. I went downstairs and some young men led me to the dining hall. They already had three dining tables put up, one above the other. They helped me, quite politely, climb up to the highest table. Then a crowd gathered around and denounced me, asking me why I was against Chairman Mao, why I was defending Khrushchev and so on. Since I was over ten feet above ground, my only fear at that time was that they might turn rough and start kicking me or pushing me down from that height in their anger. Then I might break my arm or leg. Fortunately nothing like that happened. They helped me down after an hour or so of denunciations and let me go. After that I had a whole series of struggle meetings, either singly or together with other bureau leaders. I disliked those meetings when I was the only target, because then I had to answer all sorts of ridiculous questions, many of which were unanswerable. When I was being struggled against with other bureau heads, it was more fun. Those young people had a game called "riding the jet plane". We were told to line up standing on a platform with bowed heads; then we had to stretch out our arms to the back and raise them high above our bowed heads. In this way we looked like children imitating jet airplanes. My arm muscles were quite flexible, so I could perform this feat quite easily. For some other comrades it was rather agonizing after a while, and then with trembling legs they would fall to their knees and the masses would hoot with laughter. This sort of game would go on during the struggle meetings, sometimes lasting two or three hours. Since my legs were rather strong, I could feel detached and secretly watched the others in fun. It was all very childish and ludicrous. These struggle meetings usually were called every other day and went on till the end of the year. Then the young rebels got tired of them. After the spring of 1967, there were very few such struggle meetings. However during that time I remember the young rebels in the bureau decided that there should be a parade on the streets of all those functionaries who were being denounced, myself included. There were about two truckloads of us, with just about over one dozen people. We were put standing in open trucks and driven through the streets in the west city. From time to time the trucks would stop and some young rebels would shout slogans and printed leaflets they had prepared were scattered over the crowds of onlookers. The printed leaflets gave our names and other particulars, like our positions in the bureau, the crimes we had committed, and the like. The onlookers on the streets just looked apathetic and slightly curious, but hardly anybody joined in cheering or shouting abuses, except that some children laughed. Those street people had witnessed too many such scenes those days, with many other offices doing the same. When we reached another organization's office buildings with which our bureau had had contact, like the radio broadcast station and the Xinhua News agency, we would be told to come down and line up in the building's compound. Then we were introduced in turn and denounced, the hotheads shouting slogans like "Down with all of Chairman Mao's enemies" and so on. The whole parade took practically all morning, but it was not too uncomfortable, except that the day was rather chilly and I had forgotten to wear an overcoat. When I came back home, I was shivering from the cold.

34

Red August

Red August had a frightening effect on everyone. During that August of 1966 and afterwards, the struggle meetings and the loud speakers blaring denunciations of people day and night worked on the nerves. I felt I had suddenly become a social outcast. When I went home in the evening I found Gladys and the children living their lives as usual and quite cheerful, sometimes even enthusiastic. They were not molested and their lives were different from mine. I had little conversation with them. In the daytime I was in the office and nobody would talk with me or greet me. I suppose during the month of August, I too was truly frightened.

I usually don't frighten easily. I did not feel frightened when Kuomintang soldiers aimed their rifles at me on my way to Chengdu in the interior. I did not get frightened when people panicked on our boat and said the boat was sinking in the Yangtze during the night of our voyage to Nanjing. But this time I was nervous and frightened. When I sat by myself in the office alone, I thought I heard colleagues discussing plans for struggle meetings and whispering how they would beat me to death. I also thought I heard them talking about how so-and-so had already been beaten to death during interrogation. Actually they had been discussing things next door, trying not to let me hear. But I had tried hard to catch their words and must have imagined things. This was the beginning of a period of auditory hallucination brought on by my nervous tension and fear. When I went home I told Gladys that my colleagues were planning to murder me and asked her to send a letter for me to the head of the Party's United Front Department to ask him to save me. The minister of the United Front Department in the Party Poliburo was Comrade Xu Bing, whom I knew from the old Chongqing days during the war, and I had called on him once after Liberation. I do not know whether the letter ever reached him in those days or not. Later I realized that he was not in a position to help me anyway. He was also being struggled against during the movement. Later he committed suicide after being accused of being a revisionist. It is funny nowadays to reflect on how I got so frightened at that time, but this was the beginning of a few months during which I was schizophrenic and had constant auditory hallucinations. I heard later that many people had the same sort of trouble during the movement. I knew one fellow, a "jail-bird" in my own cell when I was imprisoned, who had visual hallucinations as well. He imagined that from time to time he could see people standing in front of him staring and peering at him. Later his madness became worse and he died after being taken to hospital. That happened sometime in 1970. Fortunately I never had visual hallucinations, but I certainly had auditory hallucinations. I would hear the voices of people who were not there. This went on from the end of August until the beginning of the next year, 1967. During that period the woman Party secretary of the Press was staying at home on the pretext of illness, so a new woman Party commissar was assigned to take temporary charge. Once when I thought I heard that someone I knew was being interrogated and later beaten to death, I mentioned this to her and said I was sorry for his untimely death. That woman commissar laughed and said I was out of my mind. She said that this comrade was fine and that during lunch time I could see him at the canteen for myself. I did so, verifying her statement. Then I began to doubt whatever I heard. However the voices I heard were so clear that I could not believe I was imagining it all. Then I thought it must be sinister people hidden somewhere in the Press who had sinister wireless machines transmitting messages which I alone could hear. But how could messages be transmitted only to me and not to others? I was very ignorant of scientific matters. In my middle school days, I was very good at biology and chemistry but I had never studied electricity, and certainly in those days one had never studied electronics or anything about radios. I only had the common idea that to transmit a message through the wireless, one had to use the same wavelength, otherwise the receiver would never receive the  message. Then I thought that I had heard of some exotic substances called isotopes. I never bothered to find out what an isotope was, but judging by its name, which meant equal places or equal directions, it must be the chemical substance which the hidden evil-doer or doers had succeeded to get into my system. In that way I could receive the messages without others doing the same. All these lunatic ideas seem extremely laughable, but at the time, in my half crazy state, the idea seemed plausible. It had to be so because I was not the evil-doer plotting against my country. So when I was all alone, I tried to argue against that hidden enemy or tried to track him down. At night when I was alone in my sitting room and Gladys and the children had gone to sleep, I would talk aloud to that hidden enemy and try to debunk him. Once Gladys had not yet gone to sleep when that happened and she came out. She thought I had gone raving mad. Actually at that time I was on my way to madness.

Probably it was because I still retained some elements of sanity — I still had faith in myself — or because the mass hysteria of this period of the Cultural Revolution was dying down and I was less persecuted and feeling more relaxed, that by the beginning of 1967 I no longer suffered from the auditory hallucinations, and things became more normal. I had never dared venture out of the Foreign Languages Bureau during the latter part of 1966, but now I started going out into the city on Sundays. Every Sunday morning I would take a walk to the east or west city to look at all the big-character posters on the streets and learn about things outside. That was my only pastime. I still did not dare take a bus, because it was said that the public buses would not take counter-revolutionaries. Anybody who was considered a "monster" could summarily be thrown out of the bus. So I just spent my time in long-distance walks, and that was probably good for my health. During weekdays I had to go to the office to sit at my desk. Of course there was no proper translation work for me to do, but every morning I would be sent to do some manual labour, and that I found more enjoyable. I was sent for some time to clean the lavatories. The public lavatories in our bureau used to be very dirty and smelly, but I did a good job, scraping off the left-over excrement from the lavatory basins and rinsing them with water. After a short while, I was praised for my diligent and scrupulous work. The *Chinese Literature* section's lavatories became the cleanest in the whole bureau. Later I was sent to the kitchen in the back compound to pick unburnt coal cinders from the garbage heap. This was a more tiring job, but I enjoyed it because during that time I could have some fresh air, and it was better than sitting in the office. This sort of work lasted throughout the year to the first part of 1968. During the whole period I only had one struggle meeting, and that was in the company of my bureau chief. The young rebels by this time had split up into different "fighting groups" and they had started fighting amongst themselves. Thus they had no time to make sport with people like us, who were called "monsters". While picking coal cinders, I often thought about the fairy tale of Cinderella, and I wondered when a fairy godmother would turn up to put me in a pumpkin carriage and take me to the palace. However it turned out that this Cinderella never had the chance of going to a palace. I was sent to prison instead. Now a prison is not as comfortable as a palace, but it was not as frightening as people think. Lots of my colleagues later were beaten and quite a few were killed or forced to commit suicide during the next few years. Being in prison I was spared all that. Perhaps prison was not such a bad place after all.

35

Prison

Prison became our home on the eve of May Day (May 1st) 1968, when Gladys and I were arrested. We were there until May Day 1972, a period of exactly four years. Since the beginning of 1968, there had been quite a number of foreign experts arrested as foreign spies and put into prison in Beijing. It all started because Jiang Qing, Chairman Mao's wife, made a speech at the beginning of that year saying that we must watch out for foreign spies. She said there were spies who had come into China for many years, even before Liberation, but they had been pretending to be friends and experts working for us. After that speech, a number of our foreign experts were arrested. In our bureau, one American Jew named Israel Epstein and his English wife were arrested one night less than one month before it happened to us. I did not think we had to worry, though, because Epstein had been very active during the Cultural Revolution, while we had been very passive. That evening before we were arrested, I was gloomily drinking a bottle of Chinese liquor, at home with Gladys. Then Gladys went to bed, and I went on drinking. We finished two thirds of that bottle. Then I heard some gentle knocking at the door. I opened the door and found it was a young colleague of the personnel section who just said he wanted to talk to me outside. I thought nothing of it, since in those days he had been around sometimes in the evening to ask me to give some information about some other colleagues and I was used to that. I went out with him, still wearing my slippers, because I thought it would only take a few minutes in another room. However he went on across the compound towards the office in the front building without a word and I had to follow him. I regretted then I had not changed into a pair of proper walking shoes, but I did not think it was worth bothering. We went upstairs to the office. The room was semi-dark with only a table lamp switched on, so I could not see clearly who was in the room. Anyway there were quite a number of our young rebels with a few men whom I did not know in army uniform. When I came in, one man in army uniform came up and asked:

"What is your name?"

"Yang Xianyi."

"Where do you come from?"

"My family came from Anhui province, but I was born in Tianjin."

"How old are you?"

"I'm forty-eight."

Then his expression suddenly changed. He barked out:

"By order of the Beijing Military Control Commission you are under arrest." He seized my wrist and expertly put a pair of hand-cuffs on my two wrists. Several other soldiers crowded around me, fearing that I might resist. Actually I had no such intention and I did not feel frightened. Although it came as a surprise, I was not perturbed because after all the things that had happened the last couple of years this seemed rather tame. The soldiers themselves looked more tense than I. After a couple of minutes of silence, since I did not protest or ask questions, they produced a sheet of printed paper which said that I gave them permission to search my house and told me to sign it. I did as I was told, still saying nothing.

Then after another couple of seconds of silence, the officer nodded to his soldiers and said:

"All right. You can take him away now."

Then they took me away down the stairs. I was still handcuffed. My slippers were two sizes too large so I could not walk very fast. My only thought at that time was "Why didn't I change into proper shoes?" Outside the bureau I was shoved into an army jeep accompanied by two soldiers, one on each side of me. They pushed my head down to my knees so that I could not see where we were going, and I complied meekly and fell half asleep. Actually it was totally unnecessary. I could tell by the streetlights that were reflected into the taxi that I was taken to the west city, to the prosperous district with lots of neon lights. Then the car went south-west to a prison which I had never visited before. It was a very big compound, with a huge iron gate which opened and closed automatically. The car drove us to an office and stopped. When they took me to the office, they took off my handcuffs and I was thankful for that. I had thought that I might be handcuffed all the time in prison, and that would be very inconvenient. The officer at the desk did not ask any questions. He just gave me a form to fill in with my name, address, sex, age, etc., then told me to leave my trouser-belt, my shoelaces or any other rope and things with which I could hang myself. I also had to leave everything in my pockets on the table, especially metal things with sharp edges, like penknives and the like. They put those small belongings of mine into a large envelope and kept them, to be returned when I was released. Then they took me to my cell. It was in a separate building. Each room was locked from the outside. The room had nothing but two long wooden beds. Prisoners slept not in lengthwise fashion but packed one next to the other like sardines. In that way about ten people could share one bed. When I went into my cell, the two beds were

already full. They had about twenty people in them (actually the next morning I found out there were already twenty-one prisoners there, not counting me). Anyway they told the other prisoners to make room for me on one bed, and I squeezed myself in between them and slept. I forgot to mention that when I first went in, I asked the guard where I could go to the toilet if I wanted to pee, and they pointed me to a tin bucket between the two beds, and I promptly relieved myself. After I squeezed myself in between the other prisoners on the bed, I just took off my jacket and trousers and settled down to sleep. It was by then already midnight, and there was nothing to do anyway, since we were not supposed to introduce ourselves to each other and make conversation. There was an electric lamp on the ceiling quite out of reach and it was kept on all night. There was a small peep-window on the door so that the guards could peep in and see what we were doing at any time. Since I had had some drinks after supper and was feeling quite drowsy, I immediately fell asleep and slept soundly till nearly seven o'clock in the morning. In the morning when we got up, an oldish jailbird whispered to me:

"Hey, why did they put you in here?"

"I don't know."

"We thought it was so late and you smelled of alcohol, you must have had a few cups too many and got into trouble on the street, so they nabbed you."

"No, it was nothing like that. I was arrested at home."

He was silent for another couple of seconds, then he said wistfully:

"Your alcohol smelled so wonderful. It must be good stuff. I haven't had that for years. How much did it cost you per ounce?"

I told him I did not buy it by the ounce, but I bought the whole bottle. How much it had cost I had forgotten. Then he said:

"Did you finish the whole bottle?"

I told him that when I left there was still one third left in the bottle. He sighed and said:

"Will it still be there when they decide to send you back?"

Actually after four years when I returned to my flat, I found that bottle still on the mantelpiece, and there was still alcohol left in it, but I did not drink it. I gave it away to a young colleague.

So this was how I started my new life as a jailbird. I found out from my fellow prisoners that normally we would not have so many people in one cell. Usually it would be about a dozen or so, but recently they had arrested too many and they were going to send some to the provinces to relieve the burden. But the army truck had failed to turn up the day before. True enough, in the afternoon they took away seven or eight prisoners from the cell and life became more comfortable. Every morning the prisoners would be up by seven, and then they were supposed to tidy up their bedding and things. About an hour later they would be sent out of the cell, escorted by guards, to the lavatory to relieve themselves. They were only allowed less than ten minutes, no longer. Some of the prisoners had constant constipation and suffered great agony, but I never had any trouble. Then we had less than quarter of an hour to wash our faces. We often managed to wash our handkerchiefs and socks or underpants at the same time. About ten o'clock every morning we would have our first meal. Another evening meal would arrive in the afternoon about four o'clock — two meals a day. The evening meal was simple: two large maize buns and a bowl of soup with vegetables in it, either cabbage or turnips or beans, depending on what was the cheapest that season. There might be a slip or two of pork in the soup during national festivals. I found the food quite adequate for me since we had no exercise anyway, but some young prisoners were always hungry.

So I usually ate one and a half buns and left half of a bun for my fellow jailbirds. For the rest of the day we had two sessions of political study and reading the Party newspaper, *People's Daily*, every day, once in the morning and once in the afternoon after two hours afternoon nap. Then about eight or nine o'clock in the evening we went to bed. For political study, we read some of Chairman Mao's articles: "On Norman Bethune", "Serve the People", "The Old Man Who Moved Mountains", "On the People's Democratic Dictatorship", and that was all. We were not allowed to read other books. I was elected leader of the study group in our cell most of the time, and I could more or less memorize these few articles by heart. Our study consisted of memorizing these readings; there was no discussion nor debate. How could one argue against those sacred dictums? We were never allowed to go out of our cell, except once in a fortnight, if our guard had not forgotten the date, we were led out to the compound to breathe some fresh air. We would be taken to a walled-up place with no roof, to march up and down or in a circle for about a quarter of an hour. Then we would be led back and locked up again in our cell. This happened throughout the year. We were led out to have a communal bath with hot water once a month, and that lasted about half an hour each time. As soon as a prisoner arrived in prison, his head was shaven clean, and once every month or so we were shaven clean again. We certainly did not have to worry about our hair or beards.

36

Worries

Worries over my lot in prison were only over what would happen to Gladys and the children. Two or three days after being put in prison I was given a chance to see my jailer. He told me that if I needed any clothes and bedding or other daily necessities like tooth-brush, soap, etc., he could ask my family to send it to me, since I would be staying there a very long time. Then he asked me if I had other requests. I said my only worry was about Gladys and the children. I said that Gladys was easily frightened. When she found out that I had been taken away, she might have a nervous breakdown or attempt to commit suicide. Of my two daughters, one was graduating from university, the other from middle school, what would happen to them? He smiled and said that Gladys was all right, she was in a safe place. As for my daughters, my crime had nothing to do with them, so they would be well looked after. I guessed from his words that Gladys had probably also been arrested. Sometime later, I heard from fellow prisoners that many foreigners were actually also imprisoned in the same compound, but in a different building, and Gladys was probably among them. Then some young jailbirds told me that sometimes one could peep through the cracks of a barred window and see those foreign women prisoners walking towards the bathhouse. One day he said he actually caught a glimpse of someone who looked like Gladys according to my description. After that I felt more assured. Actually after I left prison in 1972, I heard that my son, who had graduated from university and been assigned as a young engineer to a factory in Hubei province, had not got on too well with his outfit and had become mentally unbalanced. My two daughters were left without anybody to look after them and they were sent to the countryside. They too had a hard time those four years. If I had known that in prison I would have been more worried. However I did not know all that at the time, because even then I still trusted the Party too much. I was spared a great deal of worry in this delusion. Gladys, though, had a hard time. She was arrested the same night after they arrested me. Some women even had her thoroughly searched, taking off all her clothes. I was not searched at all. I suppose they felt she was a foreign spy and thus very crafty and sinister, perhaps carrying secret codes or special devices with her. She was placed in solitary confinement, a much harder sentence than mine. I at least had plenty of company all the time. She was given better treatment in that she had much better meals and more varieties of food. She could read Western "progressive" magazines and books, while I never was allowed anything. She even read some of Karl Marx's *Das Kapital* in jail, a book she would never have read otherwise. But after she left jail, she had the habit of talking to herself when alone, for a year or so, a habit picked up during the long days of solitary confinement. I never had that feeling of loneliness. I got on very well with my fellow jailbirds, and learned a lot of things about Chinese society which I had not known before.

In Chinese prisons, important prisoners were usually given solitary confinement. Unimportant prisoners would share a cell with many others. During the Cultural Revolution, however, it was not necessarily the case that prisoners who shared a cell with others were all people with lighter offences. I myself witnessed two or three people in my cell who were told to go out with their belongings to another destination. Later I heard from latecomers that they were given a summary sentence and executed publicly. The prisoners who were sentenced to death were taken by soldiers to a district outside the east city which was called Jiuxianqiao ("Wine God's Bridge"). The culprit would be given a kick behind his knees so that he kneeled to the ground. Then a soldier would come forward and shoot him in the back of his head. He died instantly, with only one shot. The body would be wrapped up in straw matting to be collected by his relatives. If nobody came for the corpse, the body would be buried near that place, with no sign on the grave. That district in those days was desolate, isolated so as not to disturb Beijing citizens. When relatives came to collect the corpse, they had to pay forty Chinese cents for the cost of the bullet. I heard all this from a fellow prisoner who had himself witnessed such a scene. He was threatened with the same fate if he failed to confess his crime. So they took him there to see the whole execution process to frighten him into confession. I proposed to him that he must have confessed, that was why he was still alive.

The prisoners in my cell were all sorts, from different walks of life. Quite a few were young rebels who had simply resorted to hooliganism during the movements, some were crafty pickpockets, some suspected murderers. There were two middle-ranking government officials, one, according to some other prisoners who knew, had raped his own daughters. Then there was an official from the Coal Ministry whose only crime was defending his disgraced minister and writing disrespectful comments on the *Collected Writings of Chairman Mao*. I got on very well with him, and after he was released, he helped me transfer my eldest son-in-law from a coalmine in the north-east to Beijing.

There was also one peasant from the suburbs, an elderly man who had a son in the army. The son had been away for several years. During this time the son's wife, the old peasant's daughter-in-law, who was fond of her father-in-law but hated her mother-in-law, often quarrelled with her mother-in-law. One day the daughter-in-law in anger took up the chopper from the kitchen and chopped off the mother-in-law's head. The neighbours suspected that the father-in-law was behind all this, so he was dragged off to jail. It was probably a groundless charge, and after a few months he was released. During the time he was in my cell, the lice on his padded jacket got into all our clothes. The guards took great pains to exterminate the lice. All of us had to strip and our bedding and clothes were taken away to be steamed. In the meantime we were given temporary garments. Later, we still found a few live lice crawling around and we used them to play games. One of our fellow prisoners said that he knew the lice in north China always liked to crawl towards the north. So we put those few lice in a row, all facing south. Sure enough, after a couple of seconds they all turned around and crawled northwards, and we all marvelled at that. One day that old peasant played me a dirty trick. He had been mentally distraught and suddenly in the middle of the night he wanted to get up and pee. But instead of getting out of bed, he just stood up on the bed and peed on my bedding. Fortunately he missed my face. Since we all sympathized with the old man, we did not scold him. Soon after that, he was told to go home. We were not sorry to see him go, since he was the dirtiest of us all. After he left, we were not pestered with lice.

During these four years, I only knew of two men who were taken away and later executed. Another in my cell died of illness.

One had heavy iron shackles around his ankles and he was handcuffed all the time. People said he was a murderer. He only stayed in the cell for a few days, then was taken away and shot. The guards from time to time changed our cells. Once I was in a smaller cell with only four other prisoners. One of them was a young man who used to work as an accountant in a plastic surgery hospital. He told me that he used to be a soldier and during the Korean War in 1950 he had been sent as a volunteer to Korea. During his stay in Korea he fell in love with a Korean girl. After he came back to China, he got married locally but did not like his wife and was thinking of that Korean sweetheart all the time. He made up his mind to go back to Korea. Since he knew the terrain very well, he went back to the north-east, swam across the Yalu River and managed to enter North Korean territory. He was caught by the Korean frontier guards, but he thought at that time North Korea's relationship with China was not so good. The Soviet Union had just broken relations with China and the Koreans were on the Soviet side. So he took out the "little red book" of Chairman Mao's quotations from his uniform pocket, threw it to the ground and stamped on it with his foot. Then he said he did not like the Chinese government but wanted to seek asylum in Korea. He was put in detention for a few days. Unfortunately for him, during the same period, Sino-Korean relations got better again and North Korea sent a delegation again to Beijing. So they sent him back as a defector, in a big postal bag. When he told us his story, he did not think he would get into serious trouble. He said the security guards had been very good to him since he was a PLA soldier before and had had a good record. He said he had only taken a couple of Chinese yuan from his office, and once he returned it, he would be leniently treated and released. One morning he was told by the jailer to pack up and go. He said goodbye cheerfully and left. A

few days later we heard from some latecomer that he had been charged with high treason and executed.

The one in our cell who died was that young man I mentioned earlier, from some government office, who had suffered from hallucinations. He always suffered from constipation and every day he had to be driven back from his toilet with curses, the guards just thinking him crazy and disobedient. Later his legs and the lower part of his body all swelled up and he could hardly walk. The guards only realized he was ill when it was too late. Finally he was carried out on a stretcher and died.

Otherwise all the prisoners were treated all right. Those who were ill and got a fever were sent to the clinic. The guards were very disciplined. They had strict orders never to beat or kick prisoners, nor to commit any form of bodily assault. When a prisoner became troublesome, he was handcuffed for a day or two. I saw this happen two or three times, but it never happened to me. Once, a prisoner refused to take food for two or three days. They put the man in a straight jacket, then forced a tube down his throat and pumped some maize porridge with beaten egg into his stomach. It looked rather painful. After that the prisoner never refused food again. Of course the guards were told that all these men were the scum of the earth. Prisoners were treated with great contempt, as lower forms of life, but the guards never dared to apply torture. It was against the rules.

37

Prisoners

Prisoners would quarrel amongst themselves. When they came to blows and caused a commotion, the guard outside would come in and stop them. Sometimes the younger hooligans would bully and make fun of some silly old men whom they disliked. There was an old Chinese Catholic, over sixty, who sometimes would mutter prayers and sing to himself the "Ave Maria", and this got on their nerves. Then the young hooligans would throw bedding over his head and beat him up. They would not beat him too viciously or cause him any harm, because he was too old and frail; but then afterwards the old man would sing to himself the "Ave Maria" again. I think that old Catholic was later released. The young hooligans never had any trouble with me. They all liked and respected me, and thought of me as their teacher. They asked me to teach them Chinese poetry and some English to while away their time, and I taught them to sing some Scottish songs like "Loch Lomond" and "Auld Lang Syne" and the English song "Drink to Me Only with Thine Eyes" based on Ben Jonson's poem. I could recite by heart a long ballad by the Tang poet Bai Juyi called "The Song of Eternal Regret", which ran into dozens of lines. They had the whole poem copied on some paper secretly and would read it from time to time. Those young hooligans were very ingenious. We were not allowed to have any pen or paper, but sometimes we were given something on which to write out confessions. They would keep one or two sheets of paper to copy out things they liked. Because they were hungry most of the time, they would memorize restaurant menus and copy out names of delicious meaty dishes to console themselves during confinement. Sometimes the guard would come and search their things and confiscate these writings. One young prisoner, who used to be a factory worker, admired me very much. He managed to make a needle out of a slip of wood from the window. Then he sewed a painting of a pine tree on a handkerchief and gave me this painting as a souvenir. Unfortunately after I was released, all my clothes and underwear in jail were thrown away by my maid because they were too dirty and I forgot to keep that handkerchief.

I had my first interrogation after I had been in jail a week. I was told to get up by the guard one day after midnight. Then they took me across the compound to an office. All the time they had two soldiers carrying automatic rifles with fixed bayonets walking behind me. I suppose that was for the purpose of frightening me into a confession. When I was in the office, I was told to sit down on a bench, facing a platform where two officers were sitting. Then one of them said:

"Now, Mr. Yang, you had better come clean about all the crimes you've committed. We know everything about your case. Every detail of it has been thoroughly checked and rechecked. There is no need to deny anything. You know our policy. You'll be leniently treated if you confess, but if you resist, you'll be severely dealt with."

I said I was willing to confess all I knew, but I did not know the nature of my guilt. The officer said:

"There was a case when a criminal committed grave crimes

against the state. His case was even more serious than yours, but because he confessed, he was allowed to go back to work in the same office as before. On the other hand, we have sent others to public trial and execution because they refused to admit their guilt. You had better think carefully about this. There will be a public trial in a few days time. If you do not confess, you'll be sent to the trial and sentenced to execution. We give you till tomorrow to think it over."

Then I was sent back to my cell. After that I had several more interrogations, and I had to write out confessions. Each time they became more angry and said I was not confessing my real crimes. Then in desperation I started writing out a whole list of names of relatives and friends I knew before Liberation and after, telling them what connections I had with those people. I gave them one hundred names of my Chinese connections and fifty names of my foreign connections, in case any of these names might be of interest to them. Finally they asked me about my past connections with the British embassy, and with the former military attaché Adrian Conway Evans in particular. So I began to realize that they were suspecting me of being a spy working under Adrian Conway Evans, and I started giving them more details about him and about our trips together to Hangzhou, Yixing, Shanghai, Suzhou, Wuxi, and so on. Then the interrogations were over. I was left alone for a long time and I felt more relaxed. Many years later, after the Cultural Revolution, I was told that at that time a young man named Xiong, who had been driving Adrian's car, a Volkswagen, and who had spent many days with him, had been arrested during the Cultural Revolution and charged with the crime of being a spy working under Adrian. That young man, who was in jail somewhere in the interior, had admitted his crimes, but he had said that Gladys and I were with Adrian much of our time, so we must be spies too.

So there was reason in their madness after all. After the case had been cleared up, the police told me that I should be thankful to them for having taken so much trouble. They had gone to several provinces and cities to clear up this matter. However, having been in jail for four whole years, I cannot say that I felt very grateful for that wild goose chase. I was only glad that it was finally over.

Towards the end of 1971, in September, when the Lin Biao affair occurred and he and his followers were shot down over Mongolia, our jail life gradually improved. I had no more interrogations. All this was happening outside, and we of course knew nothing about it. Normally on October 1st, National Day, we prisoners would be allowed to listen to the wireless to hear the celebrations on Tiananmen Square, and Marshal Lin Biao, who was to be Mao's successor, would be there ranting like a lunatic over the loudspeaker. This year, however, Lin Biao's hoarse voice was not to be heard and there was no mention of him. I picked up the Party newspaper, *People's Daily*, and looked among the congratulatory telegrams from foreign countries and noticed that the Cambodian leader Prince Sihanouk's greetings were only addressed to Chairman Mao and Premier Zhou Enlai. This was most unusual. Prince Sihanouk at that time was considered China's closest friend, spending most of his time in Beijing. He could not have made such a grave mistake if Lin Biao was still a favourite. I had already noticed in the newspaper over the previous few months that some of the names of Lin Biao's followers appeared to be missing, one after another. This could not be coincidental. After thinking to myself, I took up my "little red book" of Chairman Mao's quotations and tore off the front page. Now, on the front page of the "little red book" was a preface written by Lin Biao. We were supposed to memorize it by heart, as if it was holy gospel. Since I was convinced that Lin Biao was no longer in power, I felt it was time to get rid of that page. Other prisoners in my jail did not notice it and I did not tell anybody about it. About a week later, our guard suddenly came into our cell and asked us all to hand over our "little red books". He turned over the pages quickly and confiscated them all. When he took my book, he found the front page with Lin Biao's preface missing. He was puzzled, then he turned over the pages again and still could not find the preface anywhere. He said nothing but threw my "little red book" back to me, and took away all the others. After he had gone, the other prisoners were puzzled and asked me:

"How is it that all our 'little red books' were confiscated but not yours? Why this special favour?"

"My 'little red book' is different. It does not have the front page." I smiled and answered. They were even more mystified and asked me to explain. I just said:

"Things are changing outside. You'll know in due course."

We sometimes got some news from outside when a new prisoner was added to our cell and would tell us recent news. Sure enough, a fortnight later, a new young prisoner came and told us that he had heard Lin Biao was dead. At that point I told them why I tore off that front page from the "little red book". The other prisoners all thought it was marvellous. This was a feat, performed in jail, of which I was very proud.

After that, life in prison became more relaxed. I had no more interrogations, and some young prisoners felt I would be released soon. However nothing happened for several months. Then it was the spring of 1972. One day I was suddenly told by the guard to come out. He took me to a big room, told me to sit in a chair, then he fastened on my neck a cardboard placard with my name written on it. After that he turned on all the lights and a cameraman came and took a photograph of me. Then I was sent back to the cell.

When I told the other prisoners about it, they looked grave, some even looked very sad. They told me that it looked like I would be sentenced very soon, otherwise they would not take my photograph like that. I also thought it looked ominous, but I paid no attention to it, because after so many years in jail, I was past bothering what might happen next. Another two weeks passed with nothing happening. Then one day I was told I should pack up my belongings and go with them. I went into an office. The officer sitting there told me that my "detention" was over. When I had first gone into prison four years earlier, they had declared that I was under arrest, and I was handcuffed. But now they apparently had changed their decision and called it "detention" instead! The officer said they had spent a great deal of effort to clear up my case. They had been to twenty-one provincial cities to ascertain every detail of my case, and now they were in a position to say that my case was cleared up and I was innocent. So I could go back to my organization and resume my work there. Then he added:

"As Chairman Mao always said, 'Nobody is perfect.' You have done good work for the Party, but you have also done bad things. There are always two sides to a man. We hope that in the future you will keep doing good things and avoid doing bad things. You are free to go home now. And by the way, we have notified your office that you are released, and your Party secretary has come with a car to take you back. You can go now."

I just stood there silently and said nothing. I still did not know what bad things I had done. So I did not thank him for his leniency. Then he said he must return to me some of my property they had confiscated four years earlier, when they had searched my flat. Actually these things were only two books. One was the confessions of Qu Qiubai, a veteran Communist captured by the Kuomintang in the early 1930s and later executed. This book was privately printed by students of Beijing Normal University. The other book was Ovid's *Art of Love* with an English translation, published in the Loeb Library series. Another thing was a small notebook. The officer suggested that they were nothing valuable, perhaps I could leave them behind. I told him that I did not want to keep Qu Qiubai's confessions, but I would like to take the Ovid back, because it was not pornography but a Latin classic, and he agreed. I also told him that the small notebook he could throw away since it was my son's notebook and had nothing to do with me. The officer said they had only kept it because it had the wavelength of some Taiwan broadcast. I told him that I never listened to the Taiwan broadcast, I only listened to English and American broadcasts anyway, and the officer nodded. So I shook hands with him and left with Ovid in my pocket.

38

Freedom

Freedom from prison arrived with a ride home in the car of the Party secretary. This was not the same woman Party secretary of several years earlier. The Party committee had appointed someone new. He opened the door to our flat, which had been sealed with two strips of white paper. It had remained sealed these four years, and everything was intact. The only difference was that they had piled up all the furniture and books in one room, so it was a mess. As I entered the room, several rats scuttled away in alarm from the wardrobe and the bookcases. They had been gnawing away bits of my cotton padded jackets and rugs to make comfortable nests for a long time. They were rather angry about my sudden arrival. I had not received any change of clothes from home for about two years in jail and looked like a scarecrow, my old clothes in tatters. I was not surprised at giving those rats a fright. Most of my garments still left in the house were half eaten by moths and rats. I finally found a slightly presentable jacket and changed into it. On the mantelpiece I saw that one-third bottle of Chinese white liquor I had been drinking the night of my arrest. There was still a dead man's skull nearby, with a hole in the top and a now-dead cactus planted in it. I remembered how, before going to jail, I had picked up that skull in the Press compound and

for fun had planted the little cactus in it. The cactus had grown to over one foot high but was long since dead for lack of water. It must have struggled for sunshine and water for a long time. It was still standing erect but when I touched it with my finger, it crumbled to dust. I tried to clean up the room a little, but it was getting dark so I decided to go out for some supper. The Party secretary had left me some money, so I decided to dine in a restaurant first then buy some new clothes to look more respectable. I picked up an old cap to put on my head to hide my shaven head and went out to look for a restaurant. I remembered that the Soviet exhibition centre was within walking distance, and it had a restaurant serving cheap semi-Western food, so I went there. I ordered a set meal with one small piece of beefsteak and potato chips, costing only one and a half Chinese yuan (less than fifty cents U.S.), and a bottle of beer. Before I left prison, I had been thinking of expensive juicy meat dishes all the time, but now that I was out of prison, I suddenly lost my appetite and no longer craved food. As I was enjoying my meal, a young man came and joined me at my table. He was a young Uighur from Xinjiang, China's central Asian province. He began to talk to me about all the atrocities he had witnessed in the interior and cursed the Chinese Communist Party. I felt it was rather imprudent of him to talk to a stranger like that, so I stopped him and gave him some friendly advice, warning him against talking too freely in public. I also took off my cap to show my shaven head and told him that I had just been released from jail. Then I said goodbye to him and went back. It was a strange feeling to be free after such a long time, but I was not in the mood to go into town to enjoy my freedom. I went to bed and slept soundly. The next morning I went to the office. My colleagues greeted me warmly as if nothing had happened during the last few years. I was told by the Party secretary that Gladys would also be released within a week, but he would ask some young colleagues to help me tidy up the flat before she came back. I was also told that the manuscripts of translations I had been working on were still intact and I could resume my work whenever I liked. A new chapter in my life had begun.

I was released the day before May Day 1972, so I was exactly four years in jail. Gladys was released about five days later. I supposed the timing was because our flat was in such a mess. I was to return first to tidy it up a little so that Gladys would not find it in such a sorry state. The office told some young colleagues to come and help me move furniture around and throw away a lot of garbage. After this the flat looked a bit habitable. The office also told me to buy some flowers and chocolate to welcome her return. I added some cigarettes and two bottles of Chinese brandy. After Gladys came back, she still felt the place was too dirty, and we had to do some more tidying up for about a week. Since all our children were away in the provinces, the office suggested that our younger daughter Zhi should be transferred back to Beijing to help us with the daily family chores. Zhi was then working as a peasant in the north-east. She was transferred back without difficulty. Then we heard that our son Yang Ye was not doing very well in his factory in Hubei province. In fact, because of our trouble, he had not been trusted politically by his colleagues and he had become slightly deranged. So we asked the office to have him transferred back to a Beijing steel plant. Then we had our elder daughter Ying transferred back to Beijing to work in the city's motor works. She had studied engineering in her university before and this was a logical move. All these transfers of our children back to Beijing took about a year. Our youngest child Zhi decided to go to Peking University as she had only graduated from middle school when the Cultural Revolution broke out and scattered everyone. She

had wanted to study archaeology but was directed to study world history instead. Then we found that our son's mental illness was getting worse. He kept hallucinating that he was an English boy and making a lot of trouble gatecrashing the British Embassy. We wanted to take him to a mental hospital, but the hospital felt that since Gladys was a foreigner they could not take the responsibility. Finally we decided to take him to England for treatment. He stayed some time in the house of an English friend Felix Greene, then moved to stay with Gladys' sister Hilda. Unfortunately, when Hilda was away visiting relatives during the Christmas holidays, he bought some petrol and set fire to himself, dying in the blaze. This happened after he was already in England a couple of years. We had thought he was recovering. Our son's death was our saddest loss, especially for Gladys, and her health deteriorated soon after that. Our two daughters both married, but later found their husbands unsatisfactory and divorced. Both went to the United States for advanced study, one in Seattle and the other in Chicago. Ying changed from engineering to studying linguistics, while Zhi studied Assyriology. Ying is now teaching Chinese in Harvard. Zhi came back to China and is now teaching in Changchun in a university there. She has married again, to a Canadian husband whom she met while studying in Chicago.

So from the time of my release in 1972 to the end of the Cultural Revolution in 1976, we mainly spent our time solving family problems. Sending our children abroad cost a lot of money. Fortunately I got back my back pay for those four years in jail. Then the Party secretary of *Chinese Literature* magazine asked the Foreign Languages Press to pay me for our translation of the novel *Hongloumeng* (*A Dream of Red Mansions*) since I was no longer on their staff. In this way we just escaped getting into debt. I had never had any savings at home, but now that my history had been cleared up, I was no longer under the cloud and the office was willing to help. Many of our friends abroad also helped us solve our family problems. Though the Cultural Revolution was still continuing at the time, my fortunes had changed. I was allowed to take part in all office meetings and discussions of how to resuscitate *Chinese Literature*, which was in a sorry state. Among the young rebels in our press, there were still a lot of struggle meetings going on against certain people, but I participated now as an onlooker, taking things cynically. Chairman Mao's wife Jiang Qing by then had assumed the role as leader of all Chinese cultural affairs. She had the simple and ludicrous idea that all past historical personalities could be classified into Legalists and Confucians. Legalists were the radicals or "goodies", and the Confucians were the conservatives or "baddies". Her real intention was to overthrow the late premier Zhou Enlai, because he represented the more sober faction of the government. She was always hinting that Zhou Enlai was a modern Confucius. However, after the death of Lin Biao, Zhou's position in the government was too strong and all she could do was attack Zhou's assistant Deng Xiaoping, who was following Zhou's more realistic, pragmatic line. Just before her downfall, she and her followers started a movement against Deng, and all government functionaries were told to join in a demonstration on the streets to denounce Deng. I was told to go also and I did not refuse. By this time I had become quite hypocritical, and I did not make any unwelcome comments. The mass demonstration turned out to be a complete fiasco. There was absolutely no mass enthusiasm or hysteria on the streets, nothing like the wild frenzy at the beginning of the Cultural Revolution. She also staged an exhibition of black art, denouncing certain Chinese artists whose works she considered decadent or anti-Communist. One old artist who had drawn a rather pink-looking sun was denounced as having

attacked Chairman Mao. Another young artist, Huang Yongyu, whom I knew fairly well from the 1950s when we had translated a folk poem called Ashma and he had made some beautiful illustrations for the book, was now accused of drawing an owl with one of its eyes closed. This was supposed to represent looking with a jaundiced eye on Chinese socialism and was therefore anti-Communist. All government workers like myself were supposed to go to this black art exhibition to re-educate ourselves, so that we could see that there were still hidden counter-revolutionaries everywhere in society. Of course all these things were gibberish nonsense, but I went obediently. I had learned that there was no use in making any protest. Fortunately, nothing more happened to those poor artists. They were not put in jail or persecuted anymore. After that, because of our sympathy with this young artist friend Huang, we used to call on him in his home quite frequently. He and his family, a wife, a son and a daughter, were living then in a shabby dormitory with only one and a half small rooms, near the railway station. We became good friends and we would visit him and chat and share their meals almost twice or three times a week. Through him we got to know and became friends with many other artists. We had very few friends at that time among Chinese writers because most of them had had a worse fate than Chinese artists. They were either in jail or sent to the countryside as rightists. Some just did not dare make friends with anybody.

39

Going Back to Work

Going back to work meant finishing up items started before prison. Between 1972, when we were released from jail, and 1976, when the Cultural Revolution came to an end, the only serious piece of translation work we did was to finish the translation of the well-known Qing dynasty novel *A Dream of Red Mansions*. This book was very popular in China, so its translation brought us a lot of credit, much more than we deserved. There was an old Chinese scholar, Wu Shichang, an authority on the novel. He helped choose among the various manuscripts and editions and helped edit this translation. There was also a society devoted to the study of this novel and scholars devoted to it are known as "Redologists" in China. Thus I became rated a "Redologist" as well. Apart from this work, some of our earlier translations were published during this period, including my translation of *Le Chanson de Roland* from medieval French and Plautus' *Mostellaria* from Latin. My translation from the Greek of Aristophanes' comedy *Peace* was lost during the Cultural Revolution, so I had to do that translation over again. But up to the present I have only translated half of it. Gladys and I also published two volumes of Lu Xun's early writings, one was his prose-poem collection called *Wild Grass*; the other was a collection of reminiscences called *Dawn Blossoms Plucked at Dusk*. We also translated Lu Xun's two short story collections, *Call to Arms* and *Wandering*, but they were not published during this period, awaiting the early 1980s. Gladys and I also published a selection of Lu Xun's writings and entitled them *Silent China*. These were published by Oxford University Press during this period, but this was not a new set of translations, just selections made from our four-volume edition of Lu Xun's *Selected Works*.

The year 1976 can be called the Annus Mirabilis in modern Chinese history. Lots of things happened during that year. In January Premier Zhou Enlai died. He was well loved by the majority of the Chinese people because of the many good things he had done to save the country from ruin on several occasions. The country's spontaneous mourning for his death was obstructed by Madame Jiang Qing and her followers, and this aroused the people's indignation so much that in early April, with the Chinese festival to mourn the dead, there was a mass demonstration. Tens of thousands of wreaths, as well as slogans and poems denouncing Madame Jiang Qing and her three topmost supporters, nicknamed the Gang of Four, spontaneously appeared on the streets. Many people were brutally beaten and arrested at this time. In March the veteran Marshal Zhu De died. He had been Chairman Mao's closest comrade in arms. During the early Civil War days, his name was always linked with Mao, and then was even more prominent than Mao. After Liberation he lived a quiet life, but the people all admired and liked him. At the end of July there was a devastating earthquake in Tangshan which destroyed the whole city. The death toll rose to over a quarter of a million people. This city is fairly close to Beijing and Tianjin, and there were casualties in these two places as well. My eldest daughter Ying, at that time still married to her first husband, a graduate of her university and former classmate of our son, was visiting her husband in Tangshan at the moment of the quake. They had some hair-raising adventures after being stranded at the railway station. They had to make their way to Beijing on foot from that devastated area, walking for two days amidst many corpses, before they arrived safely back home. On the night of that earthquake, I was sleeping with my daughter's baby in my bed in Beijing. I was awakened by a continuous grinding sound underground, as if some tank was driving over pebbles or sand. Then there were three or four sudden jolts. After that there was another shake and it was over. I realized that this must be an earthquake, so I just put the pillow over the baby's head and stretched myself over it lest the ceiling fall down on us. Then I went to sleep again. After a couple of minutes there was general pandemonium outside, with people jumping out of windows and shrieking, and people calling each other to leave the buildings. I decided to do nothing. Then after five minutes someone called from outside the window, telling us to get up. It was somebody from the office. I had to get up and put on some clothes, woke up Gladys, then went out to the compound together with the baby wrapped in some blankets. There were already a lot of people huddled there, some scantily dressed. We waited till dawn and the night was rather chilly. The next morning we were told that it was not safe to stay at home but we must move somewhere in the open. The bureau mobilized a few empty buses and cars, and we stayed in a bus at night for a couple of days. Outside on the streets temporary sheds or shelters were erected for families. Within a few days the whole city looked like a refugee camp. Actually very few houses in Beijing collapsed and there were not too many casualties. The city of Tianjin, being closer to Tangshan, was in a worse state. But the city of Tangshan was levelled to the ground. It was rebuilt a few years later.

In the month of September Chairman Mao Zedong died. There had been rumours of his death sometime before that, so it came as no surprise. Some young Communist Party members showed grief, as did some old veterans, but there were few visible signs of grief among the ordinary city population, unlike with the late Premier Zhou Enlai. Of course there was a period of state mourning. I had to go with other government workers to Tiananmen Square to pay homage to Chairman Mao lying in state. I bowed to the body lying in its glass coffin. Before his death, Chairman Mao had already appointed Hua Guofeng as vice-chairman and his successor. This Hua Guofeng had been in charge of the security forces and was instrumental in suppressing the students and civilians who had come to mourn the death of Zhou Enlai at Tiananmen Square in early April. Now, with the chairman dead, he turned around and allied himself with other veteran generals to arrest Jiang Qing and her followers. This happened in early October, less than a month after Chairman Mao had died. There was general jubilation among the masses in celebration of the end of the so-called Cultural Revolution and the downfall of the Gang of Four. My friend Huang and other artists drew paintings depicting four already cooked red crabs fastened together by a string. The crabs consisted of three males and one female, signifying Madame Jiang Qing and her three leading followers. It is customary for Chinese to eat crabs in autumn, when the crab meat becomes most succulent. After the end of the Cultural Revolution Hua Guofeng temporarily became chairman of the Republic, but Deng Xiaoping, whom Zhou Enlai had already made vice-premier and whom the Gang of Four feared most after Zhou, was leading the military commission and it was he who had the real power. Within two years, Hua Guofeng was deposed and Comrade Hu Yaobang, a child of the Party organiza-tion, was made chairman, with Zhao Ziyang, the governor of

Sichuan province, the premier. This happened in 1980. After that, Deng Xiaoping, with the help of Hu and Zhao, became the new supreme leader and a new era began. The new triumvirate did very well until 1985 or 1986, and had the support of the Chinese people. During the Cultural Revolution, many innocent people had been sent into exile or put in prison. Now they were reinstated. The country's economy was in ruins, but now it began to recover. China's reputation abroad had been very poor during the Cultural Revolution, but now it was recovering too. There was a change of fortune in my case also. It must have been 1978 or 1979 when some officials from the Security Ministry came to the Foreign Languages Bureau to make a formal apology to us. They said that during the Cultural Revolution there had been a lot of unwarranted arrests and this was all the Gang of Four's fault. They realized now that they had done harm to us and wanted to make amends. They said that they could have all the dossiers destroyed before our eyes to assure us that these charges would no longer exist. I just smiled and said nothing. Then we shook hands and they left. After that we suddenly became good and trusted comrades. I was no longer considered just a hack translator in the Press. In 1979 I was made associate chief editor of the *Chinese Literature* magazine; the year after that I became the chief editor. I spent most of the time doing editing and administration work and presiding over meetings, and had little time for translation work myself. Because many of our magazine readers had asked us for selections of classical Chinese literature and contemporary writing in book form, I decided to produce a whole series of paperback volumes apart from *Chinese Literature*. Since in the West the Penguin series of paperback books were popular, I decided to start a whole series of Panda Books, of which I made the selections myself. In the 1980s we produced quite a few dozen of these paperbacks and they sold

very well and were translated into several other languages, including French and several Asian languages. Among the more popular items were the selection of writings by contemporary Chinese women writers, tales of old Beijing, reminiscences by a Chinese actress Xin Fengxia, whom we knew quite well, stories and reminiscences by the well known writer Shen Congwen, stories and reminiscences by the well known writer Lao She, a novel about the Cultural Revolution by the young contemporary writer Gu Hua, several works of classical Chinese literature from the Han dynasty to the Qing dynasty, and many other volumes. Outside the Foreign Languages Bureau I was elected a senior research fellow of the Academy of Social Sciences, in their Institute of Foreign Literature, helping them in their research on Greek and Latin literature. When the government decided to produce a Chinese encyclopaedia in many volumes, I was made the chief editor of the section on ancient Greek and Latin literature, and I succeeded in producing two volumes on foreign literature together with many other scholars within two years. So from 1979 onwards I was kept quite busy with my editing work for several years and received many laurels. During this period I was elected executive committee member or adviser to many academic and political societies, such as the Chinese Writers' Union, the Chinese Pen Club, the Society for the Study of Foreign Literature, the Chinese Encyclopaedia, the Society for the Study of *A Dream of Red Mansions*, and so on. It is an interesting social phenomenon in present-day China that Chinese intellectuals are judged not by their academic or artistic merits but by their political or social status. If a person is persecuted politically, he becomes a social outcast, a good-for-nothing; but once he is exonerated and honoured, he is given all sorts of honorary titles and considered good for everything. My own ups and downs attest to that.

By the end of 1983 I decided that since I was nearing seventy, it was time to give up my work as editor-in-chief of *Chinese Literature*. So I resigned and passed on the editorship to a talented young Chinese writer by the name of Wang Meng, who had just been appointed Minister of Culture in the government. However his ministerial duties kept him too busy, so he never did any actual editing work for the office, and I still had to help for a few years until about 1986.

In 1985 I was elected a member of the PPCC (People's Political Consultative Conference), a position I hold until now. This is a representative body from all circles, including democratic parties, leading scientist writers and artists, and the like. Its function is to give advice and suggestions to the government, something like the British Parliament. I was elected because by that time I was already elected as member of the Central Committee of the Revolutionary Kuomintang Committee, which I had joined before Liberation, and also because I was a leading member in the Chinese Writers' Union and the Federation of Chinese Writers and Artists. I also applied to join the Chinese Communist Party in 1980. It was delayed for several years for various reasons, partly because I was already a veteran member of a democratic party. But in 1984 they granted my request, and in April 1985, one month after I was elected to the PPCC, I became a formal member of the Chinese Communist Party. I decided to join the Party because this had been my wish ever since before Liberation. Back then, I was disillusioned with the Kuomintang Party and thought only the Chinese Communist Party under the leadership of Mao Zedong and others could save China from ruin. After Liberation, although I was rather disillusioned by all the silly Party-organized mass movements which did China a lot of harm, I felt that the new Chinese democracy needed a period of tutelage under some political party and the

Chinese Communist Party was the only choice. I also believe and now still believe in the Marxist historical materialist interpretation of history based on the ideas of Darwinism. The division of people into classes is a historical fact. Later I came to realize that the class struggle theory was over-emphasized in Marxism. But it is understandable in Karl Marx's case since he was in an oppressed and exploited social position in nineteenth-century Europe. In China I felt there were many oppressed and exploited people who must be liberated as well. That is why I came to accept Chinese Communism. I must also admit that the Chinese Communist Party, despite all the faults committed in those years of rule, had also done many good things for the Chinese people, especially for the poor and uneducated masses. In the end, therefore, I decided to become a Chinese Communist.

40

Journeys

Journeys came our way once again after 1979. Between 1979 and 1986 Gladys and I went abroad many times and visited several foreign countries. I had not been out of China since we came back to China in 1940, a gap of nearly forty years. During the war years before Liberation, several friends advised us to go abroad again to teach in several foreign universities but I never considered such offers. Though conditions were hard in the interior and later in Nanjing, with the rampant inflation, I felt we could not leave China after having once made up our minds to come back. After Liberation, since most of the time we were under a cloud, the authorities would never have agreed to let us go, even if we had applied to go to any foreign country. So I never made such a request. After my name was cleared and after the end of the Cultural Revolution, it seemed that the Chinese Communist Party had regained some sanity and things were looking more hopeful. So in 1979, when Gladys wanted to go back to England to visit her family, I decided to go with her. During that year the British Association for Chinese Studies was holding an annual conference at Leeds University and we were invited to join in. So we went there and stayed with friends. I was probably invited by the British Council to give a talk in London on contemporary Chinese literature. Anyway, during the next few years I went to England about four times, each time giving talks in London on the contemporary Chinese literary scene. I do not remember the exact dates now. Once I attended a Bookman's annual dinner, and other occasions were organized by the British Council. The Council of the British Association for Chinese Studies later also conferred on me and Gladys an honorary life membership. Incidentally the Italian Dante Alighieri Society also conferred on me a diploma *di benemerenza*, though I had never been to Italy and could not speak Italian. I received the diploma because during this period I had written an article on the origin of the European sonnet, tracing its origin to Italy and to Tang poetry. This happened in 1984, after an international symposium on comparative literature in Beijing when I talked on that subject. In 1980 Adelaide University in Australia and other cultural organizations there held a festival and a Writers' Week. The Chinese Writers' Union was asked to send a delegation of Chinese writers, and I was chosen to head this delegation. So Gladys and I went to Australia and spent three weeks there. We visited Canberra, Sydney and Melbourne as well, and I gave some talks on contemporary Chinese literature and on the translation of Chinese literature into English at these universities and made many new Australian friends. There was a brilliant young Australian sinologist, Geremie Barmé, whom we got to know very well. He had studied Chinese in China and we spent some time with him when we were in Australia. The following year he went to Japan to study Japanese. We were invited to visit Japan at that time and Geremie was there to look after us, and we had a very good time together.

Our visit to Japan in 1981 was very odd. An American professor, David Kidd, happened to be in Beijing soon after the end of the Cultural Revolution. He had been in Beijing before and during the time of the Communist takeover in 1948 and 1949 and had married a Chinese wife. He got to know some Chinese professors in Peking University and thought he knew me then. Actually it was a mistake because I was in Nanjing at that time, so we had never met before. Anyway in Beijing he called on us, and we got on very well. This David Kidd at that time was the director of a cultural institute for the study of traditional Japanese arts in a town called Kameoka near Osaka. So he invited us to visit Japan. In my youth I used to feel very prejudiced against Japan, but since the Sino-Japanese war was already something of the past, and I had come to realize that we must separate the Japanese people from those military leaders who had started the aggressive war against China, I decided to accept the invitation. In spite of my prejudice against Japanese militarists, I was always very interested in ancient Japanese culture and wanted to see places like Kyoto and Nara, which had so much in common with China's ancient past. Geremie Barmé's presence in Japan added to the attraction. This institute of Japanese traditional arts in Kameoka was organized by the Omoto Foundation, which belonged to a pacifist Shinto sect that had been persecuted during the war by the government. It holds summer seminars teaching foreign visitors Japanese traditional arts, such as the tea ceremony, floral arrangements, the practice of Japanese calligraphy, Japanese swordplay, and Japanese Noh drama. Gladys and I attended all these classes and got diplomas at the end of the seminar. The rest of the time we visited monasteries and museums and shops in Kyoto and Nara and thoroughly enjoyed ourselves. Geremie also took us to a hill called Karashiyama in the district called Samano, where a memorial tablet had been placed for the late Chinese premier Zhou Enlai. Towards the end of our stay in the Kameoka Institute, I also gave a lecture on the common cultural heritage between

Japan and China in ancient times. It was well attended and well received.

In 1981 the Chinese Association for Friendly Relations with Foreign Countries sent a delegation to Western Europe and I was included in this delegation. We visited some friendly associations in Luxembourg, Holland, England and Wales, and the Irish Republic. Because our delegation head was a veteran Communist comrade named Wang Bingnan, who was China's first ambassador to Poland after Liberation and whose former German wife was then living in Switzerland, we also included Geneva in our visit. In Holland I was invited by the University of Leiden to give a talk on the translation of Chinese classics. I had been to Leiden in my early student days so I was glad to have the opportunity to revisit the university. In London, the British defence minister then was Lord Carrington. He heard that our delegation leader was China's first ambassador to Poland, and he wanted to have a private talk with Wang about Polish politics. So I had to act as Wang's interpreter during their private chat. We also visited the British House of Commons to hear a debate between Margaret Thatcher and members of the House, but we did not have an interview with the Prime Minister. In Ireland we had tea and a conversation with the Irish President of the Republic and First Lady. Because our hosts had heard that I was interested in Irish literature, they gave me some books on early Irish literature and asked me to visit the Abbey Theatre in Dublin to see a performance of Sean O'Casey's play *The Shadow of a Gunman*. Before we left Ireland, our hosts arranged an evening for the delegation and got a professional singer to sing the haunting and very moving Irish folk song "Danny Boy". Then they asked our delegation to sing a Chinese song. Our delegation leader then suggest we should sing a patriotic song, "The Five-star Red Flag Flying in the Wind" which we all knew.

We went up onto the platform and sang that song, and the audience applauded politely but not too enthusiastically. After all, none of us was a professional singer so naturally the reception was very lukewarm. I thought it was rather a shame to end the evening like that, so I suggested that I too would like to sing the Irish folk song "Danny Boy", but I could not remember the words. They immediately supplied me with a printed score, and I sang loudly without inhibition, because by then I had already had a few drinks. It was extremely successful, and the audience responded with thunderous and long applause. They all got up and joined in the singing towards the end. Some of the ladies were even moved to tears. This may give my readers the wrong impression that I have a good voice, but actually this was not the case. It just happened that I caught the right spirit of that evening, which was very friendly and merry, and I chose the right song. I was given that song score afterwards and I still keep it as a memento. I was presented with a huge bottle of Irish whiskey at the airport when I left. Though our delegation's visit to those Western countries was a success and I contributed a lot to that, after I came back to Beijing, I heard from the Party secretary of *Chinese Literature* that she had received a report from the Friendship Association that, though I behaved generally well in the delegation, they considered my behaviour abroad as a Chinese official to have been too liberal on several occasions. At that time I had already asked to be a member of the Chinese Communist Party. After this trip they deferred my request for several years before they granted my request in 1984. So I decided to keep clear of official delegations as much as possible in the future.

In 1982 I was invited by the Indian government as the guest of the Indian Cultural Commission to make a tour of India. This was between February and March. At the same time, Jawaharlal Nehru

University in Delhi was holding an international conference on the translation of literature and I was also invited. I went first to take part in that conference in New Delhi. I gave a talk on cultural relations between ancient India and China during the seminar, chaired one morning's meeting, gave another talk on translation in the university, then went on my tour. We did a lot of sightseeing and saw the Red Fort and the Taj Mahal by moonlight in Agra, then went south to Bangalore, Madras and the caves, then to Calcutta. In New Delhi I paid homage to Gandhi's grave and laid a wreath of flowers, took part in some Punjabi folk dancing, and got my hair all sprinkled with coloured water during the Holi festival. In Madras I gave another lecture in an artist's house, and in Bangalore a young guide and I rescued a boy from a lake. The boy was standing on the bank and when he saw us approaching, he gaped in fascination but slipped and fell straight into the water. Our gallant young guide immediately jumped into the lake to rescue the boy, who was also carrying his one-year-old younger brother. He slipped also and fell. I was near them on the bank, so I first pulled the child out, and the guide and the older boy scrambled out of the lake by themselves. I only got my sleeve and part of my shirt wet, but the other two were completely drenched. The older parents of these two children hurried along and we passed the rescued child to them. They looked very grateful, shook hands with us, and went away. We had a good laugh over that. The Indian weather was so warm that our clothes were dry in no time. It was altogether a most enjoyable visit. Gladys and I were both invited there because of our past friendship with several Indian ambassadors in China.

In 1983 we were invited by the Great Britain-China Association and the British Council to visit England again. We gave some talks in Oxford, Leeds and York universities, then London. Some of my talks were fine, but I was dissatisfied with my first talk at Oxford University. I felt rather inhibited and did not know what to say that day, probably because I felt the audience was rather mixed, with some young students, some of them Chinese who had not been long in England. So I did not know to whom to talk. In 1984 we were invited again to England. Merton College invited me to stay in Oxford for Michaelmas Term as a visiting fellow, because in the late 1930s I had been a student of that college. The college gave me a nice flat not very far from Merton College for the duration of my stay. It was on Holywell Street in the centre of town and very close to Blackwell's, other bookshops, and the Bodleian Library. I could have my meals in the college and have coffee and chats with the other dons. Actually during those two months I did not do anything academic and did not make use of the Bodleian. I had a copy of Aeschylus' *Prometheus Vinctus* with me and I translated about half of the text into Chinese rhymed verse but failed to finish it. In most afternoons I just pottered around the shops and watched TV, enjoying a relaxed and indolent time. I gave an evening talk on Chinese literature towards the end of my stay. In 1985 I did not go abroad. In 1986 I only went to Hong Kong twice, staying in the University of Hong Kong. The first time was to take part in a conference on East and West relations. I gave a talk on China's early contacts with the Western world in Greek and Roman times. The second time was on the occasion of being conferred an honorary fellowship by the Hong Kong Translation Society. After 1986 I did not go abroad again until the early spring of 1989, when I went with a small press delegation to Spain for two or three weeks. We were invited by the University of Granada in Andalusian Spain on the occasion of the publication of the Spanish translation of the Chinese novel *Hongloumeng* (*A Dream of Red Mansions*) which had been based on our English

translation. We visited Madrid, Toledo and Barcelona, as well as Malaga and the beaches in the southern coast. I found the Alhambra rather disappointing, since it was too occupied by tourists. However I liked Andalusia very much and wished we could have also seen Seville, but our time was too short. I was asked to give a speech at Granada University but it was cancelled at the last minute, so I could not pay my respects to Garcia Lorca's college.

So much for my visits abroad in the 1980s. This state of euphoria could not last long. Though China made a remarkable recovery after the end of the Cultural Revolution, thanks to the policy of reform in the economy and in culture and the general opening-up policy, contradictions in the political situation began to appear as early as the mid-1980s. These contradictions culminated in the student demonstrations and the Tiananmen massacre, after which things were different again and I got involved in subsequent political events which forced me to leave the Chinese Communist Party.

41

Feudal China

Feudal China used to divide the Chinese people into four main categories: intellectuals, peasants, workers and merchants (*shi, nong, gong, shang*). Intellectuals were ranked first because they were in charge of the examination system and the civil service. This was essentially the basis of the political structure. Merchants were despised and therefore ranked last. After Liberation, when the Chinese Communists seized power, in the beginning they divided the people into three main categories: workers, peasants and soldiers, ignoring the intellectuals and merchants. This was because in the old revolutionary base of Yan'an, there were very few intellectuals and little commercial activity. Workers were placed before peasants for Communist ideological reasons, although there were few industrial workers in the revolutionary ranks of economically backward north-western China. Later the powers that be divided the people into five main categories: workers, peasants, merchants, intellectuals and soldiers. The order was significant. The Communists never considered intellectuals important. In New China intellectuals were always subservient to politics. For that reason less attention has been paid to education and culture after Liberation. During times when radical tendencies in the political line predominated, the government would revert to the old practice of placing the people into three categories, ignoring the intellectuals and the merchants altogether. After the end of the Cultural Revolution, since economically China was practically bankrupt, they began to realize that commerce was also very important. Thus under the new premier, Zhao Ziyang, commerce became all important and even culture began to be considered a commodity. For a short period there was a rapid growth of capitalism and China became prosperous again and everything looked well. China was on the path towards a Western type of capitalism under the guise of socialism, called by Zhao Ziyang, "the initial stage of socialism". Actually this was nothing but the initial stage of capitalism. The new growth of capitalism brought about new contradictions within the revolutionary ranks and brought about a new bureaucratic capitalism which endangered the existence of the old privileged class. That class had been based on the idea that the veteran Communist leaders who had won political power through the barrel of a gun represented the elite of the working class and were the natural masters of the state. That was how Stalinism came into being in Russia. In the same way, the old Chinese Communist veterans like Mao, although they had distrusted Stalin, came to become Chinese Stalinists. The opening-up policy which came with economic reform also brought in the Western ideas of democracy and the demand for human rights. The old Chinese Communist die-hards just called it "bourgeois liberalism". The conflict between the old and the new became inevitable. As early as 1982 or 1983, some young hotheads were already demanding more democracy and respect for human rights. They even put up big-character posters on walls in the western part of the city, but these were soon suppressed by the government under Deng Xiaoping. Their demands did not have much public support. By the mid-1980s, Deng began to move towards the conservative side, and there was a split between Deng and the reformists headed by the chairman of the Communist Party Hu Yaobang and Premier Zhao Ziyang. Deng, who always had the army behind him, easily defeated the other two and Hu Yaobang was dismissed from his post. Of course this was unconstitutional. Most of the people were sorry to see Hu go, especially since Hu was a genuine good revolutionary who had done many good things for them after the Cultural Revolution. In the latter half of the 1980s, the over-emphasis on commercialism and the over-heated economy began to show faults. Corruption and nepotism within the ranks of the Party increased, and there was a greater discrepancy between the haves and the have-nots, with inflation and unemployment beginning to be a serious problem. The people began to voice their discontent with the Party. In early 1989, Hu Yaobang died of heart trouble after the conservatives in the Party politburo criticized him for failure in economic reform. The majority of the people, however, felt that the real trouble was that economic reform had not been followed up by radical political reform: too many veteran Communist leaders were becoming corrupt and the Chinese Communist Party needed a thorough cleaning up before it could maintain its leading position in this period of tutelage. A spontaneous mass funeral for Hu's death was staged in Tiananmen Square by university students in Beijing in May 1989. This coincided with Gorbachev's visit to Beijing, and the mass demonstrations that followed ended in the Tiananmen massacre on June 3rd and 4th. This was the background of the events in which I also got involved. Many of my readers probably have some idea of this period of contemporary Chinese history, so I feel there is no need for more detail.

As I mentioned earlier, in the early 1980s, after the end of the Cultural Revolution, things were looking up and I wholeheartedly supported the new line of economic reform and opening-up policy, just like most of the Chinese people. There was a greater democracy and freedom of thought than had ever been seen in China since the 1930s. It was as if we were having a new May 4th Movement. The May 4th Movement started in 1919 when the intellectuals, especially university students, rose in protest against the warlords who were siding with foreign imperialist powers to subjugate the Chinese people. The May 4th Movement, which had been anti-feudal and anti-imperialist in character, also brought in the liberation of the mind. The slogans then, and again this time, were for more democracy and science and were aimed against tyranny and ignorance. I was amused to find that many of the same Western books suddenly became popular again among the young people of the 1980s, the same books I had read as a student in Tianjin in the early 1930s. People were again reading and discussing books by Freud, Morgan's *Ancient Society*, Frazer's *The Golden Bough*, D. H. Lawrence's *Lady Chatterley's Lover*, T. S. Eliot, Marcel Proust's stream of consciousness and Virginia Woolf, nihilism, fascism, totalitarianism, and so on. It was as if I had gone back to the days of my youth half a century ago, as if I were about to live my whole life all over again and history had gone a complete circle. However this was just my illusion, not the reality. History can never repeat itself, it can only progress. The Chinese intellectuals had been isolated from Western ideas for half a century, hence the new generation hankered after them as if they were all new. But the new generation had matured, it was no longer so naive. They could not have the blind faith in a political leader that we had had in our younger days for Chairman Mao. In 1983 when Deng Xiaoping suppressed the "democracy wall" in western Beijing and put a few dissenters in jail, I still made excuses for him, and felt that all these big-character posters stuck on the wall reminded one of the practices in the Cultural Revolution, which I found childish and distasteful. Though I sympathized with those dissenters who were put in jail and thought they were punished too harshly, I never at that time added my name to the petitions organized by other intellectuals. I still had hope in Deng's line of reform. In the late 1980s, however, when it was clear that the conservatives in the Party were in the ascendant and economic reform without political reform was in a crisis, I began to feel that the people must rise up and support the healthy elements within the Party and combat against the few moribund and corrupt conservatives who were trying to stop political reform. Such was also the feeling of the Chinese people in general in those days. People were dissatisfied with the situation. They were demanding genuine political reform in order to eradicate the corruption and nepotism within the top échelon of the Party. They were not asking to overthrow the leadership of the Chinese Communist Party in the government. Everyone knew that there was no other political party to replace and take its place in China. The unconstitutional dismissal of Hu Yaobang and his subsequent death were only the spark that started the new revolution. What happened later in the spring of 1989 was inevitable. It was not caused by a few conspirators or accidentally through a series of events. The tragic Tiananmen massacre marked the beginning of a new period. The Chinese Communist Party needs a radical reform if it is to continue to assume leadership. It has lost the faith and support of the people, and no army, however powerful, can save it, unless it admits to its past crimes and makes a radical change now. They are wrong if they think they can delay the reform any further, after what happened in 1989.

42

Tiananmen

Tiananmen is a name which will forever resound in Chinese history. I remember that in mid-May 1989, when it was announced that the Soviet leader Gorbachev was coming to visit China to mark an end to the estrangement between the Soviet and Chinese Communist parties started in the early 1960s, most Chinese people, including myself, welcomed the event. This was especially so with intellectuals, since most of us also welcomed the reform in the Soviet Union and Gorbachev's new line. Some old Party die-hards were dubious about Gorbachev's new line, thinking it a betrayal of Stalinism. But even such people had to admit that it was a good thing for the Soviet Union and China to be friends again. Anyway, at the time it was considered a major international event, and foreign newspapers were all very keen to watch the developments. One day in mid-May I suddenly received a telephone call from the Canadian TV office saying that their correspondents in Beijing would like to interview me. They said that through friends they had heard of me as a Chinese intellectual who had been interested in Soviet-Chinese relations and was in favour of this new rapprochement. They wanted to hear my views about the visit. I was not too surprised about this request, since during the past few years I had had several such requests from foreign correspondents, especially from the BBC asking me to express my views on Chinese cultural affairs and I had always agreed to talk to them because I felt it was the duty of a Chinese citizen to do so. On this occasion, however, the changes in the Chinese government and Hu's dismissal from office were the subjects that occupied most people's minds. Ever since the beginning of the year, university students in Beijing had been demanding political reform and there had been demonstrations. Hu Yaobang's death and the public mourning brought things to a head. When the Canadian correspondent came to the Foreign Languages Bureau and asked me about Gorbachev's visit, I said that of course, as a Chinese citizen, I was very pleased with the turn of events, but at the moment we were more occupied with the events inside China. The university students had finally come out of their lethargy and were demanding political reform and their movement was gathering momentum. This was something more significant for China's future than Gorbachev's visit. The foreign correspondent who questioned me did not pursue this issue at the time. Some weeks later, though, they rang me up again and said that they were very pleased with their last interview. It had been well received in Canada, but would I agree to another interview about the student demonstrations. I agreed and this time we only discussed the student demonstrations. This was towards the end of May. At that time the demonstrations were gaining momentum. Every morning, students from different colleges and universities were going to the centre of Beijing, to Tiananmen Square. There they demonstrated for political reform, demanding more freedom of speech and freedom of the press, demanding a thorough clean-up of corruption and nepotism within the top échelon of the Party, and demanding the curbing of a privileged class. They also demanded to be rid of certain incompetent officials, including the newly appointed premier, Li

Peng. On his part, he refused to have a dialogue with the student leaders.

The students did not ask for the overthrow of the Party. These were totally peaceful demonstrations. However the government refused to have any meaningful dialogue with the students and Deng became threatening, imposing a military curfew and bringing in the armies from the provinces. The people of Beijing became very angry and themselves began to support the students' peaceful demonstrations. Ordinary citizens began going to Tiananmen Square and the number of peaceful demonstrators increased from the initial few hundred, to a few thousand then to several tens of thousands, and finally nearly a million. But even with such a massive demonstration, it was all very orderly. There was no disruption of traffic and business in the city went on as usual. People were in a festive mood. Finally, the students, with no satisfactory answer coming from the government, staged a hunger strike at Tiananmen and this incensed the people of Beijing even more. Everybody tried to do something to help those students starving to death on the square. The Beijing government was adamant, even trying to stop the supply of drinking water to the students. Many Beijing civilians went to the square carrying bottles of drinking water. I never went to the square myself, but I also carried out several big bottles of drinking water to the street corner near our bureau to pass them to students to take to the square. Many shop owners and peddlers contributed food voluntarily to those demonstrators in the square.

All of Beijing sympathized with the students. I never went to the square myself, although most of my younger colleagues in the office went with banners and slogans to the square. The government's attitude towards these patriotic students made my blood boil, but I felt so helpless, not knowing in what way I could help. I only sent a small sum of money through a friend to the students as my contribution towards the costs of the demonstration, but being an intellectual my contribution was a mere pittance. I also added my name to four or five petitions sent to the government through various organizations — the PPCC (People's Political Consultative Conference), Association of Chinese Writers and Artists, Kuomintang Revolutionary Committee, and so on, asking the government to listen to the voice of the people, to continue the political reform, and to have some freedom of the press. Beyond this, I did not know what else to do. Then my interview with Canadian TV gave me an idea: I could at least speak through the foreign TV and newspaper correspondents to the people outside China and tell them the true situation in China. So I made up my mind to speak to as many TV stations and foreign correspondents as possible. It happened that soon after my interview with Canadian TV, an American TV station in Beijing also rang up and asked me for an interview. I went to the Shangri-la Hotel, which was nearby, and gave another interview. I compared the turn of events at this moment to the May 4th Movement of 1919 and to the rise of the Paris Commune. I was in a confident and elated mood. I said that it had been unconstitutional to have Hu Yaobang removed from his post as General Secretary. I noted that what had happened in the government was, in fact, a fascist coup engineered by a few die-hards against political reform, and I predicted that their attempt to delay progress was bound to fail, even if they could suppress the popular demonstrations for the time being. After this interview with the Americans, I was interviewed by a young man from a Hong Kong magazine, who had come to Beijing to ask the reactions of certain Chinese intellectuals. We chatted a bit in the backyard of our flat and he took some photos of myself and our family. Then Australian TV came and interviewed me; then a young correspondent from Reuters, whom I had known years before, came without warning and asked me some questions about the turn of events. BBC even called me long-distance from London and asked me my opinion. There may have been one or two other calls from foreign correspondents, I don't remember, but with each interview I spoke in English and spoke without inhibition. I never heard their reports myself nor saw any of those interviews on TV, but other people heard them and were very excited about them. Some of my intellectual friends rang me up afterwards and praised me for my courage in speaking out for the students, saying that they all had the same thoughts but did not have the courage to speak. I don't know about my "courage", but I felt at that time someone had to speak out in support of the students' courageous actions, and if I did nothing but remain silent, I would feel ashamed.

By the end of May the student demonstrations had reached their highest pitch and the Beijing citizens were all out in support. Other students from the provinces were coming to the capital by train or on foot to join in the demonstrations. It had become a demonstration on a national scale, something unprecedented in modern Chinese history. However the government remained stubborn in its die-hard stance, threatening the students with a military curfew and calling these patriotic students rioters and hooligans. There was clearly a stalemate. After nearly a million people had gone on the streets protesting against the government and demanding reform, the demonstrators had become exhausted, and many of those students on hunger strike were taken to hospital. It was obvious that the students had to adopt different tactics in their demands. Many students began to return to their colleges and the demonstrators dwindled in number, with finally only a few tens of thousands remaining in the square. However, some of the students who had come later from other provinces remained, as well as a few stubborn students from Beijing universities and colleges. Had the government used more persuasion and adopted a more conciliatory attitude, the demonstration would have eventually come to an end. But the die-hards in the government would not bend and it led to the tragic and infamous Tiananmen massacre.

During the 1980s I had met a young man named Hou Dejian, a composer and singer of popular songs from Taiwan, who had decided to defect to mainland China. His famous song, "Descendants of the Dragon", was a patriotic song that was very popular in Taiwan and on the mainland; many young people loved him. We became very good friends soon after he came from Taiwan. By the end of May 1989, when the student demonstrations were at their highest pitch, Hou, who had been planning to go to Australia,  suddenly decided to join in the hunger strike in Tiananmen Square to support the student demonstrators. About this time he had become very friendly with a young college associate professor named Liu Xiaobo, somewhat of an anarchist and a crazy idealist. Liu had just come back from Europe and Hou was very much under his influence. Hou consulted me on his decision but I was against the idea because I had met this young professor Liu and knew that he was impractical and crazy. I also felt that the mass demonstration had already served its purpose to arouse the people, and that it should not go on indefinitely. However this was not the idea of some hotheads like Liu Xiaobo. I did not like to dissuade Hou too much because Hou's motives were patriotic. I just commented that I thought it was rather pointless and would interfere with his plan of going to Australia. Hou would not be dissuaded and said he would only stage a three-day hunger strike with some of his young friends and then he would go to Australia. On the evening of June 1st he came to my flat, bringing the professor Liu Xiaobo with him, and asked me to translate a manifesto written by Liu Xiaobo which would be distributed to foreign correspondents on the square. I read their manifesto and found it all gibberish, so I told them that it was too long and should be drastically cut, mentioning only the demand for more freedom of the press. They agreed and I reduced the manifesto to half a page and gave it back. The following night Hou and his friends started their three-day hunger strike on the square. This was June 2nd. On the following night the crackdown began.

The government had lost patience. The armies they brought to Beijing were ready. Armoured cars and tanks started to move towards the square, followed by soldiers. The civilians of Beijing, never before confronted with so many armed troops, showed extraordinary courage. They put up temporary barricades and tried to stop the army's advance with their unarmed bodies. Some old men and women even lay down on the streets to stop the trucks and tanks. They were the true heroes. The soldiers first tried to disperse the crowds with tear gas, but failed. Finally some soldiers fired real bullets at the crowd and the massacre began. It is impossible even now to give an accurate number of the people killed on the streets leading to the Tiananmen Square. Perhaps it was a few thousand, perhaps less. But this was a cold-blooded massacre of innocent, defenceless people by an army which had called itself the "People's Army". The event will go down in history as the most heinous crime committed by the Communist Party of China. Hou himself managed to escape with some students on the square by negotiating with the troops. It is quite likely that he himself did not witness any of these killings on the road.

After the Tiananmen massacre on the night of June 3rd and the early morning of June 4th, the government tried to cover up their terrible crime by claiming that the situation had gotten out of hand, with rioters causing disturbances all over Beijing, beating soldiers, setting fire to lorries and trams, and causing general havoc so that the troops had to come to restore order. Actually on June 3rd the city was still in a peaceful, festive mood, and although there were rumours that a crackdown was imminent, the citizens of Beijing never dreamed that their own government would react as it did. Around midnight, when we heard the distant shooting from the main streets leading to the centre of the city, some people thought it was just the sound of firecrackers let off by the Chinese on festive occasions. Then we heard that they were actually massacring unarmed civilians and the students who were trying to stop the troops' advance. Nobody in Beijing could sleep soundly that night. At dawn the firing gradually died down, with only sporadic sounds of shooting heard in different parts of the city. Then various people came to report that lots of people were killed on the main street leading to the square and that the soldiers were patrolling the streets and shooting people at random if they dared venture out of doors. Some soldiers were even shooting at windows if they saw people peeping out, and some innocent people, including children, were shot and killed as they peered out of their homes. I heard of several such cases. Early that morning a young friend of mine, also named Yang, dashed into my sitting room wild-eyed with grief, pale and dishevelled. He was a young Chinese from New Zealand who had used to work in the Foreign Languages Bureau and I had known him for years. He had taken out New Zealand nationality papers and was working then as a foreign expert in the Chinese Academy of Social Sciences. He was nearly hysterical with grief and horror and could only talk incoherently. I made him a cup of coffee to calm him down. This young man had come back to China after the Cultural Revolution and had thought everything was going well. That morning he kept muttering to himself in anger and disbelief: "But how could the government... how could they...

murder their own people?" He told me that he had gone into the city the night before to see the student demonstration. He had not gone as far as Tiananmen Square when the massacre began, but he had seen people shot and lying by the roadside. He had seen a girl student shot point-blank in the eye. Later he calmed down and left. I was full of helpless rage and grief. At midday the BBC office rang me up from London and asked me what I thought of the massacre. I was still in a towering rage and through the phone I denounced the people responsible for the crime, calling them fascists. I said there were a few die-hards in the top échelon of the Party who could not represent the whole Party. I repeated what I had just heard in the morning and I said that these people were worse than the northern warlords in the early days of the Republic, and worse than the Japanese invaders. Even those earlier fascists had not committed such a heinous crime like this, though this group called themselves Communists. Some days later I heard from friends that they had heard my denunciations through the BBC loud and clear. Many people even made copies of my outbursts. It had made quite a strong impact abroad and I was glad.

43

Running

Running from trouble does not particularly suit my character. But because many people in China and abroad had heard my angry denunciations through the radio, my friends and relatives began to worry about my safety in case the government would come to settle accounts with me. In those early days after the massacre, many people who voiced support for the students and denounced the government were arrested and taken away to prison. People said that those who got arrested were usually brutally beaten and some were even killed. One heard all sorts of stories. It was impossible to tell which ones were true or exaggerated. Anyway many people disappeared during that period. Some may have gone into hiding while others might have been arrested or killed. For over a week Beijing became a ghost city under the reign of white terror. One evening when Gladys and I were just chatting with a neighbour, an American expert, an old friend of mine who worked in the Foreign Languages Bureau but in a different section, suddenly sent his maid over with a note. The note said that he had heard from reliable sources that the security police might come and arrest me — either that evening or the next. In those days we heard that most people arrested were taken away at night, after ten o'clock, so that it would not cause

any commotion. He suggested that I should go into hiding at once. He would send someone to fetch me at the corner of the street, and I should leave immediately, taking no luggage at all, so that it would not arouse suspicion at the bureau. I then called Gladys to come out of the sitting room and whispered to her the content of the message. I told her not to worry, that I would come back in a few days, and there would be people passing news of my whereabouts to her. Then I left. I was met by that friend's son at the corner of the main street. It was getting dark and had started raining a bit, but there were still some old people on the roadside chatting about the recent events. My friend's son made me sit on the back of his bicycle and took me to his house. I was given a room to stay in and told not to come out. They looked after me very well for two nights and told me the news they heard from outside. In those days, there were still sounds of sporadic shooting at night. Then they heard there had been soldiers searching a peasants' hotel nearby and some people there were arrested or shot. They decided it was not safe for me to stay in that district. I must leave Beijing, either to hide myself in another city or get a false passport and get out of China. I told them that I had no intention of leaving China, and certainly not with a false passport. They insisted that I must not go home for the time being. So I said I would take a trip to Changchun in the north-east to see my daughter Zhi, who had just had a new baby, and they agreed. My friend then got me a the train ticket and arranged to have a young man escort me to see that I arrived safely. They even advised me to wear dark glasses and a cap to disguise myself. The journey went without mishap. I did not wear the cap nor the dark glasses. During that period the train authorities did have to check up on a passenger's identity so I showed them my PPCC card with my name and photograph and they examined it, but nothing happened.

I stayed with my daughter and son-in-law for three nights, then decided to return home. When I came back I found Gladys was all right, but she said she had had a trying time the last few days with telephone calls and unwanted visitors. In those days, many people dared not call on or phone each other, but news that I had suddenly disappeared from home had spread, so many of my foreign friends from embassies and some foreign correspondents had called or telephoned, wondering whether I had fled or had been arrested by the security police. As soon as I came back to Beijing, I wrote a note to the Party secretary of our *Chinese Literature* office explaining that before and immediately after the Tiananmen incident I had spoken to foreign radio and TV stations and correspondents about what I felt. I had done that without asking the Party's permission, and this was a breach of Party discipline since I was a member of the Party. I asked for disciplinary punishment. I did not say that I was sorry or regretted what I had done. I told the Party secretary the contents of my TV talks and what foreign TV stations I had contacted. The Party secretary did not make any comment but just asked me whether I could give them the names of those foreign correspondents I had contacted. I told him that I did not remember their names and during my absence Gladys had thrown away all their visiting cards. The Party secretary just said that it was good of me to tell the Party about what I had done, and she would give my note to the Party group in the Ministry of Culture for them to consider my case, and that was all. They never summoned me again after that, and I was never criticized in a meeting, which was the usual approach. I suppose the Party was shocked and embarrassed to hear what I had done, but I had been an exemplary good Party member ever since I had joined the Party and they did not want to dismiss me from the Party or send me to prison. This would cause a lot of unnecessary repercussions. I

attended my Party meetings as usual as well as other meetings in the PPCC, the Kuomintang Revolutionary Committee, and the like, and nobody asked me about the Tiananmen incident. Some friends whispered to me in secret that they had all heard what I had said on the BBC broadcast and approved of it, but that was all. By the end of the summer and early autumn, when the government was trying hard to distort the facts and convince the people that the crackdown had been necessary, the Party group in the Ministry of Culture sent a vice-minister to see me. He was an old friend whom I had known for years, before he became vice-minister. He himself had only joined the Party a few years earlier, about the same time as I. He is a very talented man, very intelligent and versatile in his accomplishments, and a good actor in the People's Theatre in Beijing. When he came, he told me frankly that the Party had asked him to come to discuss things with me and hoped that I would change my mind. We chatted freely, without inhibition, since we knew each other quite well as fellow intellectuals. We talked about Marxism, about Lenin and Stalin, as well as about Trotsky, Bukharin, and Brezhnev and Gorbachev. He never argued with me about what was the "truth" of the Tiananmen incident, nor did he talk platitudes. I assured him that I still had faith in socialism, but not Stalin's or later Mao's type of socialism, and he said he agreed with me. He came three times to visit me during that period, about once every month. Gladys did not take part in our conversations since he had not come just as a friend, but had been sent by the Party. These were sort of Party meetings, and Gladys was not a member of the Chinese Communist Party. However Gladys in the inner room could hear everything we were discussing, and she was rather amused. She told me later that we were just "shadow-boxing", not touching the main issue. Our final meeting made him realize that I could not be persuaded to think in a different way so he said: "I have already come three times. This is like the story of *sangu maolu* ('calling on a thatched hut three times') during the Three Kingdoms period." This was an allusion to a story from the second century, when Liu Bei, King of Shu, called on the wise man Zhuge Liang three times before the latter agreed to join him as his prime minister. I smiled and answered: "To compare me to Zhuge Liang is too much of an honour. I cannot accept such a comparison. You had better compare this to the story of *qi qin Meng Huo* ('capturing Meng Huo seven times'). In that case you have to come back four more times." We laughed and he left. What I had said was another allusion to an episode during the same period when Zhuge Liang, as Prime Minister of Shu, led his army into south-western China to subjugate a rebellious Miao group. He captured and then released a Miao chieftain named Meng Huo seven times before the Miao chieftain decided to obey his rule. The stories of that historical period are well-known in China in popular novels and in popular operas.

After that the vice-minister did not come any more. We met sometimes at various functions, but he did not try to brainwash me again. By the end of the year, when things had calmed down a little, the Party announced its decision that all Communist Party members should reregister themselves and give an account of their behaviour during the Tiananmen incident and make self-criticisms. Since I felt that I could not admit that I had done anything wrong, and I still condemned those in power who were responsible for the tragic incident, I decided I could not take part in this reregistration process. So I wrote a note to the Party secretary saying that I still felt the same as I did before, so I was asking to leave the Party. My Party secretary then told me that they considered that what I had done was a very serious offence. They might consider pardoning me if I repented, but as it was, they had to call a meeting

and dismiss me from the Party. Then a Party meeting, consisting of members of my own group, only about a dozen people, was held. About half of my colleagues who attended felt that they had to criticize me for what I had done. They did not try to convince me that it was justified to have the army crackdown or that there was nobody killed in Tiananmen Square. They only criticized me that as a Party member I should not have spoken out against the Party's decision, especially as it was a breach of Party discipline to speak to foreign correspondents and arouse so much international attention. I was also criticized for comparing the Party to the former northern warlords and the Japanese aggressors, which they felt was outrageous. The other half of those Party members remained silent. Then they put my case to a vote, and those who felt that I should be expelled from the Party should raise their hands. After a short hesitation they all raised their hands. I was asked to speak, to say whether I wanted to defend myself against the criticisms or express repentance. I only said briefly that I abided by their decision, and the meeting was over. About a week later the Ministry of Culture summoned me and that vice-minister friend and another vice-minister for an interview. They expressed regret and said that after all the time they had spent waiting for me to change my mind, it was regrettable that I should ask to leave the Party. They asked whether I felt any of the criticisms my colleagues gave me were too harsh or unjustified. I said that I bore them no resentment and I would accept the decision. They warned me that though I was no longer a Party member, as a non-Party citizen I must still abide by the constitution and not act in any way against the Party and the State. I nodded, then we shook hands and I left. And that was the end of my career as a Party member.

This happened in February, in early 1990. After I was expelled from the Chinese Communist Party, I still retained my membership

in the National PPCC and was still a leading member in the Kuomintang Revolutionary Committee, the Writers' Association, and other
organizations. My colleagues and friends behaved the same towards
me as before and I was treated just the same as before in society.
So I never felt in any way persecuted. I have just had my seventy-
seventh birthday and my health remains good. I may still live long
enough to see the beginning of the twenty-first century. What the
future has in store for me I do not know. I think I shall end my
autobiography here. If I live much longer and experience and
witness more interesting things in future, I may add another one
or more chapters to this autobiography, but for the time being,
enough is enough.

It is always difficult to give an honest and fair account of one's
life. There are always many interesting facets and episodes. What
to choose and what to skip over and leave out is a difficult question.
One can never claim to be truly objective and one always makes
decisions according to one's own subjective ideas about what is
significant and interesting. It is even more difficult to try to write
an honest autobiography about oneself. I started this account six
months ago at a friend's request. Since I started writing it for fun,
after writing a few dozen pages about my early life, my study and
travels abroad and the like, I read it and thought it read like a
picaresque novel or romance. Later when my life got more involved
with contemporary politics, I felt this autobiography was more
like a political manifesto or apology for what I had done or self-
justification or defence. I have no intention to write a picaresque
novel or romance. I hope all that I have written about my early life
is true to fact. I certainly hope I have not shown a tendency towards
narcissism or self-glorification, an excessive tendency to praise my
own perfection. I certainly have no intention either to write a
political apology or defence, since I am not ashamed of, nor do I

feel sorry for, my past actions and behaviour. If I could live my life all over again, I would still behave as I did before. What shortcomings exist in my writing, I leave for my readers to judge.

Postscript

In February 1990, when asked to do so by an Italian friend, I started writing this autobiography in English, which he translated into Italian and published. My autobiography stopped in the year I turned seventy-seven.

From 1990 until now, my wife Gladys' health has gradually deteriorated. My younger daughter originally lived with us. Her husband is a Canadian expert. After moving out, they moved to the foreign experts' apartments in the Friendship Hotel in the western suburbs. She wanted us to move to the Friendship Hotel too because it had more convenient medical facilities and she could be closer to her mother. The Friendship Hotel's foreign experts' apartments were built in the 1950s for Soviet experts. For Gladys' sake we moved there in June 1994.

In the earlier part of the last few years, I went abroad several times. At the end of 1989, I received an invitation from Oxford University, so we went to England for three months. Later we returned to Oxford once more, when my autobiography was officially released (in Italian). In September 1992, the Humanities Institute of the Australian National University in Canberra invited me to give lectures for three months. In March 1993 the University of Hong Kong gave me an honorary Ph.D. Others who received the honour at the same time included Nobel Peace Prize-winner

Mother Teresa. At the end of the same year, the Chinese University of Hong Kong invited me to lecture, actually giving me an opportunity to meet many old friends in Hong Kong and to make many new friends. I have not been abroad since 1994.

Currently my health is still good, but my memory is failing. Occasionally I want to write something, do some research, but I can't sit down to it any more.

I am eighty-five this year.

Beijing, June 1999